City Ubiquitous

Place, Communication, and the Rise of Omnitopia

THE HAMPTON PRESS COMMUNICATION SERIES
Urban Communication
Gary Gumpert, *series editor*

The Urban Communication Reader
Gene Burd, Susan J. Drucker and Gary Gumpert (eds.)

Diaspora, Identity, and the Media: Diasporic Transnationalism and
Mediated Spatialities
Myria Georgiou

City Ubiquitous: Place, Communication, and the Rise of Omnitopia
Andrew F. Wood

City Ubiquitous

Place, Communication, and the Rise of Omnitopia

ANDREW F. WOOD

San José State University

HAMPTON PRESS, INC.
CRESSKILL, NJ 07626

Printed in the United States of America

Library of Congress Cataloging-in-Publication Data

Wood, Andrew.
  City ubiquitous : place, communication, and the rise of omnitopia / Andrew Wood. — 1st ed.
      p. cm. — (Hampton press communication series)
  Includes bibliographical references and index.
  ISBN 978-1-57273-884-3 (hardbound) — ISBN 978-1-57273-885-0 (paperbound)
  1. Urban ecology—United States.   2. Consumption (Economics)—United States.
3. Shopping malls—United States.   4. Lifestyles—United States.   I. Title.
  HT243.U6W66 2009
  307.760973—dc22   2008053705

Hampton Press, Inc.
23 Broadway
Cresskill, NJ 07626

Contents

Images

Acknowledgments

City Ubiquitous was founded in an Ohio University classroom.

Working to complete a graduate course assignment for Jenny Nelson more than a decade ago, I wrote a paper about the opening theme to *The Simpsons* and concluded my draft with some nascent thoughts about Springfield as a sort of all-place. Wrapping up the paper, I mused that the cartoon city that seems to exist simultaneously in multiple places ought to be called "omnitopia." Offering that playful *portmanteau*, I submitted my paper and moved on. A few weeks later, I was surprised to find that my professor, not one for effusive praise, had written some marginalia next to that word, inviting me to explore it further. A scratched line on a graduate paper set forth the process that led to this book.

Even so, my first years on the tenure-track drew me far from omnitopian fields; I'd chosen to dabble in all manner of smaller projects. But Lela Noble, my dean at the time, recommended that I focus forthwith on producing peer-reviewed publications (assuming I still hoped to earn tenure at San José State University). Sharing a meal with my former office-mate and continued close friend, Phil Wander, I reviewed a number of incomplete manuscripts that might serve this purpose, and I received encouragement that omnitopia was a worthy site to apply my efforts. His advice, most notably to abandon lengthy literature reviews before I could first say something meaningful in my own voice, inspired me to imagine the omnitopian framework.

Before long, concerns about tenure gave way to a scholarly agenda that continues even now. The journal publications that followed offered me the space to try out ideas that became the foundations of *City Ubiquitous*. I gratefully acknowledge a number of editors and publishers who encouraged me and allowed me to reprint portions of several articles for this book. Specifically, a substantial amount of Chapter 4 and a small part of Chapter 5 first appeared in *Communication Theory*, *13*(3), published by Oxford University Press/Blackwell. Other parts of Chapter 5 also appeared in *Space and Culture*, *8*(4), published by Sage. And a substantial amount of Chapter 7, the Part II overview, and some of the introduction first appeared in *Text and Performance Quarterly*, *25*(4), published by Routledge/Taylor & Francis (informaworld.com).

Regarding this last journal, I am particularly grateful to Michael Bowman, who recognized the undeveloped nature of my initial manuscript submission and chose nonetheless to offer me an opportunity to grow as a scholar. Professor Bowman's willingness to provide a list of essential readings, a veritable master's class in tourism and performance, reflects the highest caliber of collegiality, one I hope to emulate.

I am also indebted to Anne Marie Todd, co-author of the *Critical Studies in Media Communication, 22*(3) piece that introduced much of the omnitopian framework I adapt in chapter 3.

I would add that some preliminary materials have also appeared on my blog, *Woodland Shoppers Paradise* (woodlandshoppersparadise.com), and from class notes maintained on my personal website, *Wood Valley* (omnitopia.com).

A number of other professional colleagues guided me to this place. Specifically, I thank Greg Dickinson, Hanns Hohmann, Wenshu Lee, Carolyn Marvin, and Matthew Spangler for their advice, support, and inspiration.

I also offer special appreciation to Roger Aden, Judith Yaross Lee, Raymie McKerrow, Tim Simpson, and Julie White, who collectively opened the door to the world I still love to explore; Anita James, whose tough question at a colloquium on my research pushed me into fruitful and necessary directions; and to my department chair, Dennis Jaehne, who demonstrates a balance of gentle humor and ferocious intelligence that continues to boggle my mind.

I also would like to recognize the SJSU Department of Communication Studies and College of Social Sciences for grants and assigned time through the years that made this book possible.

Thanks also to students of my classes, particularly Rhetoric and Public Life, Visual Communication, and Communication in the Age of Mobility, where I developed ideas that led to this book. Special thanks to Dana Morella, who helped me think more carefully about Starbucks, and to Alison Perez, who provided thoughtful commentary on Chapter 6.

I offer my gratitude and admiration to Susan Morreale (Partners Composition) for her seemingly limitless patience, kind support, and expert skills in crafting this effort. I am also grateful to Barbara Bernstein at Hampton Press for her creation of a collaborative environment in which I could work productively and sanely. And, of course, I thank Gary Gumpert for taking a chance on this manuscript.

I also wish to express my love, respect, and appreciation to Jenny Wood and Vienna Wood. Our conversations in airports, on highways, and at the dinner table helped shape the contours of omnitopia. I should add that Jenny's willingness to plow through various drafts of this book saved me from countless errors. Naturally, any mistakes that remain are my own.

One final note: For purposes of illustration, comment, and scholarly analysis, I refer to a number of trademarked names throughout this book. I affirm that these marks remain the property of their respective owners, and I emphasize that my opinions and interpretations (excepting those otherwise cited) do not reflect those of any other person or entity.

Introduction

The true has no windows. Nowhere does the true look out to the universe. And the interest in the panorama is in seeing the true city. "The city in a bottle"—the city indoors.

—Walter Benjamin (1999, F°, 24/840)[1]

Nostalgic images of public life reside within hazy fantasies of place: the village green, the town hall, the local pub. We celebrate these places with some fondness, even while employing a certain degree of strategic ambiguity in recollection. Our images of these places involve families listening to brass bands on a cool summer evening, neighbors working together to fashion public policy, a friendly greeting at a favorite café where the pie is homemade. In this reverie, one may choose to obscure the darker aspects of those places: the provincial fears of outsiders, the incessant obligations of social life, and the petty exclusions wrought by small-town prejudices. In this forgetting, many people yearn even now for a place "where everyone knows your name." Yet these sorts of places have receded from contemporary life, replaced by the multiplex, the shopping mall, and the office park, and we wander the broad boulevards of a new sort of polis that is more enclavic than any small town, even as its borders and contours become more difficult to discern. We know the names of today's common places, but we do not know the name of this "place."

I reflected on this one evening as my students and I discussed Starbucks.[2] In this conversation, we debated whether this ubiquitous coffee shop chain might be considered a "meaningful place," a locale that exists for purposes beyond mere commodity exchange. Some students replied that this site of commodity exchange *is* meaningful. They had a point, especially because Starbucks seems hell-bent on inserting itself into every crevasse of urban life (a goal that, despite fierce battles with McDonalds and Dunkin' Donuts, the company is beginning to realize). More intriguingly, my students proposed that Starbucks should be viewed as a broadly open place, a contemporary agora where anyone from corporate executives to construction workers to soul-patch poseurs with a few bucks to spare may grab a caffeine jolt. That broad spectrum of personalities must mean something. Yet something about this conclusion felt wrong to me. With the fervor of one whose faith was not yet firm, I replied that this kind of "agora" is meaningless, or at least it should be viewed as such. Meaningful places require human interaction, not just the passing of dollars for things, I argued. "Why," I said, "I could buy a cup of coffee at Starbucks without uttering a word to a single person. And if I could, that would illustrate my point. How meaningful can a place be that would permit such anonymous exchange?" I felt that I had made my point, but my students called my bluff. Okay, professor, engage the ritual of coffee at Starbucks without uttering a word. Just try.

Soon after accepting my students' challenge, I found myself waiting in a Starbucks queue, wondering whether I could maintain a vow of silence in even this forcibly social place. Grinding along with a multiclassed queue of caffeine lovers, I knew that my solitude could be pierced by psychological interrogation. Am I smooth or intense, elegant or bold? Do I possess a sparkling acidity or am I caramelly sweet? Surely someone might ask, "May I suggest Ethiopian Yergacheffe?" Staring at the huge price board that demanded some manner of interaction, I wondered whether I could order a coffee without a word being exchanged. Perhaps this experiment was destined for the growing pile of promising notions that fail in execution. But then I got an idea. What if I attempted some form of anticipatory disengagement? With a mobile phone cupped to my ear and detached gaze in my eyes, I would manage the exchange by placing my Starbucks debit card and a cardboard coffee holder on the counter. On the cardboard I wrote "T" and "CM," the universal symbols for a "tall" Caramel Macchiato, and my name. I smiled at the kid who received my paper and plastic before turning my gaze toward the phone. The phone was not even switched on, but its presence provided a potent aural enclave.

I can't help but laugh at the self-indictment inspired by the term for this practice. I have become one of a growing cohort of "cellphonies" (Harmon, 2005), and as a southerner by birth and culture, I feel guilty for this subterfuge. Where I was raised, one learned to "know one's place," yes, with all the history stirred up by the phrase. This place calls for at least some kind of human interaction, doesn't it? When I ride the bus, I create another aural enclave with the aid of my iPod earphones. But I remove one bud to say thanks to the driver when I depart. It is a small gesture, but one that is important to me. So I stood there in Starbucks, feeling guilty about more than my purchase of overpriced coffee. But the kid behind the counter was well versed in this exchange. He merely smiled and swiped my card, his eyes already searching the line behind me as he passed my cardboard instructions to the barista. Using the recycled coffee holder saved me a dime, and I didn't have to spend a word on communication with strangers. A few minutes later, I heard my name called, but the coffee sat atop the counter alone. I picked it up without the need for thanks. Finding a seat amid an amalgamation of laptop and mobile phone users, some reading, others chatting with friends, I gazed through the plate glass window: Wal-Mart to the right, an interstate highway straight ahead. I sat in the California town of Salinas along Highway 101, but I could be anywhere.

Looking down the road, surveying its bland interchanges, I began to think of my Starbucks exchange as a first step on a larger journey, and I wondered: Could I extend this experiment beyond the walls of a single stop along the highway? Perhaps with some luck, I would not simply visit this continuum; I would inhabit it. With a little planning and a willingness to travel a long distance, I could visit a place marked by disparate structures and common practice, a ubiquitous city. Finding this place would require a fair amount of research and planning, and some funding, too. Fortunately, around my university, I am known as a road tripper. Although my scholarly pursuits attempt the kind of esoteric musings befitting an academic trying to go places, my passion involves long journeys down rural highways. I will bypass 100 chain restaurants to savor a humble cup of coffee at a small-town diner. I have driven 1,000 miles over a day to photograph an exquisite piece of motel signage. To the many colleagues who asked whether I saw the Disney/Pixar film *Cars*, I replied: Sure I did, and I loved it unabashedly. My eyes glistened when the sleepy town of Radiator Springs transformed itself into a neon Route 66 fantasy. I thrilled to each image from the Mother Road that I could spot in the film; every shimmering piece of architecture glowed like one of William Gibson's (1981) semiotic ghosts that only a fortunate (or haunted) few could see. But this trip would not be about visiting those sorts of places or living those kinds of media-fed fantasies. Instead, this drive would call forth a structural and perceptual enclave whose apparently distinct locales convey inhabitants to a singular place, a place I call *omnitopia*.[3] I planned to travel the country without leaving the confines of this place.

My itinerary called for me to fly from San José, California to New York City; rent a car; and drive west toward the Pacific coast along Interstate 80, a cross-country trip of approximately 3,000 miles over $4^1/_2$ days. My goal was simple: I would cross America without speaking to anyone. After all, omnitopia is a place where human communication follows different rules, when it does not become irrelevant. To accomplish this task, I employed a growing range of mediating technologies such as online registration, self-service kiosks, and after-hours key dispensers. Assuming that these technologies could not help me avoid all human interaction, I allotted myself 10 words to speak with other people per day. As it turned out, I greatly overestimated my word budget. Instead of requiring 10 words a day, I spoke 5 words to other people during the entire trip. As a student of human communication, I found the effort to craft an itinerary that would remove me from human interaction to be personally difficult. I also found the trip to be lonely and disorienting. I cannot say it was a pleasant trip. Even so, I believe the trip was necessary to illustrate my growing unease at the design and practice of omnitopian expansion that increasingly works to make strangers of us all. To describe omnitopia, not merely as a brief coffee shop vignette, but as an embodied performance, I will assume the voice most appropriate to discussing this kind of experience, always in the present tense.

On the Road Again

My trip begins by passing through the regulated terrain of San José's (SJC) international airport. Unlike other airports, SJC is woven into the urban fabric, practically downtown, and a convenient node to the Silicon Valley network. Entering that node, however, demands a remarkably complex interplay of electronic and physical identity checks. The spectacle of search and frisk marks this place, more than the personal interrogations ("Are you carrying any explosives") that reflect a sadly naïve pre-9/11 age. At various checkpoints, technologies of surveillance are woven tightly into the labyrinth. The traveler learns to pack light, wear flip flops, and carry major documents at all times, even to wear them around the neck like a chain of office. Once admitted into the inner sanctum, the airport traveler senses a muffled silence as people become isolated cars on a snowy day, trying to avoid collisions. Airports transform us into strangers even in the midst of the cities we call home. Passing through the whooshing doors, passing the ticket-dispensing kiosks, and breezing by the skycaps, frequent travelers embody a kind of corporate asceticism marked by a new set of values: keep moving. Airborne, I cross the continent, either asleep or watching satellite TV. A smile and curt headshake evade the possibility of a drink order. The cabin lights dim, and I sleep, lulled by the hum of distant iPods. Hours later, I arrive in New York, gliding on moving pathways while raindrops beat against plate-glass windows.

I now will find and occupy my mobile enclave, a mid-size rental car with no deductible, and start heading west. At the car rental site, I am known by my credit card. Only four words, my name spoken twice, put me in the driver's seat. Passing through New Jersey, where legally mandated full-service gas pumps would threaten my bubble of silence, I head for Pennsylvania in search of a fast-food shop where I can use an electronic kiosk to purchase a deli sandwich. Hundreds of these shops have begun experimenting with kiosk technologies, and the larger fast-food restaurants like McDonald's rolled out prototypes in Chicago and Denver. Although the larger fast-food chains have been slow to expand the use of this technology, convenience stores such as Royal Farms, Sheetz, and Wawa have embraced self-service kiosks to increase order accuracy, improve efficiency, and enhance sales (Liddle, 2004). Learning the rules of the machine, I discover that each selection branches into contextually connected choices such as size and condiments until I have assured the machine that, no, I do not want a side order. Okay, yes, I want fries. I receive a receipt printout while the folks behind the counter race to complete my order. Incidentally, the fifth word of my trip, also on the first day, is the most banal: "sauce." When I select horseradish for my roast beef sandwich in a Wawa, the teenage deli chef leans over the counter to clarify what the kiosk does not convey: "real or sauce?" In omnitopia, it is best to keep your tastes simple.

That night, I sleep in an extended-stay hotel in Cleveland. I arrive after the lobby has closed and find that my key resides behind a button punch-pad. Just type my name and a comfortable bed awaits me. The next day, I stumble back onto the interstate in the pouring rain. That afternoon, traveling west of South

Image 1: Signs of the Times. *Photograph by Andrew Wood*

Bend, Indiana, I am delayed by a traffic jam with virtually no movement for about a half hour. Referring to my map, I discover that I can leap onto Highway 20. Before long, I am cruising along a great old road through the downtowns of the Hoosier State with red, orange, and yellow leaves of fall scattered among the front lawns. In New Carlisle ("A nice place to visit, a great place to live!"), the porches are festooned with jack-o-lanterns. I dial my iPod to John Mellencamp and sing about little pink houses while rolling past a main street café decorated with American flags. I yearn to stop for a hot cup of coffee and some friendly banter and cherry pie. But tonight I will sleep within a maze of office parks with tinted glass, a culture colored beige. I will dream scenes from *Office Space* and rise the next morning without remembering where I am.

My Internet tendrils connect me to distant beds, secured with credit and opened through key combinations when the lobbies have closed. Upscale hotels have begun to employ the same kiosk technology to provide plastic keys that open multihundred dollar doors to a night's rest. But all manner of hotels have begun to acknowledge that folks do not want conversation after a day on the highway; they want cable TV and wireless Internet access. I awaken to *Cable News Network* and *USA Today*. One day I am in Omaha, the other I am in Cheyenne; another, I am in Salt Lake City, but I am never really there.

I travel self-contained, dropping my keys in the slot before heading back to the highway. Only rarely does anyone invite the heat of what Kenneth Gergen (1991) calls a *microwave relationship*: one that pops quickly but cools fast and offers little nutritional value. In an edge city ringing the Omaha downtown, after I have processed my plastic-sheathed chicken Caesar salad through a UPC scanner at a Wal-Mart self-service checkout stand, an older woman drops her bag. My southern instincts call for quick action, but she is faster. As she scoops up her possessions, she glances at me and smiles: "It gets harder when you get older, huh?" What follows is an invitational silence, not a demand, but an opportunity. I smile back with falsely knowing disengagement, and the moment is gone. After a couple of days, I discover a frantic love for talk radio. Using my mobile phone to e-mail text messages and blurry photos to my wife fails to fill the void I feel. I hunger for human voices. Rush Limbaugh speaks and for once I listen. The lack of conversation has transformed me into a deep ocean diver feeling that panic of oxygen deprivation. I catch gulps in discrete rest stops, listening to families squabble over ill-folded road maps. My nods to strangers become more pronounced, my smiles more apologetic.

One evening in Cheyenne, I take pictures of gas stations drenched in rainy fluorescence and head for a motel. This place has no kiosks, no mediating technology between me and the counter person. I have dreaded this night. I could not find an extended-stay inn nearby, and I am certain that I will spend scarce words from my budget speaking with a friendly manager who has just returned from a motivational conference. I signal my anticipatory disengagement with a

Image 2: Cheyenne Gas Station. *Photograph by Andrew Wood*

mobile phone covering one ear. I think about college students who signal the degree to which they are willing to engage in conversation by whether they leave one of their earphones dangling. We are building a practical etiquette in this new world of aural enclaves. Fortunately in Cheyenne, the manager is also on the phone. I provide my tokens: a driver's license, my reservation printoff, and my credit card. She hands me a receipt and room key without a word.

The ritual is fixed now. I drive a few hundred miles, swipe my card at a gas station, navigate the cavernous expanses of a Wal-Mart in search of deli food and bottled water, and cruise a few hundred miles more toward an extended-stay hotel where my room key awaits my tapping of a keypad. Dropping into Salt Lake City, I have grown so accustomed to the continuity of anonymous travel that I decide to take a vacation from my vacation. It is time to see a movie. If my instinct is correct, omnitopia has expanded away from the highway into more presumably public places. By chance, I park near a metroplex and peer into the lobby. Sure enough, I can use a kiosk to purchase movie tickets in the lobby and even check my e-mail at an Internet terminal. Before the show starts, teenagers tap away on mobile phones, and the darkened arena glows purple and green. Returning to the hotel, I visit a "cupboard" room where all manner of snacks are on display. I can drop my money in a box, charge the food to my room, or not pay at all. No one would know my choice. I am on the honor system. The next morning as I prepare to head for Nevada, I drop my plastic key in the basket. The lobby is empty.

Driving through the Nevada desert on my way toward sunset and the Pacific coast, I spot anonymous words written in the piles of stones. Lovers and enemies leave markings on the near-moonscape, telling us they were there. Apparently "Doug + Rita." Along the roadside, simple crosses mark violent deaths. Voices remind even the silent traveler that we all pass each other through the eternities. These monuments and memorials convey a similar need to affirm our mutual humanity, to leave traces that might prove permanent. I smile to think of Doug and Rita, whomever they are. I contemplate the death of a stranger whose life is marked by whitewashed wood and a teddy bear. I enter California with confidence that no one will ask my business at the agricultural inspection station. Sure enough, no one is there.

Across 3,000 miles of interstate over some 108 hours, I have bypassed America even as I crossed its length. I have never met a single person who could touch me, and I rarely get the sense that one might try. This post-public America does not resemble the alienated strangers of an Edward Hopper painting; we are not lonely nighthawks in an after-hours café. In fact, we are more connected to more people in more ways than any other civilization in human history. However, the nature of those networked communications, their ubiquitous nature and simultaneously Balkanized specificity, has fashioned a new kind of polis: not an agora where strangers mix and mingle, but something entirely new. This ubiquitous place, this omnitopia, is growing beyond interstates and airports. It is colonizing coffee shops and bookstores, and it is changing the rules of discourse. This place reflects a certain degree of wealth and privilege, but it is growing beyond the rarified pleasantries of airport "clubs" and hotel concierges who efficiently rid the road of its bumps and surprises. In this city ubiquitous, we can carry countless voices with us, but we never must speak with a neighbor. Aided by peripatetic technologies, we are never lost, but increasingly distant.

A Rhetoric of Ubiquity

This book offers an effort to understand omnitopia as a lens upon our age of ubiquity, a period in which all peoples, places, and things become accessible from any point in a global network. In the age, traditional distances recede, enabling a sphere of interaction that renders each point equidistant from every other point.[4] This age of ubiquity is both structural and perceptual. It requires physical places and technologies to collapse those distances into manageable relation. But it also demands perception that these points are accessible and desirable. Such an age is consequently a rhetorical notion, enacting a vision of public life that one enters through communication, specifically the identification of oneself as an occupant of an idea.

Given its rhetorical origins, this work draws most directly from a subset of communication scholarship focusing on space and place. This kind of scholarship owes a special debt to Yi-Fu Tuan (1977) and Michel de Certeau (1984), who, while arriving from different directions, helped introduce the field of communication studies to cultural geography. Presaging the field's embrace of that framework, Darryl Hattenhauer (1984) argued for the embrace of semiotic theory to read human-made structures, stating, "[a]rchitecture not only communicates, but also communicates rhetorically" (p. 71). From this dictum, Hattenhauer advocated the study of ceremonial and memorial architecture while proposing that postmodern sites would play a role in our inquiries as well. Thereafter, communication scholars have sought to study the structure, design, and planning of place and the psychological, social, and improvisational components of space, the intersection of these two being mediated through authorizing discourse, unspoken ideology, and human interaction.

So far, the results are promising. One of the richest lines of communication scholarship emanating from this study has focused on the Washington, DC Vietnam Veterans Memorial as a place that intersects with a space of overlapping narratives about the war and our public memory (Blair, Jeppeson, & Pucci, 1991; Carlson & Hocking, 1988; Ehrenhaus, 1989; Foss, 1986; Haines, 1986). Inspired by this conversation, communication scholars have focused on other memorials, about the Holocaust (Hasian, 2004), the civil rights struggle (Armada, 1998), Martin Luther King, Jr. (Gallagher, 1995), Buffalo Bill (Dickinson, Ott, & Aoki, 2005), and Israeli settlements (Katriel, 1994). Adding to this commemorative turn, communication scholars have also broadened their focus on even more complex constellations of texts related to the meaning of World War II (Biesecker, 2002), the "place" of Sojourner Truth (Mandziuk, 2003), and the ways in which we mourn at sites of violent death (Jorgensen-Earp & Lanzilotti, 1998; Trujillo, 1993). Beyond commemoration, communication scholars have also investigated places as intersections of tourism, community, and media-fantasy fulfillment (Aden, Rahoi, & Beck, 1995; Clark, 2004; Goodstein, 1992; Makagon, 2003), not to mention sites of consumerism (Dickinson, 1997, 2002). From this perspective of communication scholarship, we find that places do not simply contain the stages on which we speak; they are messages themselves. Although these works inspire this book, I believe we can also focus less on sites as locales, differentiated places of time and character, and learn more about the process through which places become omnitopia.

Expanded Definition of Omnitopian Framework

As noted earlier, omnitopia enacts a structural and perceptual enclave whose apparently distinct locales (and locals) convey inhabitants to a singular place. For a growing number of people, it is like a wireless "cloud" that is accessible to some and invisible to others. The typical omnitopian may be the conventioneer who flows from international airport to atrium hotel to shopping mall to theme restaurant without ever walking the streets. Moreover, as our archetypal omnitopian flows from convention to convention, she or he begins to view them as terminals to the same place. An imperfect amalgam of Greek and Latin roots constructing an "all-place," the term *omnitopia* draws its lineage from utopia (not-place) and heterotopia (other-place) to reveal the shift from totalizing narratives to overlapping contradictory narratives. A key distinction from heterotopia, however, is the shift from separate locale (park, church, graveyard, motel) to a complete enclave that approximates all of urbanity. Omnitopia does not reside elsewhere, but "everywhere." Whereas heterotopia offers a social safety valve from public life (Foucault, 1986; see also Hetherington, 1997; Soja, 1995, 1996, 1997; Wood, 2003a, 2004), omnitopia constructs a reproduction of the world that is necessarily and strategically incomplete. Although the "entire world" cannot reside within the omnitopian field, one glimpses enough of the world to ignore what has been elided. As we will see, that smaller mirror world reflects much about the larger one; the connection flows both ways.

I have surveyed the contours of omnitopia in several venues, trying to develop a coherent yet flexible framework for this concept. In previous efforts, I studied "aspects" of omnitopia in airports (Wood, 2003b) and "strategies" of omnitopia in motels and hotels (Wood, 2005a). I have expanded on this notion of strategies by surveying depictions of omnitopian urbanity (Wood & Todd, 2005) and unpacking performances of omnitopia within tourist enclaves (Wood, 2005b). Most recently, I have revised the initial omnitopian framework by its application to the film *Dark City* (Wood, 2008). In these works, I have proposed five components to omnitopia: dislocation, which detaches a site from its surrounding locale; conflation, which merges disparate experiences into a whole; fragmentation, which splits a singular environment into multiple perceptions; mobility, which orients a place around movement rather than stasis; and mutability, which enables the perpetual change of a place. However, in this book I transcend mere categorization. Instead, I hope to survey the design and communication of this ubiquitous age, revealing its troubling implications for meaningful human interaction while also noting the bounds and limitations to this phenomenon.

Reflecting on the limitations of this project, I freely admit that my efforts to offer a name and grammar for omnitopia risk creating a lens that is custom designed. This lens may reveal only what I choose to see. Henri Lefèbvre (1991) offers fair warning:

> When codes worked up from literary texts are applied to spaces—urban spaces, say—we remain, as may easily be shown, on a purely descriptive level. Any attempt to use such codes as a means of deciphering social space must surely reduce that space itself to the status of a *message*, and the inhabiting of it to the status of a *reading*. This is to evade both history and practice. (p. 7)

Respecting this concern, it is my hope that this project will reflect a way of seeing modernity that does not create a sensibility, but rather illuminates what might otherwise be obscured. If successful, writing about omnitopia will result in a moment of recognition that renders the familiar to be profoundly strange and therefore worth our attention.

Here we must consider the limits of that recognition. Being intentionally limited, omnitopia is inevitably limiting. Two people moving through the same geographical location may nonetheless occupy entirely different spaces: one in omnitopia, the other being elsewhere. Certainly both are subject to similar globalized flows of commerce and power, "[b]ut even if . . . bourgeois travelers can be 'located' on specific itineraries dictated by political, economic, and inter-cultural global relations (often colonial, postcolonial, or neocolonial in nature), such constraints do not offer any simple equivalence with other immigrant and migrant laborers" (Clifford, 1997, p. 35). The "world" afforded the inhabitant of omnitopia is essentially an enclave of privilege, its fluid mobility enabled through the totems of successful credit checks, keycard swipes, password confirmations, and security profiles, at least when seeking entrance into its domain. As such, an inquiry into omnitopia appears to valorize an artificial world of "a few itinerant elites," employing James Weiner's (2002) caustic reading of Clifford's (1997) *Routes*, a project that Weiner dismisses as "ludicrously subjective, superficial, and . . . irrelevant . . . a meditation that can only take place within a corklined room or a tastefully-appointed museum foyer, under privileged conditions of institutional support which can afford a total disengagement from the world" (pp. 25–26). While reminding such critics that most any kind of academic prose rests on a foundation of privilege, I would emphasize that the study of omnitopia does not covet some sort of business-class disengagement from the real world. Instead, this project arises from a passionate concern about the consequences of an omnitopian sensibility that has begun to colonize itself beyond the domains of well-heeled movement, metastasizing into all manner of everyday places. This analysis, this act of naming, follows a personal belief in the value of meaningful places, particularly those that reside outside the realm of privileged mobility. Accepting Larry Ford's (1998) comment that "we see what we have words to describe" (p. 528), I would add that to name a thing is to propose its undoing, even if the act seems to perpetuate its power for a time.

In naming omnitopia, I should share a final comment on its similarity and simultaneous distinction from a related term: *non-place*. Omnitopia can be situated in conversation with non-place, but it should not be confused with the term that French anthropologist Marc Augé (1995) deploys to represent fleeting sites of "supermodernity," in which place becomes distilled into text without human meaning.[5] Augé writes, "[i]f a place can be identified as relational, historical and concerned with identity, then a space which cannot be defined as relational, or historical, or concerned with identity will be a non-place" (pp. 77–78). Certainly, journalistic accounts of new media are replete with descriptions of such non-places that seem interchangeable with omnitopia. For example, Parvaz (2005) of the *Seattle Post-Intelligencer Reporter* laments the implications of *techno-cocooning*:

> This eliminates the charm of being on a trip, the chance meetings we have with each other, the jokes we overhear, the serendipitous connections that make leaving one's home and going outside worth it. It wipes off all social fingerprints from ourselves, leaving us untouched and alone. (¶ 14)

Writing about the introduction of fifth-generation video iPods, *New York Times* columnist David Carr (2005) adds:

> So this is how we end up alone together. We share a coffee shop, but we are all on wireless laptops. The subway is a symphony of earplugged silence while the family trip has become a time when the kids watch DVD's in the back of the minivan. The water cooler, that nexus of chatter about the show last night, might go silent as we create disparate, customized media environments. (p. 3)

I am drawn to these perspectives; they make plenty of sense to me. But my project does not concentrate on discrete non-places. Rather, I articulate a perspective of "the world" that has become condensed (for a growing number of people, yet hardly all) into an enclosure of the *same place*. This is not to announce, literally, the death of specific cultures. Although a number of places certainly resemble one another, the study of omnitopia does not assume that all places are the same (except, perhaps, to the lazy tourist who never leaves the hotel pool). Any serious traveler of even the most banal places can spot unmistakable utterances of "here" and "now" anywhere, and, undoubtedly, all places are real and meaningful to someone (Kincaid, 1989). Thus, omnitopia is not about the alleged homogeneity of globalization. Instead, this project advances a perspective in which, for many people, a growing number of places are becoming nodes[6] to an enclave that is designed to resemble the real world, but not so accurately as to hinder consumer behaviors.

Omnitopia is the cavernous, airy enclosure that presumes to contain the world entire in an endless interior, a world seemingly without frontiers. Perhaps a more appropriate inspiration for this project comes not from Marc Augé but from Jean Baudrillard (1989):

> America is a giant hologram, in the sense that information concerning the whole is contained in each of its elements. Take the tiniest little place in the desert, any old street in a Mid-West town, a parking lot, a Californian house, a BurgerKing [sic] or a Studebaker, and you have the whole of the US—South, North, East, or West. . . . The hologram is akin to the world of phantasy [sic]. It is a three-dimensional dream and you can enter it as you would a dream. Everything depends on the existence of the ray of light bearing the objects. If it is interrupted, all the effects are dispersed, and reality along with it. (pp. 29–30)

Although I would define *omnitopia* as a smaller version of the world than Baudrillard's holographic "America," including only enclosed simulacra of the totems he cited within its entirety, I find it useful to employ Baudrillard's emphasis on ephemerality. Omnitopia, after all, appears and fades in a manner dependent on perception. To bring omnitopia into sharp relief, this book advances along three vectors: its historical origins, its structural performances, and its inevitable collapse.

In that spirit, this book is organized into three parts: Imagining Omnitopia, Visiting Omnitopia, and Challenging Omnitopia. Part I outlines a historical trajectory of omnitopia, noting its appearance in 19th-century arcades, department stores, and world's fairs (chapter 1: Emergence), its United States expansion along the ribbons of prewar and interstate highways (chapter 2: Construction), and its contemporary manifestation as a constellation of components illustrated by cinematic depictions of urbanity (chapter 3: Framework). Part II shifts our attention from historical and conceptual perspectives to a survey of sites that currently demonstrate an omnitopian way of living. The tour begins with a study of air terminals as detached enclaves (chapter 4: Airports), pauses to examine highway and city spots of temporary domesticity (chapter 5: Hotels), and then enters the urbanized simulacra of fantasy and commerce found in various shoppers' paradises (chapter 6: Malls). Part III advances a postomnitopian agenda by first considering the potential for pleasure, if not resistance, illustrated by Las Vegas-style post-tourism (chapter 7: Performance), the gradual abandonment of heretofore totalizing places by way of placeless enclaves (chapter 8: Convergence),

and the remaining desire of people to exit omnitopia in search of genuine locality (chapter 9: Reverence). As a whole, this book offers an evaluation of design,
performance, and transcendence that rests on confidence that no place is more
powerful than the individual and collective will of those who carve windows
from walls.

Notes

1. Unless noted otherwise, all quotations from Walter Benjamin are taken from
Howard Eiland and Kevin McLaughlin's translation of *The Arcades Project* (cited as
Benjamin, 2004). These quotations include in-text references to the Tiedemann notation
system and page numbers from the English translation.

2. All trademarked terms are used for purposes of academic analysis. None of
their uses represent the opinions or policies of their owners.

3. After deciding to organize my research around the term *omnitopia*, I learned
that Nintendo used the same word in its 1995 game, *Secrets of Evermore*. My usage of
the word does not reflect any connection to that company or its game.

4. I am drawn to Sorkin's (1999) description, "In this new city, the idea of distinct
places is dispersed into a sea of universal placelessness as everyplace becomes destination
and any destination can be anyplace" (p. 217), although the notion of "placelessness"
does not quite jibe with the omnitopian conception of dislocation. In this enclave, one is
detached from local geography, but the experience of "place" is not necessarily "dispersed."
It is more appropriately viewed as being transformed into a "place unto itself."

5. It bares merely a brief reiteration here that, although Augé has popularized
study into non-place, he continues a well-established intellectual tradition advanced from
different trajectories (and subtly distinct articulations and translations) by Roland Barthes,
Michel de Certeau, Jacques Derrida, Michel Foucault, and Paul Virilio, among others. In
fact, Bosteels (2003) reminds us, "almost *all* contemporary French thinkers whom Eng-
lish-language commentaries associate with so-called poststructuralism and the critique
or deconstruction of humanism, at one point or another in their trajectories, assign a
central role to a certain notion of the nonplace" (p. 119). Meanwhile, in the United States,
Melven Webber employed non-place (specifically the "non-place urban realm") as a way
to articulate the means through which communities arise via media of common interest
more than the limits of local geography, whereas Paul Fussell employed the term when
commenting on the placelessness of contemporary tourism. See Gumpert (1987) for
another fruitful application: "In the contemporary urban/suburban world most people
are potential members of a series of 'non-place' communities. Such multiple membership
in non-place communities constitute a person's 'media community.' Such communities do
not require the simultaneous physical presence of its members since they are connected
by print an electronic media" (p. 178).

6. My reference to node is not original. In a recent example, Jenkins (2002) describes
buildings as nodes within a network, arguing that individual spaces are less meaningful
than their flowing relationships with other spaces: "The building as a permeable entity
becomes less an individual building block in a collection of blocks, but rather it becomes

an unstable assemblage that is intimately connected to and renegotiated by the surrounding buildings, streets, communities, and economies and the world beyond" (p. 232). As such, nodes are malleable, easily edited according to whims of design or perception. Nodes are pliable entrances to fixed locations.

References

Aden, R. C., Rahoi, R. L., & Beck, C. S. (1995). "Dreams are born on places like this": The process of interpretive community formation at the *Field of Dreams* site. *Communication Quarterly, 43*(4), 368–380.

Armada, B. J. (1998). Memorial agon: An interpretative tour of the National Civil Rights Museum. *Southern Communication Journal, 63*(3), 235–243.

Augé, M. (1995). *Non-places: Introduction to an anthropology of supermodernity* (J. Howe, Trans.). New York: Verso.

Baudrillard, J. (1989). *America* (C. Turner, Trans.). New York: Verso.

Benjamin, W. (2004). *The arcades project* (H. Eiland & K. McLoughlin, Trans.). Cambridge, MA: Harvard University Press.

Biesecker, B. A. (2002). Remembering World War II: The rhetoric and politics of national commemoration at the turn of the 21st century. *Quarterly Journal of Speech, 88*(4), 393–409.

Blair, C., Jeppeson, M. S., & Pucci, E., Jr. (1991). Public memorializing in postmodernity: The Vietnam Veterans Memorial as prototype. *Quarterly Journal of Speech, 77*(3), 263–288.

Bosteels, B. (2003). Nonplaces: An anecdoted [sic] topography of contemporary French theory. *Diacritics, 33*(3–4), 117–139.

Carlson, A. C., & Hocking, J. E. (1988). Strategies of redemption at the Vietnam Veterans' Memorial. *Western Journal of Communication, 52*(3), 203–215.

Carr, D. (2005, December 18). Taken to a new place, by a TV in the palm. *The New York Times*, Ideas & Trends, p. 3.

Clark, G. (2004). *Rhetorical landscapes in America: Variations on a theme from Kenneth Burke.* Columbia: University of South Carolina Press.

Clifford, J. (1997). *Routes: Travel and translation in the late twentieth century.* Cambridge, MA: Harvard University Press.

de Certeau, M. (1984). *The practice of everyday life* (S. Rendall, Trans.). Berkeley: University of California Press.

Dickinson, G. (1997). Memories for sale: Nostalgia and the construction of identity in Old Pasadena. *Quarterly Journal of Speech, 83*(1), 1–27.

Dickinson, G. (2002, Fall). Joe's rhetoric: Finding authenticity at Starbucks. *Rhetoric Society Quarterly, 32*, 5–27.

Dickinson, G., Ott, B. L., & Aoki, E. (2005). Memory and myth at the Buffalo Bill Museum. *Western Journal of Communication, 69*(2), 85–108.

Ehrenhaus, P. (1989). The wall. *Critical Studies in Mass Communication, 6*(1), 94–98.

Ford, L. R. (1998). Midtowns, megastructures, and world cities. *Geographical Review, 88*(4), 528–547.

Foss, S. K. (1986). Ambiguity as persuasion: The Vietnam Veterans Memorial. *Quarterly Journal of Speech, 34*(3), 326–340.

Foucault, M. (1986). Of other spaces. *Diacritics, 16*, 22–27.

Gallagher, V. J. (1995). Remembering together? Rhetorical integration and the case of the Martin Luther King Jr. Memorial. *Southern Communication Journal, 60*(2), 109–119.

Gergen, K. J. (1991). *The saturated self: Dilemmas of identity in contemporary life*. New York: Basic Books.

Gibson, W. (1981). The Gernsback continuum. In T. Carr (Ed.), *Universe 11* (pp. 81–90). Garden City, NY: Doubleday & Company.

Goodstein, E. S. (1992). Southern Belles and southern buildings: The built environment as text and context in *Designing Women. Critical Studies in Mass Communication, 9*(2), 170–185.

Gumpert, G. (1987). *Talking tombstones and other tales of the media age*. New York: Oxford University Press.

Haines, H. W. (1986). "What kind of war?": An analysis of the Vietnam Veterans Memorial. *Critical Studies in Mass Communication, 3*(1), 1–20.

Harmon, A. (2005, April 14). Reach out and touch no one. *New York Times*, p. G1.

Hasian, M., Jr. (2004). Remembering and forgetting the "Final Solution": A rhetorical pilgrimage through the U.S. Holocaust Memorial museum. *Critical Studies in Media Communication, 21*(1), 64–92.

Hattenhauer, D. (1984). The rhetoric of architecture: A semiotic approach. *Communication Quarterly, 32*(1), 71–77.

Hetherington, K. (1997). *The badlands of modernity: Heterotopia and social ordering*. London: Routledge.

Jenkins, L. (2002). 11, Rue du Conservatoire and the permeability of buildings. *Space and Culture, 5*(3), 222–236.

Jorgensen-Earp, C., & Lanzilotti, L. A. (1998). Public memory and private grief: The construction of shrines at the sites of public tragedy. *Quarterly Journal of Speech, 84*(2), 150–170.

Katriel, T. (1994). Sites of memory: Discourses of the past in Israeli pioneering settlement museums. *Quarterly Journal of Speech, 80*(1), 1–20.

Kincaid, J. (1989). *A small place*. New York: Plume.

Lefèbvre, H. (1991). *The production of space* (D. Nicholson-Smith, Trans.). Oxford: Blackwell.

Liddle, A. J. (2004). Computerized kiosks let c-store customers help themselves. *Nation's Restaurant News, 38*(2), 48.

Makagon, D. (2003). A search for social connection in America's town square: Times Square and urban public life. *Southern Communication Journal, 69*(1), 1–21.

Mandziuk, R. M. (2003). Commemorating Sojourner Truth: Negotiating the politics of race and gender in the spaces of public memory. *Western Journal of Communication, 67*(3), 271–291.

Parvaz, D. (2005, February 7). Living in a bubble: Our love of techno-gadgets is insulating us from the real world. *The Seattle-Post Intelligencer*. Available from http://seattlepi.nwsource.com/lifestyle/210821_popoff210807_copy.asp.

Soja, E. W. (1995). Heterotopologies: A remembrance of other spaces in the Citadel-LA. In S. Watson & K. Gibson (Eds.), *Postmodern cities and spaces* (pp. 13–34). Oxford: Blackwell.

Soja, E. W. (1996). *Thirdspace: Journeys to Los Angeles and other real-and-imagined places.* Cambridge, MA: Blackwell.

Soja, E. W. (1997). *Postmodern geographies: The reassertion of space in critical social theory.* New York: Verso.

Sorkin, M. (1999). See you in Disneyland. In M. Sorkin (Ed.), *Variations on a theme park: The new American city and the end of public space* (pp. 205–232). New York: Hill and Wang.

Trujillo, N. (1993). Interpreting November 22: A critical ethnography of an assassination site. *Quarterly Journal of Speech, 79*(4), 447–466.

Tuan, Y.-F. (1977). *Space and place: The perspective of experience.* Minneapolis: University of Minnesota Press.

Weiner, J. (2002). Between a rock and a non-place: Towards a contemporary anthropology of place. *Reviews in Anthropology, 31*(1), 21–27.

Wood, A. (2003a). The Middletons, Futurama, and Progressland: Disciplinary technology and temporal heterotopia in two twentieth century New York world's fairs. *New Jersey Journal of Communication, 11*(1), 63–75.

Wood, A. (2003b). A rhetoric of ubiquity: Terminal space as omnitopia. *Communication Theory, 13*(3), 324–344.

Wood, A. (2004). Managing the Lady Managers: The shaping of heterotopian spaces in the 1893 Chicago exposition's Woman's Building. *Southern Communication Journal, 69*(4), 289–302.

Wood, A. (2005a). "The best surprise is no surprise": Architecture, imagery, and omnitopia among American mom and pop motels. *Space and Culture, 8*(4), 399–415.

Wood, A. (2005b). "What happens [in Vegas]": Performing the post-tourist *flâneur* in "New York" and "Paris." *Text and Performance Quarterly, 25*(4), 315–333.

Wood, A. (2008). "Small world": Alex Proyas' Dark City as omnitopia. In J. Perlich & D. Whitt (Eds.), *Sith, slayers, stargates and cyborgs: Modern mythology in the new millennium* (pp. 121–142). New York: Peter Lang.

Wood, A., & Todd, A. M. (2005). "Are we there yet?": Searching for Springfield and *The Simpsons'* rhetoric of omnitopia. *Critical Studies in Media Communication, 22*(3), 207–222.

I

Overview

When Frederick Jackson Turner proclaimed the closing of the American frontier at a meeting of the American Historical Association at the 1893 Columbian Exposition in Chicago, he envisioned a transformation of public life that would stretch beyond the United States to revolutionize the urban world. In his "frontier thesis," Turner declared the end of the American boundary between civilization and disorder that had been located in "the West." This end marked the closure of a sharp demarcation that demanded all manner of risks and privations, but one that inspired freedoms too: liberation from settled ways and outmoded norms. On the now-closed frontier, one could previously encounter:

> That coarseness and strength combined with acuteness and inquisitiveness; that practical, inventive turn of mind, quick to find expedients; that masterful grasp of material things, lacking in the artistic but powerful to effect great ends; that restless, nervous energy; that dominant individualism, working for good and for evil, and withal that buoyancy and exuberance which comes with freedom. . . . (Turner, 1920, p. 37)

With this definition, Turner differentiated the American frontier from its European antecedent, which he said merely divided militarized urban concentrations. The closing of the American frontier meant the emergence of the urbanized citizen, one more refined and less independent than in the previous era, more European perhaps. Of course, and Turner noted this also, the nation would seek new frontiers. What Turner did not imagine, however, was the enclavic nature of those new frontiers.

Frederick Jackson Turner could hardly foresee the era that would follow the closing of the frontier and concomitant rise of an urbanized nation, as the internal impulse toward expansion would be met with the need to guard the borderlands from external threats. At first, as the highways stretched over distant horizons, transforming the ragged hills into gentle slopes; as telephony offered nearly ubiquitous and immediate modes of communication, enabling regional firms to expand into national and international markets; as broadcast radio and TV blanketed the nation with a mass market, collapsing regional distinctions and even dialects; and as Internet communication emerged to provide a capsule version of the globe in its World Wide Web, both sides of the frontier became for many a romanticized and mythical site for storytelling in which even children pretending to be cowboys would fantasize also about having some "Indian" blood. Along the way, 20th-century America discovered new frontiers: in the space program, in fights against disease, and in conflicts overseas. On these newfound margins between civilization and chaos, the adventure of new discovery and the threat of disorder could still be met in the manner imagined by Turner: with innovation and grit, and sometimes with violence. Yet in the 21st century, the freedom of the frontier became replaced by the fears of the enclave as the nation rekindled its anxieties of a porous border as it faced the threats of terror attacks after 9/11 and as it considered the practicalities of building a wall between the United States and Mexico to thwart the movements of illegal immigrants. In this manner, reminiscent of European-style borders imagined by Turner, the frontier could not be defined as the limit of expansion, but rather as the site where the expansion of others would be halted.

In the next three chapters, we undertake a historical overview of the rise of omnitopia as an enclave guarded by invisible yet substantial frontiers. We summon memories of 19th-century arcades and department stores that provided blueprints for vast and complex international expositions that marked a frontier between civilization and chaos. We then trace one key product of those fairs, the U.S. interstate highway system that seemed to complete Turner's closing of the frontier, even while enacting strict delineations between meaningful and supposedly empty or dangerous places. We then conclude with a reading of two films, Jacques Tati's *Play Time* and Steven Spielberg's *The Terminal*, which provide us a framework for understanding the omnitopian enclave in contemporary life.

Reference

Turner, F. J. (1920). The significance of the frontier in American history. In *The frontier in American history* (pp. 1–38). New York: Henry Holt and Company.

1

Enclave

Arcades are houses or passages having no outside—like a dream.

—Walter Benjamin (2004, L1a,1/406)

What would be the point of an arcade in a society that is itself only a passageway?

—Siegfried Kracauer (1995, p. 342)

The apparently distinct places of public life may be termed a labyrinth of interiors, easy to enter, difficult to escape. Today still, one may find an outside, a frontier, a border, a boundary, an edge that designates the distinction between in *here* and out *there*, particularly if one is sensitive to the distinctions made manifest through differing modalities of race, class, gender, and other markers of privilege. But these sorts of horizons are astutely placed, and their bounds have become harder to discern than they once were. In an age of ubiquity, when all people, all things, and all places appear to converge within certain nodes—cyberspace, shopping malls, airports, terminals of all kinds—we witness a paradoxical balance of porous borders and rigid rules. Moreover, the bewildering spectacles found within their domains often threaten to banish the possibility that an outside world exists at all. You can tell the time if you can find a clock. You can observe the weather outside if you can find a window. Finally, you can depart at any time, but with some effort. After all, although the entrances to these places may be lit with gaudy excess, their exits often are hidden within a maze. In this way, these places may be compared to virtual worlds found in "sandbox-style" video games whose nonlinear and open-ended play renders it difficult to imagine an "edge" to the world. You may swim through an ocean of pixels, but you will never escape the confines of this place. Even so, despite their disciplinary strategies, these places cannot be confused with prisons. After all, a prison has walls that one might climb, gates one might smash, borders one might cross. These places are far subtler, their barriers more carefully concealed. Actually, these places may be better termed *enclaves*. They become entire worlds to us while protecting us from the frightening landscapes beyond their carefully crafted interiors. These places are powerful and instructive. They teach us that protection can be pleasurable and that discipline can be fun.

This lesson demands more attention than it has thus far received. We should study the rise of an enclavic sensibility that attempts to control, encapsulate, and finally eliminate the possibility of an "outside world." Here, I should note that this notion of *enclave* is significantly different from the alternative notion of *enclosure*, a term that may bring to mind the fencing of common land for private purposes. Although enclosure offers a useful illustration of the privatization of public life, enclave reflects the maintenance of a distinctive identity of a people and place apart from its surrounding milieu. I would add that contemporary enclaves offer more than mere distance from the threats of otherness. They instead pose the possibility that people may live in partial reproductions of the world built so grandly and so persuasively that the edges of their "enclosures" can no longer be found, sought, or even imagined. This kind of enclave offers a totalizing environment whose frontier is not "closed," as historian Frederick Jackson Turner announced in 1893. It is *removed* from view. How shall we undertake an analysis of these enclaves? I propose starting with a brief history of arcades, department stores, and world's fairs whose simulacra of urban cosmos did much to inspire the enclaves that followed. Collectively, these sites suggest a progenitor of omnitopia.

Rise of the Consumer Enclave:
Arcades and Department Stores

The 19th and early 20th centuries marked a period in which grand consumer spaces would portend to a new enclavic sensibility. These enclaves, unlike smaller enclosures oriented around a specific purpose, would envelop a broad spectrum of human activities to reduce the need to ever go "outside." The 19th-century arcade provides a rich example of this theme. Connecting disparate buildings and businesses, arcades facilitated the tighter integration of urban life and enabled the possibility that a consumer class could navigate its environs without being limited to the streets and shop fronts that previously defined the city. Walter Benjamin, the Weimer-era critic, translator, and philosopher of history, orients our tour of the 19th-century arcade.

Benjamin took the Parisian arcades as a starting point for his efforts to analyze the totalizing enclosure of urban life. Unlike most of his Frankfurt School colleagues, Benjamin imagined more than anesthesia inside the spectacle of capitalism. He proposed the possibility that persons cast within the urban structure may step outside of its disciplinary framework, and that such a stroll might even be pleasurable. To investigate this notion, Benjamin spent 13 years assembling a complex corpus of texts and commentaries about urban life before committing suicide in 1940.[1] Benjamin's sprawling and unfinished montage, *Das Passagen-Werk*, would later be known to readers of English as *The Arcades Project*: an exhaustive inventory of observations and quotations, types and tropes, figures and places.

Revealing the purposeful wanderings of an intellect whose journeys through the Parisian street scene blurred with his personal struggles to reconcile Marxism, Freudianism, surrealism, and mysticism, *The Arcades Project* has been described both as a ruin and a masterpiece of 20th-century writing. Touring its pages, one strolls through a phantasmagoria, a dream city of *konvolutes* whose outwardly random categories have reminded more than one reader of a "certain Chinese encyclopedia," a taxonomy that shatters "all the ordered surfaces and all the planes with which we are accustomed to tame the wild profusion of existing things" (Foucault, 1994, p. xv).[2] Describing Benjamin's aversion to grand unifying theories, Siegfried Kracauer (1995) explains, "he who faces the world in its immediacy is presented with a figure that he must smash in order to reach the essentialities" (p. 260). Wandering through the open files of *The Arcades Project*, one can vividly imagine Benjamin's wanderings, his transformations of places and people into texts as he strolled the arcades of modernity.

The word *arcade* refers to a series of arches joined along a common axis. As a structural device, the arcade can be traced to Roman architecture, illustrated by the lines of arches found in aqueducts and the Colosseum. From Roman times onward, arcades provided a way to integrate pedestrian traffic into urban design by providing covered passages along or between buildings. Although typically used in cathedrals and mosques, arcades also served as a site of commerce. This use would become essential to understanding the appearance of the French arcade in the 19th century. With the advent of iron and glass construction, Parisian planners employed the arcade (most prolifically in the 1820s and 1830s) as a covered passageway between buildings to draw pedestrians away from the streets into a consumer enclave of shopping and display. Benjamin offers a vivid description of the arcades he studied, quoting from an *Illustrated Guide to Paris*:

> These arcades, a recent invention of industrial luxury, are glass-roofed, marble-paneled corridors extending through whole blocks of buildings, whose owners have joined together for such enterprises. Lining both sides of these corridors, which get their light from above, are the most elegant shops. . . . [A1,1/31]

For Parisians of this era, the glass roof began to supplant the arch as the primary identifying characteristic of the arcade. Sieburth (1988) illustrates:

> At once edifice and street, the *passage* converts house into corridor, residence into traffic, permanence into transit. Roofing the external world of the city into a domesticized interior, bathed in the twilight of natural and artificial illumination, the arcade occupies a space that seems to offer both the panoramic openness of natural landscape and the cozy closure of a room. (p. 11)

This arcade provides an essential step in the efforts of city planners to imagine the urban world of interiors whose interactions with the outside world could be controlled or even circumvented completely. By way of illustration, Benjamin quotes Eduard Devrient:

> Rainshowers annoy me, so I gave one the slip in an arcade. There are a great many of these glass-covered walkways, which often cross through the blocks of buildings and make several branchings, thus affording welcome shortcuts. Here and there they are constructed with great elegance, and in bad weather or after dark, when they are lit up bright as day, they offer promenades—and very popular they are—past rows of glittering shops. [A3a,4/42]

From these and similar observations, one recalls the arcade as a commercial matrix of roads and rest stops laid atop the civic map of public life, a kind of interstate highway system bypassing the mean and unkempt abodes between the cities. The interstate analogy, imperfect as it is, suggests a broader purpose of the arcade: to allow passage from node to node so transparently and safely that one may forget that these interstitial spaces exist at all. The city's arcades, along with its related cafés, bistros, and shops, made it possible to conceive a miniature city that was set apart from the outside world, a sealed fantasy world of looking. Citing the *Illustrated Guide to Paris* once more, Benjamin agrees that "the arcade is a city, a world in miniature . . . in which customers will find everything they need" [A1,1/31]. To accomplish its illusion of completeness, this miniature world demanded a broad field of vision, one that would be assisted by the city's proliferation of mirrors.

Walter Benjamin's Paris, his phantasmagoria of modernity, was a city of mirrors in whose smooth reflections people could continually study themselves, and in doing so, compare themselves to each other and to the commodified ideals they saw in the city's shopping districts.[3] Moreover, the use of these mirrors as lighting devices appeared to bring the external world safely into the interior: "Where doors and walls are made of mirrors, there is no telling outside from in" [R1,3/537]. Elsewhere, Benjamin would emphasize that mirrors and other lighting devices would ultimately banish the exterior entirely. "Actually, in the arcades it is not a matter of illuminating the interior space, as in other forms of iron construction, but of *damping* the exterior space" [R1a,7/539; italics added]. This expansion of mirrored enclaves, protected from the outside and affirming the value of consumerist identity (and discipline), would almost inevitably evolve into that icon of modern urbanity known as the department store.

The rise of the department store reflected improvements in mass production, rail transportation, and large-scale accounting practices, evoking a world of consumption under one domesticated roof. Although some debate the identity of the "first" department store, most historians trace the roots of this form to Paris' *Au Bon Marché* (Clausen, 1985). As a predecessor for the department stores that would follow, *Au Bon Marché* appealed to a growing middle-class sensibility of conspicuous consumption.[4] When its assemblage of galleries of departments was collected into a city block-wide building, begun in 1869 and completed in 1887, *Au Bon Marché* offered its consumers an international exhibition of shopping, one whose iron and glass structures called forth endless vistas of consumer choice.[5] In these spaces, "The floors form a single space. They can be taken in, so to speak, 'at a glance' " [A3,5/40].[6] In *Au Bonheur Des Dames*, Émile Zola (2001/1883) used *Au Bon Marché* as a model for his literary department store and described how that endless interior represented the modern (and, to him, *feminized*) convergence of faith and commerce:[7]

> Space had been gained everywhere, air and light entered freely, and the public wandered around at ease beneath the bold vaults of the widely spaced trusses. It was a cathedral of modern trade, light yet solid, designed for a congregation of lady customers. (p. 231)

In places like *Au Bon Marché*, momentary visitors would become long-term inhabitants, training themselves to adapt to the modern ethos of endless, passive consumption: "taking it all in."

The department store offered a uniquely modern enclave of endless interiors and forgotten boundaries. In this way, department stores continued the evolution of consumer spaces inspired by the arcades, gathering together various specialty shops that had previously been segmented into walls and districts. The department store as a city, inhabited by shopping *flâneurs* who wander avenues of desire, leads inevitably to the department store as a world unto itself. Some viewed this world as the setting for a genuine improvement in the human condition. Most famously, Bradford Peck's (1900) utopian novel *The World a Department Store* proposed that the benefits of corporate society, presumably the decline in wasteful competition and painful alienation, could be easily secured "by the simple removal of the roof and the walls ...." (p. 243).[8] Rather than attempting to build utopia, however, most owners of department stores sought less ambitious goals: to draw customers into their confines by rendering the act of shopping as an extension and simulacrum of urban life without the grime, dust, and danger of the city.[9]

The 20th-century malls that replaced or enclosed their department store predecessors perfected the art of building tiny worlds to serve as surrogates for the real one. Well-known examples such as the Mall of America and West Edmonton Mall could transform the banal act of shopping into an adventure comprising amusement park-style rides and themed environments that worked to draw a version of the "outside" inward. Before the rise of the malls, however, international expositions and world's fairs offered grand views of public life that managed to be both expansive and enclosed. Let us now visit those "crystal palaces" imagined by the designers of the great fairs. Doing so, we find that these spectacles provide "worlds in miniature," enclaves against a range of natural and social threats.

World's Fairs as Enclaves of Civilization

Although I focus mostly on the 1939–1940 New York World's Fair, it is necessary to provide some historical context from earlier fairs. Initially, we should recall that international exhibitions and world's fairs arose from earlier national expositions, starting with the first industrial exposition held in Paris in 1798, the *Exposition Publique des Produits de L'industrie Française*.[10] These exhibitions would prove useful to affirming national character, not to mention the values of an industrial economy (Harvey, 1990). France, for example, employed national expositions to prove its stability after almost a decade of revolutionary turmoil and to define itself as an industrial power on par with Britain. Inspired by the French example, Prince Albert called for an even more ambitious plan five decades later: to gather together all the industrialized nations of the world for a display of empire that would define the frontiers of civilization as imagined by a European (and specifically British) vision (Philips, 2004). The resulting 1851 *Great Exhibition of the Industry of All Nations* attracted 6 million visitors to a display of architectural confidence and nationalist fervor:

> [I]t has been reserved for England to provide an arena for the exhibition of the industrial triumphs of the whole world. She has offered an hospitable invitation to surrounding nations to bring the choicest products of their industry to her capital, and there to enter into an amicable competition with each other and with herself; and she has endeavored to secure to them the certainty of an impartial verdict on their efforts. (cited in Blake, 1995, p. ix)

Surely the most significant architectural aspect of the 1851 Exhibition was its Crystal Palace. Designed by Joseph Paxton as a winter garden, the Crystal Palace gathered the grand exhibition within a huge structure of prefabricated iron and glass upon London's Hyde Park. One can fairly argue that the Crystal Palace was a grander version of the arcades found throughout Europe. Similarly, one can find public responses to the Palace's ability to manipulate nature to human ends or to eliminate nature altogether. It should be added that the building's placement drew concern from lovers of the elm groves that would presumably be removed for sake of the Palace: "But anxious onlookers soon raised a cry of alarm lest these trees be sacrificed for the sake of a whim. 'Then I shall roof over the trees,' was Paxton's answer . . ." (cited in Benjamin, 2004, G6; G6a,1/183). Like the arcade, the Crystal Palace promised a roof. But this time, the roof would cover the whole "civilized" world.

Here, one must remember that the enclavic sensibilities of 19th- and 20th-century world's fairs could *suggest* the potential for a world without frontiers. They could not eliminate the real divides that they exacerbated. For this reason, Frederick Douglass, Ida B. Wells, Ferdinand L. Barnett, and others protested racial exclusions of the 1893 World's Columbian Exposition. Writing in a pamphlet entitled *The Reason Why the Colored American is not in the World's Columbian Exposition*, Barnett offered a powerful indictment of the Fair's hidden borders: "Theoretically open to all Americans, the Exposition practically is, literally and figuratively, a 'White City,' in the building of which the Colored American was allowed no helping hand, and in its glorious success he has no share" (cited in Rydell, 1999, pp. 79–90; see also Wood, 2004). Women also faced a strict border at the Columbian Exposition. Although wealthy White women were assigned their own building, they were told that the collective art, literature, and handwork of all women would be relegated to a pavilion said to cost less than the Golden Door of the Exposition's transportation building (Miller, 1893). For those on the margins of 1893's self-proclaimed nexus of civilization, the totality of its "world" was no more than a mockery of its own rhetoric of inclusion.

Nonetheless, the 20th-century era of world's fairs and expositions continued to collect, refine, and package "civilization." One of these, the 1939–1940 New York World's Fair, provides a salient site to undertake our exploration of contemporary urbanity. Visited by an estimated 45 million people in its two seasons, the New York World's Fair helped to popularize notions of urban design and technological innovation that would seep into popular culture in ways subtle and grand. This fair added a component of time to the racial and gendered exclusions of previous fairs by casting itself as an enclave of the future. Especially in its first season, the fair promised a blueprint for "Building the World of Tomorrow With the Tools of Today." Within its confines, distinct from the surrounding challenges of a nation still emerging from the Great Depression, yet facing war clouds on both shores, "tomorrow" became a protected enclave. Ironically, the potential of that future resided atop a former dump that readers of F. Scott Fitzgerald's *The Great Gatsby* recall being named the valley of ashes. Within two of its most popular and memorable exhibits, the Theme Center's Democracity and General Motors' Futurama, the fair demonstrated the potential of the enclave to demarcate a spatial and temporal site that resided apart from the world beyond.

Democracity

Located at the heart of the 1,216-acre fairgrounds, Democracity presented a diorama of suburban living set within an awe-inspiring spectacle of light, sound, and miniature design envisioned by theatrical and industrial designer Henry Dreyfuss. The display was placed within the 180-foot diameter Perisphere,[11] which along with the 610-foot-tall Trylon marked the fair's focal exhibit of the "world of tomorrow."[12] Visitors entered the Democracity exhibit after ascending an escalator and stepping onto one of two elevated balconies that rotated slowly around the edges of the Perisphere's interior. Looking below, they gazed on an ordered metropolis ringed with satellite farmland, mill towns, and bedroom communities of the year 2039. As visitors revolved around its perimeter, changing hues would suggest that day and night passed over the city within 6 minutes ("City of Tomorrow," 1939). As a climax, lights would then project 10 groups of people along the inside of the great sphere, farmers, artisans, industrial workers, and others, showing them expand in size. At the same time, a musical chorus would mount toward a majestic crescendo. The show concluded in a blaze of

Image 3: 1939–40 New York World's Fair Theme Center. *Author's Collection*

illumination and sound, after which visitors would exit the display, walking down the curving Helicline ramp that snaked around the Perisphere to savor an aerial view of the fairgrounds.

Democracity presented the lessons of the arcades and department stores that preceded it on a grand scale. In fact, a booklet for sale at the Perisphere celebrated the presence of covered passages in their futuristic city as proof of the planners' ability to offer safety from nature: "The arcades are a blessing on very sunny days or in sudden squalls. Democracity hasn't managed to manage the weather ... but it can cope with it" (Seldes, 1939, "Balance Sheet" section, n.p.).[13] Beyond mere protection from the elements, Democracity illustrated how careful engineering and rational planning could encapsulate the entire world within one frame, transcending mere enclosure to imagine the potential for a liberating enclave: "On one side is the World of Tomorrow, built by millions of free men and women, independent and interdependent. ... On the other side is chaos . . ." (Seldes, 1939, "The Vision in the Sky" section, n.p.). On the eve of the Second World War, the need to craft this enclave was more than mere flourish. The fears stoked by totalitarians in Europe and Asia had become palpable.

In contrast to those fears of impending war, Democracity offered the illusion that the world, all of it that mattered anyway, could be captured through clever manipulation of lighting and perspective. The 1939 *Official Guide Book* enthused about the Perisphere's ability to recreate a world within the world, recalling unintentionally Walter Benjamin's insight into the role of mirrors in the fantasy construction of urban life:

> Here is the magnificent spectacle of a luminous world, apparently suspended in space by gushing fountains of liquid reds and blues and greens, over which clings a strange ethereal mist. An ingenious arrangement of mirror casings on which eight groups of fountains continuously play make the supporting columns invisible; while at night powerful lights project cloud patterns on the globe and wreathing it in color mist, create the startling illusion that it is revolving like a great planet on its axis. (pp. 43–44)

Designer Henry Dreyfuss was passionate in his belief that Democracity could point the way to a world without the social ills that afflicted his age. His enclavic city represented a frontier one would never wish to cross.

> [M]any of our modern ills, due to man's furious attempts at escape, will be eliminated in coming generations. Living in a spacious world, filled with beautiful and useful things, Man of Tomorrow will be a happy, healthy animal. Today we are born into a shell and we spend our lives fitting ourselves to it. In the World of Tomorrow *we will build a shell* to fit our lives. (Duffus, 1938, p. 23; italics added)

   The nature of this shell would be unlike any boundary previously imagined. It would not be marked by a wall, but by the impossibility of walls. Dreyfuss explained: "Now while the exterior of a sphere looks exactly like a sphere, the interior of a sphere when one stands within *it looks like nothing at all*—walls, ceiling and floor are of one surface and one appears to be standing in infinite space" ("Magic Carpet," 1938, p. 12; italics added). Democracity, that magnificent defense against chaos, both natural and human, signified the possibility of a perfect enclave whose frontiers would be all-powerful because they could no longer be seen. In this manner, Democracity offered an appeal that would find remarkable similarity with an exhibit just behind the Trylon and Perisphere, beyond the Grand Central Parkway: General Motors' "Highways and Horizons" pavilion and its glorious Futurama.

Futurama

The General Motors pavilion sought to inspire its visitors to reconsider the nature of urban life by positioning effective car and highway design at the center of an improved civilization, most notably in its famed Futurama exhibit, a world of tomorrow set within the world of 1939–1940. Conceived by Norman Bel

Image 4: General Motors Futurama. *Courtesy General Motors Media Archives*

Geddes,[14] Futurama placed its viewers in seats on a sophisticated conveyer belt that wound along a series of dioramas that approximated a tour of urban life in the year 1960, a flying journey covering hundreds of miles over mountains and lakes, towns, and cities:

> A vast countryside, drenched in blinding sunlight appeared. Far-flung orchards, rich with white blossoms; great patches of land under cultivation, but not yet in fruit; towering hillsides, tiny farmhouses, magnificent roads—all held the guests spellbound. Automobiles moved swiftly up and down the great ribbons of highway, the sun striking fire from their polished tops. ("Fair Visitors," 1939, p. 17)

The illusion required the gathering and building of 1,000,000 miniature trees, 500,000 miniature buildings, and 50,000 miniature automobiles in its first iteration (Kaempffert, 1939). Futurama was bold, daring, and unapologetic in its optimism.

As a multimedia convergence of high-minded education and corporate jingoism, Futurama was the most popular attraction at the fair.[15] Visitors sometimes waited for hours to see the exhibit of an ambitious interstate highway system.[16] Aided by tiny speakers embedded in the blue velour seats, visitors witnessed a remarkable narrative: a world of radar-controlled cars, auto-gyros, and airports that floated on pools of liquid. Listening to a taped announcer who whispered in their ears, visitors gasped and giggled at the audacious show: "Strange? Fantastic? Unbelievable? Remember, this is the world of 1960!" Most astoundingly, at the conclusion of the ride, visitors exited to a full-sized Metropolis of Tomorrow and saw, if but for a fleeting moment, the realization of the General Motors promise of better things to come.[17] As with Democracity, Futurama employed an enclavic sensibility that both delineated and eliminated horizons.

To understand that sensibility, we should investigate the Futurama exhibit in more detail. We begin as its visitors did, after waiting in long and sunburned lines that seemed endless: entering the lobby room at last. This room displayed a map and presented a recorded lecture of the failures of the 30s-era interstate highway system, of traffic tie-ups that cost money, time, and lives. No doubt, visitors who queued for hours in the human traffic jam that surrounded the Highways and Horizons building were primed to hear this message. Government support and visionary planning were needed to begin an ambitious building program of roads, bridges, and city-bypassing highways that would free America from gridlock and inspire an explosion of economic and social benefits. Although the message was compelling, the room was even more evocative as an endless open space, one whose horizons could hardly be imagined. An exhibit prospectus explained:

[T]his great Map Lobby is in subdued twilight. Its character is that of great solemnity. Everything has been done to *keep the spectator from realizing* that he [sic] is within a room at all. The gray blue tone of it helps this impression as does the fact that the walls widen out from him [sic] both in plan and section. They appear to be spreading away from him into space. (cited in Coombs, 1971, p. 15; italics added)

One may recall here Henry Dreyfuss' similar description of the interior of his Democracity "shell," whose boundaries look "like nothing at all."

Departing the Map Room, visitors entered smaller shells for their journey into a corporate future. Doubtless, these two-seater "cars" inspired some visitors to view Futurama as more of a "dark ride" than as a tour of tomorrow.[18] Adams (1976) recalls: "This physical space induced an ease and relaxation otherwise impossible in public. Each visitor participated in what seemed to be a highly personal presentation" (p. 22). Nonetheless, once visitors took their seats and began to "fly" over the countryside of 1960, they witnessed the glories of the promised interstate highway system. This advertisement for General Motors (and appeal for public support of private enterprise) drew from the modern fears of urban life and responded with an assurance that the efficient motorways of tomorrow would help clean up the cities and protect their citizens within their own little cocoons. In case some unpleasantness managed to survive the urban renewal, the threats produced by bad planning could be bypassed with little difficulty: "Whenever possible the rights of way of these express city thoroughfares have been so routed as to displace outmoded business sections and undesirable slum areas" (*Futurama* [pamphlet], 1940, n.p.). The world of tomorrow would be simultaneously grand and limiting, an intoxicating combination for a worried populous.

One gathers from period reviews of the exhibit that Bel Geddes succeeded in creating a compelling visit to the world of tomorrow. This is not to say that people in the '30s were dupes. They saw through Futurama right away and even shamed designers to adjust the ride by pointing out missing details, such as places of worship.[19] But the pleasure of the ride was not in its depiction of the future, but rather in its promise of passivity. One could watch the experts at work, confident that someone had a plan for tomorrow. One could take it all in "at a glance" as Benjamin cited in his *Arcades Project*. This pleasure of watching, the gaze that offers no rebuke, produced a guilty pleasure in even the most assured commentators. E. B. White (1939) admitted as much in a *New Yorker* essay:

When night falls in the General Motors exhibit and you lean back in the cushioned chair (yourself in motion and the world so still) and hear (from the depths of the chair) the soft electric assurance of a better life—the life which rests on wheels alone—there is a strong, sweet poison which infects the blood. I didn't want to wake up. (p. 26)

This "sweet poison," the whispering of the authority's voice from the plush confines of a moving chair, the selling of a tomorrow built by the automobile industry, and the distribution of jaunty blue and white buttons that announced "I have seen the future" all promised an enclavic sensibility that would replace the old frontier with new highways and horizons.

Leaving the Fair: The American Common and the Closing Days

Democracity and Futurama were the best-known enclaves of the 1939–1940 New York World's Fair. But the fair was also a welcome enclave against the growing fears of war oversees. In a symbolic note, fair planners constructed an "American Common" in 1940 on the spot where the Soviet Pavilion stood in the previous season, before the Soviets signed their nonaggression pact with Germany and invaded Finland. The Soviet Pavilion had been noted (and sometimes mocked) for a towering statue of a socialist worker hoisting a red star, which was razed after the USSR withdrew from the fair (Swift, 1998). In its place, and in light of the fair's budgetary woes, planners settled for a grand lawn, on which they erected a bandstand and hoisted an American flag (Shalett, 1940). Each week during that latter season, the American Common hosted a "fair within the fair," meant to symbolize the nation's careful balance of individuality and cohesion.[20] But exposition vice president Robert D. Kohn emphasized that the American Common was designed to inspire patriotism above all other considerations: "Participation in this program by people whose origins . . . are in countries now at war does not in any way ally the program with any foreign government. The American Common is only for American citizens with American ideals and political beliefs" ("Folk Fetes," 1940, p. 19). Kohn's reference to war served as evidence that the world's fair was an enclave against the violence that had begun to engulf the globe.[21] For that reason, a *World's Fair 1940* pamphlet advertised: "This summer you can go 'abroad at home'—safely, comfortably—along peaceways that emphasize brotherhood, not bombs" (n.p.). The fair's second season, anchored by such grim optimism, closed in October 27, 1940.[22] Fourteen months later, the United States entered the Second World War.[23]

Conclusion

Exiting 19th-century arcades and department stores and passing through 20th-century gates of international expositions and world's fairs, we cannot help but look back on these mammoth assemblages with some degree of nostalgia. These enclaves demonstrated a modern confidence that humankind could protect itself from the threats of natural and social disorder. Starting with grand partitions of iron and glass and stretching to capture the entire world within audacious frames, they reflected what David Gelernter (1995) termed an Age of Authority: a belief that experts and planners could lead the world to better times. From the other side of the conflagrations that followed, both in the 20th century and in our present Age of Anxiety, such a spirit may be dismissed as worse than mere wishful thinking. It may be termed *hubris*. However, one cannot fairly claim that we have departed entirely from our enclavic sensibility. We find today ample evidence that we still believe it possible to see the entire world without ever visiting it, to live instead within the omnitopian enclave. Despite our best instincts (and even best interests), many of us continue our search for spaces that connect us, even if they only elicit a shopper's view of public life. All too frequently, the interactions they follow are fleeting and transitory, our mementos merely souvenirs of a life we never lived.

When we excavate more deeply into the 1939–1940 New York World's Fair, beyond its promise of a consumer's utopia, we inevitably reach the interstate highway system. Doing so, we travel from relatively simple arcade-department store enclaves to the more totalizing enclosures found in the airports, hotels, and malls of today. I believe that the highway offers that structural and perceptual link between these nodes. To that end, I propose a brief exploration of the rhetorical distinction between the "traveler" and the "tourist" as a lens on the history of interstate mobility. This study reveals the popularization of the road as a "place," not merely a means of transit, a place that detaches the tourist from meaningful (and potentially threatening) encounters with "others," even as it promises genuine opportunities for social interaction. Like the Perisphere and Futurama, the interstate appears as a world unto itself. Like these world's fair progenitors, it enables us to bypass the world we once called "real."

Notes

1. Walter Benjamin died after an arduous climb over the Pyrenees, fleeing Vichy France. A German Jew who had already endured a concentration camp, Benjamin joined a small group immigrating to the United States. Although some historians debate the nature of his death, most believe that when Benjamin learned of his imminent return to France, he took a fatal overdose of morphine.

2. Rejecting the illusion of a "completed" textual history, Benjamin envisioned his project as a cinematic performance, opening its viewers to multiple and conflicting voices and stances: an approximation of urban life. Simon Gunn (2002) observes:

> Instead of the accumulation of empirical data and the analysis of cause and effect, he proposed a technique or method based on the idea of montage—hence, the assemblage of fragments of theory and concrete historical detail, quotation and interpretation, arranged on a principle of dis-association. (p. 265)

Mike Featherstone (1998) illustrates a common assertion about Benjamin's prescience, noting similarities between the "reading" *The Arcades Project* and clicking through the World Wide Web: "Were Benjamin alive today, one can speculate that his project could be more fully realised [sic] through hypertext and multimedia" (p. 910).

3. Benjamin extended the mirror motif to the city's interpersonal interactions: "Even the eyes of passersby are veiled mirrors, and over that wide bed of the Seine, over Paris, the sky is spread out like the crystal mirror hanging over the drab beds of the brothels" [R1,3/538].

4. Gail McDonald (2002) reminds us that, beyond their efforts to construct a high culture site of edification, where gentlemen could write correspondence and ladies might observe ethnographic exhibits, the primary purpose of the department store was to transform momentary visitors into long-term inhabitants:

> The department store invites *drift*: solid walls having been replaced by columns, the divisions between one department and the next are vague; wide aisles, like generous avenues, encourage movement along the lines of horizontal display cases and arouse flaneurlike observation of other shoppers; mirrored columns make self-scrutiny easier and, at the same time, multiply one's focus and desire. (p. 233; italics original)

5. In describing *Au Bon Marché*, Clausen (1985) expands on the link between department stores and international exhibitions:

> The new building's vast all glass-iron interior was loaded with associations. It recalled the glazed shopping arcade of the 1820s and 1830s, so too the soaring spaces of the glass exhibition hall. It drew also upon memories of the 1851 Crystal Palace, which had captured the public imagination with its light, space, and scale, or more recently Eiffel's *Galerie des Machines* at the 1867 Paris Exposition. It carried their aura of technological progress and generated the same excitement of festival or fair. (p. 24)

6. Here, Benjamin quotes from Sigfried Giedion's 1928 treatise on French architecture, *Bauen in Frankreich: Bauen in Eisen, Bauen in Eisenbeton* (*Building in France: Building in Iron, Building in Concrete*).

7. *Au Bonheur des Dames* tells the story of Denise Baudu, who makes her way to Paris after being orphaned back home. Seeking employment in her uncle's shop, she discovers that his business, as well as other small firms throughout the city, is being throttled by the emergence of a new kind of department store that gathers all manner of wares under one vast roof. Eschewing the kind of specialization that is the hallmark of the family business, Au Bonheur des Dames is the Wal-Mart of its day. The novel follows Denise's transformation from gullible, provincial waif to confident and courageous young woman, an evolution marked by her eventual conquest of the heart of the store's owner. Although ostensibly concerned with whether Denise can keep her honor and dignity amid the treacherous social environment of the store, *Au Bonheur des Dames* introduces its readers to the transformation of Paris in the era of Haussmannization.

8. Sadly, Bradford Peck's attempt to form a cooperative commonwealth along the lines of his book proved to be fruitless, largely due to his own struggles with egalitarianism: Cary (1977) notes: "Some of the cooperators chafed at Peck's authoritarianism and resented the fact that members did not democratically control the Association. Peck, it appears, attempted to conduct the Cooperative Association as he had run his store, where he headed a definite hierarchy of functionaries" (p. 382).

9. Intriguingly, Susan Sontag (2001) drew from the world-as-department store in her description of the touristic value of photography: "Whatever the moral claims made on behalf of photography, its main effect is to convert the world into a department store or museum-without-walls in which every subject is depreciated into an article of consumption, promoted into an item for aesthetic appreciation" (p. 110).

10. Carpenter (1972) recalls notable predecessors to the 1798 exhibition, including a 1683 inventions-only exhibition held in Paris and a 1754 industrial exposition held in Vienna. Carpenter adds that expositions prior to 1798 "do not seem to have amounted to much, either in size or in public interest, if, indeed, they were open to the public" (p. 466).

11. The 1939 *Official Guide Book* offered further illustration of the Perisphere's mammoth size: "Never before in history has man undertaken to build a globe of such tremendous proportions. Eighteen stories high, it is as broad as a city block, its interior more than twice the size of Radio City Music Hall" (p. 43). Even so, planners found they could not complete the sphere at its planned diameter of 200 feet. Similarly, they had to settle for a Trylon that stood 90 feet shorter than its original planned height of 700 feet.

12. The theme center became an instantly recognizable icon on par with the most successful commercial images of the decade ("Perisphere draws crowds," 1939). Nonetheless, although the geometrical simplicity of the Trylon and Perisphere offered a bold exemplar of 30s-era high modern style, some observers noted similarities between the 1939 Theme Center and the 1853 New York World's Fair building, which was known for its dome-capped Crystal Palace and neighboring triangular observatory tower ("Theme of 1853 Fair," 1939).

13. The transformation of the metropolis by way of arcades was, by this time, a well-established trope. For example, in the hugely influential Regional Plan of New York, a committee reported its vision of a city whose pedestrians and motorists would occupy separate worlds within the world:

> We see a city with sidewalks, arcaded *within the building lines*, and one story above the present street grade. We see bridges at all corners, the width of the arcades and with solid railings. We see the smaller parks of the city . . . raised to this same sidewalk-arcade level . . . and the whole aspect becomes that of a very modernized Venice, a city of arcades, plazas and bridges, with canals for streets, only the canal will not be filled with water but with freely flowing motor traffic, the sun glittering on the black tops of the cars and the buildings reflecting in this waving flood of rapidly rolling vehicles. (Adams, 1931, pp. 308–309; italics original).

In this future New York City, "Walking would become a pastime. . . . Shopping would be a joy" (Adams, 1931, p. 309).

14. Democracity creator Henry Dreyfuss apprenticed under Bel Geddes until 1924.

15. Soon after the fair opened, the American Institute of Public Opinion reported that Futurama was the fair's most popular exhibit, followed by the Theme Center's Democracity exhibit ("Futurama is voted the most popular," 1939).

16. *New York Times* columnist Meyer Berger (1939, June 7) provided ample illustration of the suffering endured by many who queued to enter the Futurama:

> If you have stood for hours on the ramps leading to the General Motors Futurama show, toasting in the sun, you will understand why a choleric old fellow blew up yesterday and bought himself a spot way up front of the line for $5 cash. Here, it seems to us, is the germ of an idea for some enterprising fellow who wants to get tanned and make some money at the same time. (p. 12)

The line cutter's payment is best contemplated when compared with the cost of an all-day ticket: 75 cents (in the 1939 season; that price was dropped to 50 cents in 1940).

17. Documents from the period list the ride as taking between 15 and 17 minutes.

18. Meyer Berger (1939, May 4) described the Futurama's unexpected use as a make-out spot: "[T]he seventeen-minute ride in the soft double-chairs ... is The World of Tomorrow's greatest gift to the gob of today. The sailors and their sweethearts do this ride over and over again. 'There's a special kick,' one of them explained, 'in stepping into the chairs in 1939 and to keep on necking right into 1960.' The ride is dimly lighted" (p. 18).

19. Meyer Berger (1940, April 9) described the addition of worship places in the fair's second season: "They built and set down in the towns and cities something like 600 new churches because clergymen had written in, chidingly, that the Futurama world of 1960 was a godless world—not enough houses of worship" (p. 24).

20. The 1940 *Official Guide Book* affirmed: "Within its boundaries you find the greatest variety of racial strains getting along with each other and living at peace. This is evident despite curious divergences of dialect, social organization, blood and economic interest that exist in the 48 states" (p. 14).

21. Describing a plan to hold simultaneous divine services at the pavilions of nations engaged in the opening salvos of the European war, *New York Times* reporter Milton Bracker (1940) noted, "The impossibility of isolating the world of tomorrow ... from the grimmest aspect of the world of today" (p. 24).

22. Meyer Berger (1940, October 28) recalled the sad last day of the Futurama exhibit: "Bob Murray, who was Lord of Creation in G. M.'s Futurama, fought back the tears when his show went dark. Mr. Murray and his crew were the last to ride in the Futurama chairs. They left with bridges and trees in their pockets for souvenirs" (p. 10).

23. The fair closed at a loss of almost $19 million: "No funds were left to complete Robert Moses's planned improvements to Flushing Meadows Park, and the fair's structures, including the Trylon and Perisphere, were torn down and their scrap steel was donated to the war effort" (Rydell, Findling, & Pelle, 2000, p. 96).

References

Adams, D. (1976). Norman Bel Geddes and streamlined spaces. *Journal of Architectural Education, 30*(1), 22–24.

Adams, T. (1931). *The building of the city: Regional plan: Vol. 2.* New York: Regional Plan Association.

Benjamin, W. (2004). *The arcades project* (H. Eiland & K. McLaughlin, Trans.). Cambridge, MA: Harvard University Press.

Berger, M. (1939, May 4). At the fair. *New York Times*, p. 18.

Berger, M. (1939, June 7). At the fair yesterday. *New York Times*, p. 12.

Berger, M. (1940, April 9). About New York. *New York Times*, p. 24.

Berger, M. (1940, October 28). At the fair. *New York Times*, p. 10.

Blake, G. P. (1995). *The great exhibition: A facsimile of the illustrated catalogue of London's 1851 Crystal Palace Exposition.* Avenel, NJ: Gramercy Books.

Bracker, M. (1940, May 23). All allies to pray at fair on Sunday; joint services for safety of their countrymen to be held in pavilions. *New York Times*, p. 24.

Carpenter, K. E. (1972). European industrial exhibitions before 1851 and their publications. *Technology and Culture, 13*(3), 465–486.

Cary, F. C. (1977). The world a department store: Bradford Peck and the utopian endeavor. *American Quarterly, 29*(4), 370–384.

City of tomorrow shown in sphere. (1939, April 27). *New York Times*, p. 20.

Clausen, M. L. (1985). The department store: Development of the type. *Journal of Architectural Education, 39*(1), 20–29.

Coombs, R. (1971). Norman Bel Geddes: Highways and horizons. *Perspecta, 13*, 11–27.

Duffus, R. L. (1938, December 18). A city of tomorrow; a new design of life design for a city of tomorrow. *New York Times Magazine*, pp. 4–5, 23.

Fair visitors "fly" over U.S. of 1960. (1939, April 19). *New York Times*, p. 17.

Featherstone, M. (1998). *The flâneur*, the city and virtual public space. *Urban Studies, 35*(5–6), 909–925.

Folk fetes to use Soviet site at fair; series of bazaars and fiestas to stress Americanism of groups of foreign origin. (1940, March 8). *New York Times*, p. 19.

Foucault, M. (1994). *The order of things: An archeology of the human sciences* (A. Sheridan, Trans.). New York: Vintage.

Futurama [pamphlet]. (1940). General Motors Corporation.

Futurama is voted the most popular. (1939, May 17). *New York Times*, p. 19.

Gelernter, D. (1995). *1939: The lost world of the fair.* New York: The Free Press.

Gunn, S. (2002). City of mirrors: *The Arcades Project* and urban history. *Journal of Victorian Culture, 7*(2), 263–275.

Harvey, D. (1990). *The condition of postmodernity: An enquiry into the origins of cultural change.* Malden, MA: Blackwell.

Kaempffert, W. (1939, September 10). Magic carpet in Futurama; seeing the world of tomorrow from a chair train. *New York Times*, p. D8.

Kracauer, S. (1995). *The mass ornament: Weimer essays* (T. Y. Levin, Trans.). Cambridge: Harvard University Press.

Magic carpet to take visitors into the world of tomorrow. (1938, July 27). *New York Times*, p. 12.

McDonald, G. (2002). The mind a department store: Reconfiguring space in the gilded age. *Modern Language Quarterly, 63*(2), 227–249.

Miller, F. F. (1893). Art in the woman's section of the Chicago exhibition. *Art Journal, 55*, xiii–xvi.

Official guide book of the New York world's fair. (1939). New York: Exposition Publications.

Official guide book: The world's fair of 1940 in New York. (1940). New York: Rogers-Kellogg-Stillson.

Peck, B. (1900). *The world a department store: A story of life under a coöperative system.* Lewiston, ME: Bradford Peck.

Perisphere draws crowds on first day. (1939, May 1). *New York Times*, p. 2.

Philips, D. (2004). Stately pleasure domes—nationhood, monarchy and industry: The celebration exhibition in Britain. *Leisure Studies, 23*(2), 95–108.

Rydell, R. W. (Ed.). (1999). *The reason why the Colored American is not in the World's Columbian exposition: The Afro-American's contribution to Columbian literature.* Urbana: University of Illinois Press.

Rydell, R. W., Findling, J. E., & Pelle, K. D. (2000). *Fair America: World's fairs in the United States.* Washington, DC: Smithsonian Institution Press.

Seldes, G. (1939). *Your world of tomorrow.* New York: Rogers-Kellogg-Stillson.

Shalett, S. M. (1940, January 2). "People's" common dedicated at fair; opening fashion building at the fair. *New York Times*, p. 43.

Sieburth, R. (1988). Benjamin the scrivener. *Assemblage, 6*, 6–23.

Sontag, S. (2001). *On photography.* New York: Picador USA.

Swift, A. (1998). The Soviet world of tomorrow at the New York World's Fair, 1939. *The Russian Review, 57*(3), 364–379.

Theme of 1853 fair recalled in exhibit. (1939, March 19). *New York Times*, p. 59.

Urry, J. (2002). *The tourist gaze: Leisure and travel in contemporary societies* (2nd ed.). London: Sage.

White, E. B. (1939, May 13). They come with joyous song. *The New Yorker*, pp. 25–28.

Wood, A. (2004). Managing the Lady Managers: The shaping of heterotopian spaces in the 1893 Chicago exposition's Woman's Building. *Southern Communication Journal, 69*(4), 289–302.

World's fair 1940 [pamphlet]. (1940). New York: New York World's Fair Corporation.

Zola, E. (2001/1883). *Au bonheur des dames* (R. Buss, Trans.). New York: Penguin Classics.

2

Construction

When we get these thruways across the whole country, as we will and must, it will be possible to drive from New York to California without seeing a single thing.

—John Steinbeck (2002, p. 70)

Today you can survey the grounds of the 20th-century New York World's Fairs and imagine, if only fleetingly, that its fantasy version of tomorrow continues to endure. Using satellite imagery through a virtual globe program such as Google Earth, you can visit landmarks from both the 1939–1940 and 1964–1965 iterations of the fair (the New York City Building from 1939, the Unisphere from 1964, and a few others), and you can overlay memories of those fairs atop the inevitably more pedestrian pleasures of Flushing Meadows Corona Park, which occupies the current-day fairgrounds. But use your mental (or computational) software to zoom upward, expanding your vision to enclose the triborough region, and zooming upward further still to grasp the snaking lines of the Eastern Seaboard, and you'll spot perhaps the most enduring memento of those great fairs: the interstate highway system. This communication network carries messages about a new kind of mobility even as it carries passengers and cargo between distant cities.

The 1939–1940 New York World's Fair contributed significantly to an evolving belief that viewed interstate travel as being synonymous with progress. The endless ribbons of highway, promising an all-weather corridor from coast to coast, signaled the death of the frontier. One could no longer imagine places in America only accessible to adventurers. The open road, typically emphasizing the word *road* even as the key to that phrase was the word *open*, would help Americans cast off their provincial small-town ways, even as it meant freedom from urban labyrinths. The interstate did not lead "no place"; it was no utopia even in the most literal sense. It created a place all its own that could not be named as easily as a locale, but it existed all the same. This "place" called for an entirely new sensibility, portending a remarkable transformation in human affairs.

Naturally, such an optimistic vision would take root in a 1930s-era world's fair before coming to fruition in the 1940s and 1950s. The 1933–1934 Chicago Century of Progress Exposition showcased new age technological improvements that would free people from drudgery. The 1939–1940 New York World's Fair extended that vision to create a fantasy vision of a utopian technocracy in which people could live, *would* live, upon their collective adoption of a rational and modern worldview. To the public imagination, that new world would be found along the highway, thanks in large part to the advertising prowess of General Motors. The company's film *To New Horizons*, a cinematic companion piece to their Highways and Horizons exhibit, promised such improvement once the new interstates were built. The 1940 version of the film, one that accounted for churches and universities that were strangely absent from the 1939 version, assured its audiences that the death of the frontier did not herald the death of new horizons, but rather assured their inevitable crossing: "Our greatest strides in providing more things for more people have been made at a time when the influence of new geographical frontiers was about over." Banishing those frontiers, the interstate system championed by Futurama designer Norman Bel Geddes would bypass decaying city centers and connect disparate markets, stitching together a nation more united than its original planners could imagine. What's more, the most amazing fact of the exhibit could not be found among its outlandish visions of radio-controlled cars and airports that rotated on pools of liquid. No, the genuine achievement of the Highway and Horizons exhibit was how quickly its fantastic vision of tomorrow became the banal reality of today:

> Although many specifics of Geddes's design were never implemented in the Interstate Highway Act of 1956, there is no doubt that this project helped popularize the concept of the superhighway and build the foundation for the eventual construction of the largest public works project in history. (Fotsch, 2001, p. 67)

For GM, and shortly for America, the promise of the interstate highway offered "new horizons" of achievement, not so much a technocratic fantasy, but a practical reengineering of urban life to suit an age of mobility.[1]

The corporate purpose of this appeal can hardly be denied. Historians of both the Fair and the Interstate Highway System recall Walter Lippman's (1939) oft-quoted evaluation of GM's use of the Highways and Horizons exhibit to popularize their vision of an interstate system: "GM has spent a small fortune to convince the American public that if it wishes to enjoy the full benefit of private enterprise in motor manufacturing, it will have to rebuild its cities and highways by public enterprise" (p. 25). Many readers of this phrase, myself included at one point, have interpreted Lippman to be dismissing this boosterism as evidence of the supremacy of Big Business over the common good. However, David Gelernter (1995) reminds us that Lippman compared General Motors' rhetorical efforts to those of the various totalitarian regimes whose nations also exhibited their wares at the fair, and that Lippman found GM's "convincing" strategy to be far preferable to the less subtle techniques employed by the Soviet Union and Italy.[2] Despite the benefits that corporations would surely reap from the construction of a modern interstate system, this transportation innovation flowed from a broader reservoir of desire to travel freely and without constraint, an affiliation between movement and modernity.

The Pennsylvania Turnpike realized that promise first, demonstrating in practical terms what fairgoers saw at the Futurama exhibit—the dream of limited-access interstates that would criss-cross the continent, bypassing congested cities and bringing progress to the nation. In 1940, that dream was fixed in a concrete toll road: a (mostly) four-lane highway stretching 160 miles from Middlesex (west of Harrisburg) to Irwin (east of Pittsburgh). In terms of size and ambition, the Pennsylvania Turnpike was the first of its kind in the United States. No longer would motorists meander around curvy hills with limited sight distances. The Pennsylvania Turnpike promised broad roads, limited curves, and level grades. As a result, motorists could zip along straightaways at 100 miles per hour, if their tires could handle that speed. Patton (1997) explains that the Turnpike was

Portal and Tunnel on Pennsylvania Turnpike

"America's Super Highway"

Image 5: Pennsylvania Turnpike Postcard. *Author's Collection* built to accommodate automobiles that had not yet been built. As a result, this road became a symbol of tomorrow.

Designed in the waning days of the Depression, the Turnpike was primarily a make-work program, transforming old railroad grades and tunnels into the new super-highway project. One early Turnpike postcard reports that 51,345 "man years of direct and indirect employment" were dedicated to the road's construction. The Second World War halted extensions of the Pennsylvania Turnpike, but the idea had been fixed in the American consciousness. After the war, the United States saw an explosion of roadbuilding that culminated with the post-1956 interstate highway system and the subsequent rise of omnitopia. Roads like the Pennsylvania Turnpike transformed the United States, for good and for ill, into so much of what it is today, while representing a peculiar kind of enclavic practice that would fundamentally alter the meaning of "place" in contemporary life.

I believe it is useful to analyze historical, architectural, and rhetorical foundations on which the interstate highway became a place on itself, one that constructed a strange sort of community shared by automobilized strangers. The highway made it possible to imagine the United States as a singular place, rather than a collection of disparate towns, dialects, and classes. By highway, one could still visit local sites, but one began to view them as manifestations of a singular enclavic sensibility. This notion of enclave derives inspiration from John Stilgoe's (1998) book, *Outside Lies Magic*, in which he describes the oddly permeable yet strictly defined nature of the modern road:

> No fences, no gates, no guards keep trespassers from the enclave intended to serve travelers, but the cluster of businesses is every bit as much an enclave as the new residential developments sprouting everywhere in outer suburban regions. The cluster seems so patently, so insistently porous that travelers understand it only as something through which everyone passes, either staying on the interstate highway or exiting for a few minutes to fuel, for five minutes to use rest rooms and buy hamburgers-to-go, maybe for a night in a room one cannot remember a week later. (pp. 162–163)

A communication network no less important than the telegraph or telephone, the 20th-century interstate enacted a prototype for omnitopia along its ribbons of asphalt that reoriented the national identity further and further away from the frontier, both the edges of home and hearth and the horizon of one's potential life travels, and toward an expectation of ubiquity. On the highway, one could travel near or far and never know the difference. I presume that most readers are familiar with the post-1956 Eisenhower Interstate Highway system that serves the needs of commuters, vacationers, and truckers. I even imagine that the reader is somewhat familiar with the history of the interstate as a cold war network of limited-access highways designed to allow for the rapid movement of troops and *matériel* in case of war. I thereby have chosen to focus on the pre-1956 American highway. I begin with the 19th-century transition of tourism from an elite affectation to its 20th-century iteration as a popular rite, considering the implications of the transition in dominant mode of travel from train to auto, before concentrating on one manifestation of interstate-era architecture and design: the Greyhound bus terminal. I have chosen to focus on Greyhound because of the bus line's success in introducing autotouring to the mass public. The bulk of this inquiry addresses three strategies of pre-1956 Greyhound advertising that helped solidify that highway as a kind of place that helped construct the omnitopian sensibility that would follow.

From Train to Auto

In the United States and Europe, and in other industrialized regions around the world, a central aspect of the 19th- and early 20th-century eras was the increasing potential for ordinary people to detach themselves from their surroundings. According to Leo Marx (2000), the dialectic that defined this period was one of the machine and the garden. The machine represented the power of human technology to reshape the world in the image of humankind, cast out the demons of the wilderness, and reorient the cosmos around the ordered grid. It was well illustrated by the 19th-century locomotive and its potential to cut through and reshape the verdant land to its human-made purposes. Marx reads students of the American character, Henry Adams, John Stuart Mill, and Alexis de Tocqueville, and finds consensus among these thinkers about the power of the locomotive.

> A locomotive is a perfect symbol because its meaning need not be attached to it by a poet; it is inherent in its physical attributes. To see a powerful, efficient machine in the landscape is to know the superiority of the present to the past. (Marx, 2000, p. 192)

In contrast to the locomotive, the garden reflected the pastoral ideal, the cyclical return to home and hearth. The Edenic call for simplicity and innocence would be recast in parks and natural places still capable of inspiring sensations of awe, the humility of humanity faced with the sublime. The industrial world managed to craft some semblance of balance between the machine and the garden, especially in the development of suburbs and the associated designs of the garden city movement. But the locomotive demonstrated a profound re-creation of the natural world into an extension of human will. The late 19th- and early 20th century would augment this vision with the skyscraper, the luxury liner, and the airplane. But the train, depot, and rail line offer the essential model for the interstate highways that would eventually reign supreme over the American landscape, training its travelers to adopt a radically different pose of pseudopresence.

The train and its network of stations created an entirely artificial notion of place, one not restricted to the natural turns of rivers or even the natural obstructions of mountains.

> The railroad differed from any preceding form of travel. Not only did it comfortably convey larger numbers of people greater distances than ever before, but for the first time, people passed through a landscape yet did not necessarily engage it. . . . They became observers, not participants, willing or otherwise, in all that rolled by outside their train window. (Rothman, 1998, p. 39)

The train traveler could cross the continent in a world entirely separate from its pedestrian strife. Beyond its impact on the rider, the train also worked to transform the sites one might visit. As economic and conceptual maps began to become reconfigured to the lines on the train schedule, places existed insofar as trains could reach them conveniently; their accessibility became less a matter of their idiosyncratic charms and more a concern of standardized grades and gauges. As a result, the railroad played an integral part in the construction of post-Civil War America, most notably in the formation of cities. Upon the arrival of the railroad, cities became arranged in an economic and mythic hierarchy: those being closest to the main line were deemed to be more important and more prosperous than those located far from a depot. In the early 20th century, railroads continued to grow as a mass-market mechanism to move an increasingly large populous, but they would become bypassed by the introduction of the automobile as the primary means of transportation for most people.

The impact of the car on American culture, myth, and sociability is nothing less than total. One may imagine a medieval town navigated solely by foot. But one can hardly visit some 20th-century locales without the car; one can hardly imagine their *existence* without a car. The gasoline station, the motel, the drive-thru, and the drive-in theatre come quickly to mind, structures built to accommodate the automobile. The car changed our perceptions of place and mobility so perfectly because, unlike the train, it became woven into our daily lives. Consider one frequently cited claim: "As late as the turn of the twentieth century, which brought the Ford Model T, the overwhelming majority of Americans lived and died within twenty miles of their birthplace" (Bernstein, 2004, pp. 39–40). With the advent of the automobile (and the bus), greater numbers of people could join those hearty travelers who had previously blazed the paths they trod by assuming the identity of the *tourist*. With this pose, this gaze, one could consume the natural and human made as one would shop in a mall.

Differentiating the tourist from the traveler (or explorer) has been a perennial activity for scholars of modern mobility. The traveler may be viewed as a person who desires to know the world with a minimum of mediation; she or he becomes immersed in local culture, language, and cuisine, and she or he hopes to become renewed in the process. The tourist, in contrast, prefers a sanitized version of the world with a substantial degree of mediation; she or he consumes facsimiles of local culture, language, and cuisine, or simply avoids them by occupying artificial places built entirely for persons of similar inclination and privilege. Most important, the tourist economy forces local people and places to adapt themselves to the needs and stereotypes of the temporary visitor; the tourist returns home rested, perhaps, but fundamentally unchanged.

The literary and academic distinction between traveler and tourist, although intriguing, often demonstrates an ironic parochialism that rests on a class-based rebuke of the masses. Fussell (1980) exemplifies:

> What distinguishes the tourist is the motives, few of which are ever openly revealed: to raise social status at home and to allay social anxiety; to realize fantasies of erotic freedom; and most important, to derive secret pleasure from posing momentarily as a member of a social class superior to one's own, to play the role of a "shopper." ... The resemblance between the tourist and the client of a massage parlor is closer than it would be polite to emphasize. (p. 42)

The short-lived luxuries of the fake "grand tour" reduce the cultured exploits of genuine travelers to the tacky search for souvenirs: cheap postcards, gaudy

SEVEN MILE STRETCH ON LINCOLN HIGHWAY NEAR GRAND VIEW POINT LOOKOUT

Image 6: Lincoln Highway Postcard. *Author's Collection*

trinkets, and gluttonous meals. Tourists, so say their more cultured critics, do not wish to visit the world, but rather to inhabit a world of their own. Later on, we consider the possibility that the traveler/tourist dichotomy has suffered the same collapse of high/low culture that marks a late modern milieu. But for now, we might be satisfied to accept that "tourism" as a concept and practice exists, and that its performance contains meaningful implications for the relationship between a mobilizing people and the places they visit.

The automobile reaffirmed the detached nature of the tourist gaze in a manner that would have surprised its first enthusiasts, the wealthy motorists who saw the cross-country road trip as a grand adventure that required a daunting degree of independence, engineering prowess, and serendipity. With poorly designed and incomplete maps, often little more than laundry lists of directional turns and mileage markers, and a dearth of supporting businesses, early 20th-century motorists often were required to repair their own finicky machines, camp outdoors, and survive on their wits; they viewed themselves as travelers whose exploits were worthy of novelization. Belasco (1997) describes these auto-gypsies as carving freedom from the soul-crushing constraints of urban life. He also notes how the early 20th-century references to the car in various forms of popular culture (e.g., advertising, song lyrics, and mass-market fiction) offered a stirring rebuke of Standard Time imposed by railroads. The car and its driver (and often its hired mechanic) promised to connect the motorist to every twist and turn of the road, a means to actually go somewhere. Not confined by the rigid grid of rails, the motorist could set any number of passages from place to place. This newfound freedom, and the romantic association of auto-travel with genuine travel, would not last long, however.

With the addition of radios and cruise control, not to mention improvements in design and fuel efficiency, automobiles grew to resemble miniature railroad cars that carved through the landscape, providing a panoramic perspective while detaching their inhabitants from their surroundings: "The fast lane of the freeway thus turned into a space for meditation and roving minds, coupled with new types of visions made possible by General Motors' introduction of the panorama window" (Löfgren, 1999, p. 60). In this sense, we find a tourist enclave that previews visions of the omnitopia to come. Tourists would quickly eschew auto camps and choose instead the individualized cabin of the tourist court, requiring a brief exchange with the owner before settling into their "home away from home." Back on the freeway, the tourist would become trained to view others in traffic as obstacles to be avoided. From this perspective, one would no longer be forced (or even inclined) to know one's neighbors, and, if one did, the cause would rarely be a happy one. In this proto-omnitopia, touristic anonymity would become an exemplar for a revolutionary code of urban antisociability.

Beyond the automobile, the highway became a "place" whose apparatus of movement and dislocation became a destination unto itself. Being "on the road" would come to symbolize an American brand of pilgrimage, in which a specific destination would be secondary to the value of movement for its own sake. Yet for every Sal Paradise who rocketed down the two-lane searching for the perfect high of perpetual speed, millions of tourists would fantasize about the same road trip that would contain stops at "local" diners and overnight stays at "quirky" motels, each of which seemed to reproduce ersatz "memories" from the same mythical vision—a highway that strings together disparate touristic nodes into an endless mall of consumer exchanges. Daniel Boorstin (1992) illustrates:

> Now it is the very "improvements" in interstate superhighways . . . that enable us as we travel along to see nothing but the road. Motor touring has been nearly reduced to the emptiness of air travel. On land, too, we now calculate distances in hours, rather than in miles. We never know quite where we are. At home as well as abroad, travel itself has become a pseudo-event. (p. 114)

On the highway, middle- and working-class motorists became accustomed to the kind of mobility reserved to wealthier tourists, and they learned new rules of mobility. The value of a place would be defined less by its originality and more by its accessibility, less by its locality and more by its ubiquity. Certainly the 20th-century tourist would take photographs and jot "wish you were here" on penny postcards, but they increasingly found themselves in the same place wherever they went, and for a time they liked it. Understanding that value calls for us to study some manifestation of the early highway. We could stop at a local diner or pull up to a drive-in movie spot. But for my money, the Greyhound bus terminal provides a usefule place to continue our journey.

Greyhound Bus Terminals

As we have seen so far, the growth of American highways inspired a postvernacular architectural form, one in which consistency and standardization would represent a newly valued aesthetic. This is well exemplified by the Greyhound bus terminal. In its initial iterations, the Greyhound terminal represented the democratic potential of American mobility. In towns, large and small, the Greyhound, symbolized by a streamlined galloping canine, promised a one-way ticket for anyone looking for better prospects, journeying to visit a distant loved one, or simply overcome by wanderlust. The depots also offered a greasy spoon for late-night burger cravings, a chance to pick up a magazine, and long benches for late night slumber. Soldiers heading for war, families heading for a new life, and loners just passing through—pretty much everyone a generation ago spent some time in a bus terminal.

Since the early 20th century, Greyhound terminals and advertising have signified American mobility. Greyhound began in 1914, when Carl Eric Wickman charged 15 cents for miners who needed a lift between Hibbing and Alice, Minnesota. By 1927, bus travelers could cross the country in less than 6 days. Despite financial woes in the 1930s and 1940s, Greyhound became a globally respected brand that personified inexpensive travel throughout North America, its terminals, from simple signs posted on the walls of rural drug stores to huge urban stations, imbued with a kind of mystique as places of danger and opportunity. One could enter a terminal and meet anyone or go anywhere. Even so, despite the nostalgia woven by preservationists, Greyhound terminals were always simple, practical places. The terminals were designed around the comings and goings of large numbers of people waiting to start, continue, or conclude their journeys, as well as purchase tickets, buy newspapers, consume meals, and welcome visitors. These places could easily be viewed as examples of Marc Augé's non-places, manifestations of text with no personal or social context. One might visit "Cleveland" or "Cincinnati" or "Chicago." But one could hardly expect to be in a place. At a bus terminal, one is always just passing through. Like similar places built around the purpose of transit, these terminals were not intended to be remembered as much as to be used.

Even so, the terminals built during the 1930s and 1940s contained more than mere means of movement; they were meant to symbolize an *ideal* of movement. Many did so through their implementation of a *streamline moderne* style, an approach toward design that celebrated the power and pleasure of mobility. This style, an offshoot of the art deco movement, reflected a Depression-era transformation of functional things into set pieces for living in the future. *Streamline moderne* may be differentiated from its deco cousin by its emphasis on horizontality and its general lack of ornament. Departing from the Jazz Age affection for chevrons, lightning bolts, and zigzags, along with the *mélange* of pre-Columbian, Moorish, and "Oriental" references, *moderne* strove to emulate the stripped-down wind tunnel silhouette of the machine whose function mirrored its form. The sleek contours of the *moderne* reflected the clean lines of the early century locomotive, aircraft, or ocean liner, or the greyhound for that matter. Typical design elements include a strong horizontal orientation, the presence of 90-degree curves, the inclusion of porthole windows, and the practice of banding: colored lines, often in groups of three, that served no purpose except to suggest motion and efficiency. These were places built for speed.

Greyhound terminals such as those designed by William Strudwick Arrasmith in Washington, DC (1940); Cincinnati, Ohio (1941); and Cleveland, Ohio (1948) represent a prominently cohesive assemblage of *streamline moderne* architecture.[3] The terminals stretched a city block or more, sleek and flatly oriented. Only a single towering marquee sign disrupted the horizontal orientation. That sign, edged with *sans serif* letters marching down its face, announced the

Greyhound moniker in a manner resembling that of a movie theatre. At least one side of the structure met the curb with a 90- or 180-degree curve, often separating the bays where passengers entered and departed from the sidewalk. Glass block occasionally lined the curve of an upper floor or climbed a parallel line that accented the marquee. The buildings invariably featured some use of banding, sometimes a colored accent, to mark the ledge of their flat roofs. The terminals drew from the same styles of nearby diners and drug stores whose ornaments of fluted aluminum and penchant for portholes suggested the realization of ocean-going steamships or Buck Rogers' escapist fantasies, not to mention the realization of world's fairs past. In so doing, they often resisted any form of communion with the more traditionally glamorous or fanciful buildings that surrounded them.

Riders with moments (or hours) to spare found terminals to be places to purchase postcards and jot down telegraphic messages about their health, weather, and surroundings. They also scribbled notes about the numbers of miles they traveled and the virtues (or miseries) of the places they had seen. Their comments were augmented with corporate prose meant to extol the virtues of the stations where they sat. The back of a postcard for the Cleveland Greyhound Terminal defines itself around large numbers of platforms, hours, states, people, and dollars:

> The beautiful new Greyhound Terminal is the largest in the world. Twenty-one loading platforms[,] busy 24 hours a day[,] provide fast bus service to all 48 states, Canada and Mexico. More than 300 people can be seated in the extra-spacious curve-lined lobby. This luxurious bus terminal cost over $1,250,000 to build, [and it] serves over 3,000,000 people each year.

These postcards generally depicted the terminals at street level, positioning the viewer as a pedestrian looking up at towering structures whose facades curved beyond the postcard frame. Occasionally, the terminals were depicted within their urban locales, situated among taller buildings and invariably blue skies. Other images suggested that the terminals stood alone, with no surrounding buildings to draw the attention of the viewer. Either way, the stations suggested a network of terminals that conveyed their inhabitant to a place that was somehow distinct from their surrounding locales. Once riders left the terminals, they discovered an interstate network composed of nodes to the same place.

The "Only by Highway" Campaign

Following the Second World War, Greyhound sought to stoke enthusiasm for bus lines that had suffered during the years of rationing, and the company benefited from the rapid expansion of highway travelers ready to enjoy the kind of mobility that had been denied them when oil, rubber, and other auto essentials were tasked for the war effort. While factories worked to retool production back to civilian automobiles, Greyhound offered inexpensive cross-country mobility through its "Only by Highway" advertisement campaign, which appeared in mass-market magazines such as *The Saturday Evening Post, Holiday*, and *Life Magazine* in 1946. I view these advertisements as fragments of a corporate construction of interstate travel as the means to enter a synecdoche of America.

Before continuing along this line, my use of the term *synecdoche* may require some clarification. A synecdoche is a figure of speech that substitutes a part of a thing for the whole, or does the reverse. Kenneth Burke (1962) explained: "We might say that representation (synecdoche) stresses a *relationship* or *connectedness* between two sides of an equation, a connectedness that, like a road, extends in either direction, from quantity to quality or from quality to quantity" (p. 509; italics original). One may certainly substitute LAX for Los Angeles, but one also may imagine all of Los Angeles in the airport. This notion of synecdoche differs from an alternative trope, *metonymy*, which reduces a thing from quality to quantity. In previous iterations of this project, I have been tempted to employ metonymy to illustrate how omnitopia reduces "the world" into a tourist enclave, a one-way distillation. Yet I have chosen synecdoche over metonymy to emphasize how the tourist enclave also can signify the whole if one is so inclined. For that reason, I analyze the U.S. interstate, that two-way road imagined by Burke, as a synecdoche for *America*. It need not be overemphasized that this version of America serves as a synecdoche for modernity and, ultimately, the world. This latter iteration promises to contain everything a tourist would wish to see. More important, this synecdoche also proves useful as a training ground for more developed manifestations of omnitopia to come.

Cruising from node to node of this proto-omnitopian network, a visitor to Greyhound's America finds it difficult to imagine borders or limitations, even as the tourist requires strict delineation between inside and outside to ensure safe passage through the potentially dangerous domains that reside beyond the tourist enclave and its invisible horizons. As we discover through a cursory analysis of "Only by Highway" advertisements, postwar Americans were invited to view Greyhound's buses and terminals as communicating doors to the kind of place that could blur "somewhere" with "everywhere." This approach envisioned the interstate as being defined as a "place," as detached from nature, and as designed to observe "others."

Identifying the Highway as a "Place"

Greyhound defined the highway as a place worth visiting, not just as a means of transportation. In this way, the company associated itself with efforts by early century highway boosters to transform miles of concrete and macadam into destinations. One may recall that, prior to the development of the post-1956 Eisenhower interstate highway system, older highways were often named. In this era, one could travel from Maine to Florida along the *Atlantic Highway*, or one could travel from New York to California along the *Lincoln Highway*.[4] And one could even find a sense of place on numbered highways such as Route 66, the great diagonal highway commemorated by John Steinbeck as the Mother Road, the road of flight for Oakies and Arkies searching for freedom from Dust Bowl miseries. These named and famously numbered highways, marked by logos and featured in songs, books, and films, helped inspire a belief that road travel need not be focused entirely on a series of destinations, but should rather be a place unto itself.

Drawing from this practice, a Greyhound advertisement entitled "Only by Highway ... You Meet the Real America" (ellipses original) sought to connect individual roads into a common conceptual space: the open range that recalls the American West. The ad depicts a bus parked next to a mountain range. In the foreground, a woman in jaunty summer clothes lifts a child up to get a better look at a cowboy on horseback; in the background, a pleasant company of tourists, including one man in a suit, gaze upward at the peaks. On the right of the image, a child can be seen sitting in the bus, staring at the cowboy and smiling. The caption reads:

> There's just one way to know and enjoy the magnificent Country in which you live. That's to see it close up, face to face, within hand-clasp range of its friendly and interesting people—in the very shadow of its trees and mountains—along its lively and pleasant residential streets. That way is the *Highway*. Which is the same as saying, By Greyhound—because Greyhound alone serves nearly all the famous-name National Highways of the U.S.A. and Canada, plus thousands of miles of other equally interesting highroads that reach to every corner of This Amazing America. (italics and capitalization original)

Another example may be found in the 1946 Greyhound Picture Map of America, an artifact that also employed the "Only by highway" slogan. The enclosed map shows a tourist's version of the United States, with states noted by readily decipherable icons: marble monuments in Washington, DC, beach balls in Florida. The brochure enthuses:

> You'll view America through wide windows ... you'll see hard-riding cowboys at work ... the American Indian of pueblo and plain ... the crops that grow in green and gold fields ... the products that flow from great industrial plants ... the deep, green forests that abound with game, and the lakes and streams that are filled with game fish. Greyhound will show

you the *real* America . . . *and you'll enjoy every moment of it*! (ellipses and italics original)

With appeals such as this, readers are invited to imagine the highway as a meaningful place, not just as a means of conveyance. More important, one must employ the highway to visit an America that is "real," presuming that places inaccessible to the interstate are not so much "unreal" as nonexistent. With this advertisement, the highway becomes a predecessor to omnitopia, each named road merely serving to lead to the same place: America. This singular place, however, contained contrasting locales, which needed some reconciliation. At this point, then, we consider a second strategy.

Detaching the Highway From the Natural Environment

Greyhound envisioned a harmonious relationship between the interstate highway and the surrounding environment, even as it detached the former from the latter. An "Only by highway" advertisement entitled "The highway . . . The Greyhound . . . They *add up* to America's most convenient transportation!" (ellipses and emphasis original) illustrates this strategy. The ad presents a diagonal four-lane interstate that curves toward a hilly horizon. At the bottom left, a clean, white overpass connects with an off-ramp. On either side, forest scenes bound the road. On one side, two deer gaze in the general direction of the viewer; both glow with an artistic affect that places them outside of the scene, drawing the eye to their presence. Behind the deer, trees curve alongside of the road. On the other side, a Greyhound "Post House" is nestled within a hillside; no cars appear in the parking lot. Toward the horizon, a church steeple anchors a small town. The lower right contains a Greyhound, its windows filled with passengers. Like the deer, the bus floats in a sea of white negative space set apart from its surroundings. In this advertisement, the viewer studies an orderly intersection of built and natural worlds. For Greyhound, postwar progress means continual growth, which means a continually finer integration of garden and machine:

> America's highway system is being (and will be) enormously expanded and improved, with multi-lane, streamlined roads criss-crossing the whole continent. Greyhound will more than keep pace with this advance—is now planning and building finer bus equipment, more modern downtown terminals, new wayside Post Houses. All this *adds up* to better transportation for you—today, and in the days to come. (italics original)

It should be noted, this addition does not mean a total convergence. Greyhound's equipment, terminals, and "houses" ensure that one may pass through this place without experiencing its effects. Aside from scheduled stops and orderly transfers, the tourist's encounter with the road is similar to that of the deer or the bus: detached.

Those places become marked and packaged as sites/sights designed for quick immersions with the natural world. In this touristic enclave, economy and efficiency measure the value of things. An advertisement entitled "Only by Highway you see these wayside wonders, close up!" depicts a giant redwood tree filling the left side of the frame, which reveals itself to contain a glass-front house within a large opening on the ground. Standing near the tree, a man steadies a woman above him who stands on a giant root; she holds one of her hands aloft in a triumphant pose. In the foreground, another woman, wearing a long skirt and a light summer blouse, aims a camera at the pair. She also lifts one of her hands upward, her index finger points straight up, directing her subject. In the background to the right, a small number of tourists step out of a parked Greyhound. The ad text announces:

> The millions who love the unspoiled natural beauty that's found *only by highway* are also practical people . . . they know that Greyhound saves them money—they appreciate frequency and convenience of schedules—they enjoy the easy riding comfort of Greyhound coaches. These things are offered by Greyhound in fullest measure. (ellipses and italics original)

The highway creates the spots that one may visit, leading its tourists from photo opportunity to photo opportunity. The images are not so much sublime (remember: the tree is notable as much for its human "improvement" as its natural splendor) as it is accessible. The "easy on–easy off" ethos alters the touristic sensibility. One does not travel with the intention to endure the real or stylizing sufferings of the pilgrimage. One tours instead to collect the same souvenirs as one's neighbors. This aspect calls upon us to identify a third strategy of the "Only by highway" campaign: observation of "others."

Employing the Highway to Observe Social "Others"

Greyhound promised that one could use the highway to tour outside of one's social group with a dependable degree of safety and detachment. Returning from the road, the tourist may then announce, "I shot a real live Indian with my camera!"[5] Greyhound fulfilled this desire in several artifacts of the "Only by highway" campaign. An advertisement entitled "Only by highway you'll find America so thrilling, so friendly!" portrays a fisherman, wearing overalls and a slicker hat, hoisting a lobster toward the faces of two touring women visiting the New England Coast along Highway 1. One of the women leans toward the other; her wide eyes, pursed lips, and extended fingers suggest her mild alarm at the sight of the lobster. Her taller friend smiles while peering through a camera at the lobsterman. The photographer frames the image, viewing the lobster and its handler as objects that will be shared as souvenirs after the trip. The advertisement reads: "The colorful, the curious, the friendly things that make America so fascinating are found in the fullest measure *along its highways*. There you'll meet them close up, at first hand . . . and in congenial company" (italics and ellipses original). In these and other "Only by highway" advertisements, a Greyhound bus waits in the background. The bus offers a moving terminal to distant places and social groups, uniting them into a series of consumer opportunities. One may photograph the lobsterman, secure in the knowledge that a ready exit away from this scene lies near at hand.

Extending from this theme, one found in Greyhound advertisements the potential for tourists to view locals from a comfortable distance. An advertisement entitled "Only by highway you'll roll through America's well-kept front yard" features a trio of young teenagers singing underneath a foregrounded oak tree filled with hanging moss. In this scene, one of the youths even plays a banjo. In the background lies a creamy-pillared plantation home whose windows are lit for the evening. Entering the tableau from the middle left, a Greyhound bus appears to cast its headlight beams on the players. The advertisement text reads:

> In the romantic Old South, as in nearly every other part of the United States and Canada, buses enter each town and city the *front way*, usually through pleasant residential districts, beside parks and stately public buildings—on highways that avoid drab industrial districts. (italics original)

Recalling the Futurama exhibit, we might recall a similar affirmation of the way in which dangerous "others" are isolated from the "front ways," bypassed by the highway that renders some places as nonexistent even while it connects "every place." Once more we recall the 1940 *To New Horizons* script:

> Here is an American city re-planned around a highly developed, modern traffic system. The parks of the city have continuity and proper placement. These areas are united into long, green strips surrounding each community. Along both banks of the river, beautifully landscaped parks replace the outworn areas of an older day. . . . On all-express city thoroughfares, the rights of way have been so routed as to displace outmoded business sections and undesirable slum areas whenever possible. Man continually strives to replace the old with the new.

This progress appeal neatly elides explanation of precisely who will reside in "the new."

As noted previously, the American West provided an open range for the national imagination. Thus, an advertisement entitled "Only by highway you'll meet these 'Amazing Americans' at home!" features a woman standing next to a Native weaver who makes a rug. The tourist looks away from the Native, placing one hand confidently on her hip while she holds the other hand near her mouth. Standing away from the two women, a man arches his back away from them to observe the scene from a distance. He smiles at his companion, staring over the Native. The ad offers its own context of this scene:

> The setting is in the vast and colorful Southwest . . . an Indian rug weaver plies her skilled fingers as her ancestors have done for uncounted centuries . . . the girl from the waiting bus tries on one of the rainbow-tinted blankets, and gives her own big-city version of an Apache war whoop! (ellipses original)

Lobsterman, Indians, and other caricatured figures define interstate America to the mobile tourist. Glimpses of genuine "otherness" become edited out of the landscape so that, eventually, one may go anywhere without necessarily leaving one's safe expectations.

Image 7: Route 66 Postcard. *Author's Collection*

Conclusion

Following the inauguration of the Eisenhower Interstate System, highways became increasingly oriented around flow, bypassing urban cores and promising unimpeded movement from coast to coast. The old numbered highways such as 30 and 40 can still be found on contemporary maps, whereas other numbered roads such as Route 66 were decommissioned. The contemporary interstate system helped usher in the rise of edge cities and exurbs, places marked by big-box stores, repetitive chain restaurants, and shimmering parking lots. We might even propose that the interstate brought forth a nation that is entirely generic and interchangeable, although such a claim fails to survive the test of experience:

> Roadside homogeneity in American culture is a common assumptive slur which does not survive close scrutiny. The commercial cluster at an interstate does follow norms of form, scale, composition, and structure, but in detail its repertoire is endless and bears witness to the regional variation which pervades and enriches American mass culture. (Norris, 1987, p. 31)

What does follow from America's embrace of the interstate is a valuation of detached fluidity, a sense that unhindered motion between places, "making time," merits more affection than the places themselves, especially when "regional variation" seems increasingly to run no deeper than surface level appearances.[6] Yes, it is true that more people travel to more places with more efficiency than ever before. However, one can fairly question the value of this transformation. Stilgoe (1998) offers a trenchant tour of the interstate when he asks, "[i]s it possible for motorists to forget whole chunks of their drive, to be unable to recall at which interchange they bought gas or stopped for a cold drink? What exactly makes interchanges so peculiarly forgettable, so exquisitely unseeable?" (p. 178). Answering this query, what makes such a large swath of public life unseeable and uncontestable, provides some purpose to this project.

To that end, we have followed the transformation of the mobile gaze to that of the tourist safely cocooned in the automobile or bus. The shift from mass transportation to individual transportation allows us to consider the perception of freedom that early 20th-century travel afforded. One could tour the entire country, seeing it all without following a restrictive schedule by personal car or even by bus. Yet as we studied the Greyhound terminals and advertisements of the pre-1956 era, we found that this freedom contained a significant limitation. The "America" afforded to the 20th-century auto traveler was a limited facsimile of the one we might call real. Once the highway became a place worth visiting, a means to consume safely caricatured versions of potentially threatening "Others," many Americans could easily forget the existence of a world beyond this enclave.

Having observed the rise of omnitopia from its arcade predecessors to its interstate prototype, we now can unpack its meaning and application in contemporary times, aided by an analysis of two films, one released in 1967 and one released in 2004, that help us complete the transition from mid-20th century to current day. From this perspective, we may propose an omnitopian framework that is useful in the analysis of contemporary sites. Our tour, if successful, should result in a decidedly nonomnitopian framework: the desire to look closely and to critique, to make strange what seems so ordinary.

Notes

1. My use of this phrase is inspired by Henry Seidel Canby's (1934) *The Age of Confidence: Life in the Nineties*: "For I believe that while the age of mobility may be better or worse than the age of confidence, there have been these definite, describable losses to check against our gains. We can put our children on wheels to see the world, but we cannot give them the kind of home that any town provided in the nineties, not at any price" (p. 258).

2. Lippman emphasizes that General Motors' futuristic interstate system will require a collaboration of public and private enterprise, rather than a monopoly of efforts by one or the other. His claim serves as a contrast to the kinds of statism exhibited by the Soviet and Italian pavilions built for the fair, but he hardly rebukes the role of private industry. Indeed, in the same essay, Lippman celebrates the spirit found in the General Motors exhibit: "Surely it is as proud an exhibit as one could find of what men can achieve by private initiative, voluntary organization, individual leadership and the personal genius of scientists and inventors. . . . [T]his is what private enterprise can do, and the best that the Italians or the Russians have to show is no more than a feeble approximation to it" (p. 25). Incidentally, one may presume that Lippman avoided reference to Germany only because that nation did not participate in the fair.

3. Wrenick (2007) notes that Arrasmith took some inspiration from Thomas Lamb-designed terminals in New York City and Charleston, South Carolina.

4. The Lincoln Highway continued from Salt Lake City to San Francisco along another numbered road, Highway 40. As Butko (2005) notes, today's motorists along the U.S. 30 and U.S. 40 can still spot remnants of the Lincoln Highway. Preservation groups line sections of the road with metal logo signs, some businesses include the word *Lincoln* in their names, and even some of the original road signage can be found in bridges and mile markers.

5. This is not a merely theoretical example. One 1956 Polaroid advertisement in my collection depicts a Native American standing next to a young male tourist (wearing the Native's ceremonial headdress). To the right of that image, its duplicate is now framed as a photograph, held by the photographer's thumb and forefinger. The caption reads: "It was one of those once-in-a-lifetime shots . . . and 60 seconds later I *knew* I had it!" (ellipses and emphasis original).

6. I am reminded of a *Simpsons* episode entitled "Fear of Flying," in which Homer announces a peculiar variant of wanderlust: "Come on, Marge, I want to shake off the

dust of this one-horse town. I want to explore the world. I want to watch TV in a different time zone. I want to visit strange, exotic malls. I'm sick of eating hoagies. I want a grinder, a sub, a foot-long hero. I want to *live*, Marge!"

References

Belasco, W. J. (1997). *Americans on the road: From autocamp to motel, 1910–1945*. Baltimore: Johns Hopkins University Press.

Bernstein, W. (2004). *The birth of plenty: How the prosperity of the modern world was created*. New York: McGraw-Hill.

Boorstin, D. J. (1992). *The image: A guide to pseudo-events in America*. New York: Vintage Books.

Burke, K. (1962). *A grammar of motives and a rhetoric of motives*. Cleveland, OH: World Publishing Company.

Butko, B. (2005). *Greetings from the Lincoln Highway: America's first coast-to-coast road*. Mechanicsburg, PA: Stackpole Books.

Canby, H. S. (1934). *The age of confidence: Life in the nineties*. New York: Farrar & Rinehart.

Fotsch, P. M. (2001). The building of a superhighway future at the New York world's fair. *Cultural Critique, 48*, 65–97.

Fussell, P. (1980). *Abroad: British literary traveling between the wars*. Oxford: Oxford University Press.

Gelernter, D. (1995). *1939: The lost world of the fair*. New York: The Free Press.

Lippman, W. (1939, June 6). A day at the world's fair. *New York Herald Tribune*, p. 25.

Löfgren, O. (1999). *On holiday: A history of vacationing*. Berkeley: University of California. Press.

Marx, L. (2000). *The machine in the garden: Technology and the pastoral ideal in America*. Oxford: Oxford University Press.

Norris, D. A. (1987). Interstate highway exit morphology: Non-metropolitan exit commerce on I-75. *Professional Geographer, 39*(1), 23–32.

Patton, P. (1997). Road to nowhere. In J. Brouws, B. Polster, & P. Patton (Eds.), *Highway: America's endless dream* (pp. 32–54). New York: Stewart, Tabori & Chang.

Rothman, H. K. (1998). *Devil's bargains: Tourism in the twentieth-century American West*. Lawrence: University Press of Kansas.

Stilgoe, J. R. (1998). *Outside lies magic: Regaining history and awareness in everyday places*. New York: Walker and Company.

Steinbeck, J. (2002). *Travels with Charley in search of America*. New York: Penguin Books.

Wrenick, F. E. (2007). *The streamline era Greyhound terminal*. Jefferson, NC: McFarland & Company.

3

Framework

[The airport] is not a place that has a defined border, but instead dissolves into a series of modalities that blend into the city—the motorway, the airport rail link, aircraft noise limits, regenerated buffer zones, and the navigational beacons that are fretted across the city landscape.

—Terry Pratchett (2004, p. 105)

Omnitopia rests on historical and structural foundations of arcades, department stores, and international expositions, which collectively construct a synecdoche of civilization. Enacting enclavic rhetoric, omnitopia produces a convincing simulacrum of the "outside world" that enacts perceptual and structural barriers between tourist-corporate enclaves and the messy and dangerous domains beyond. Although the mapping of those domains may appear to be outside of our lived experience, we recognize the interstate highway system as a prototype for the omnitopian sensibility that reflects a most subtle and sophisticated form of ideology whose moorings and manifestations cannot be seen because they are hidden in plain sight (and plain sites). The interstate highway demonstrates the transformation of omnitopia from a situated enclave into a perceptual one in which *a place* becomes a node into *all-place*. At this point, we are nearly able to enter omnitopia as both a site of contemporary life and as a mode of communicating in that supposedly broad sphere. We enter that site aided by fieldwork from three distinct nodes of omnitopia: airports, hotels, and malls. However, before we enter the omnitopian frame more concretely, we must first excavate its abstract practices, which I label *dislocation, conflation, fragmentation, mobility*, and *mutability*. These practices provide a framework for omnitopia, rather than a blueprint. Like a grammar, they propose an embryonic organization of principles whose manifestations differ from application to application. Like a grammar, they are best understood with the aid of exemplars.

Two films offer a notably useful vision of omnitopia: Jacques Tati's 1967 film *Play Time* and Steven Spielberg's 2004 film *The Terminal*. Separated from one another by language, tone, and 37 years, these films present a shared view of urbanity as enclavic. In other words, they depict contemporary life as plate-glass cities whose inhabitants reside within a protected interior of disciplined, scrutinized, and protected places. With their sprawling interconnections and commodified pleasures, these enclaves may be compared to shopping malls because they contain enough necessary features for living that one need not ever leave. However, these films reflect another dimension of enclavic urbanity that currently remains undertheorized. In both *Play Time* and *The Terminal*, we witness images of urbanity that enact the apparent convergence of all urbanities. In the Paris of *Play Time* or the New York of *The Terminal*, one is not merely isolated from the "real cities" outside the enclave. Instead, one exits a specific locale and enters a continuum that appears to contain all nodes of urbanity. In this manner, we visit cinematic versions of omnitopia through which we witness a collection of all places while occupying one location.

These films provide a meaningful lens on omnitopia by illustrating a perception and practice of urbanity that generates a sense of recognition by most viewers and a belief that places powerful enough to craft simulacra of the world may well contain the seeds of danger as well as pleasure. Naturally, other cinematic depictions of the city might offer more striking illustrations of omnitopia. Most immediately, one might survey film-noir dystopias ranging from *Metropolis* to *Blade Runner* and maybe *Dawn of the Dead* to illustrate urban enclaves that "bristle with malice" while managing to convey a sense of perfect containment.[1] I would also add Alex Proyas' 1998 film *Dark City* to the list of noir films that illustrate the fundamental omnitopian principle of enclave (Wood, 2008). Certainly, *Dark City's* depiction of a conflated city of overlapping styles and histories, its structures and characters convulsing in accordance to the hidden architecture of unseen overseers, reveals the foundation of omnitopia when a stranger announces: "There's no escape. The city is ours. We made it." However, these sci-fi/horror depictions of urban life, insightful as they are, fail to convey the banal practices of everyday life that mark omnitopia. Put more directly, one can hardly watch *Dark City* or similar films with a sense of familiarity; these examples stretch too far beyond quotidian urbanity to be useful. Hence, I turn to *Play Time* and *The Terminal* whose uncanny depictions of contemporary life, despite their own excesses, are more readily familiar to most viewers. I introduce these films in some detail before employing them to illustrate the five components of the omnitopian framework.

Introduction to Play Time and The Terminal

Jacques Tati's *Play Time* depicts an urban enclave of international-style architecture, ubiquitous technology, commodified exchanges, and alienated people that manages somehow to result in a comedic romance in which folks learn to find their way in a city that doesn't function as efficiently as its planners would hope. *Play Time* marks the return of the director's hapless alter ego, M. Hulot, who visits a glass maze of overlapping and interconnected spaces: office spaces, convention spaces, transportation spaces, domestic spaces, and pleasure spaces. Although based on the Paris of modernity, *Play Time* takes place in a film set built for Tati and labeled "Tativille."[2] Within this labyrinth, far more than a backdrop, Hulot searches for a bureaucratic functionary, meets an old army buddy, and occasionally spots Barbara, an American tourist with whom he engages in an anonymous romance. All the while, he stumbles through a city of continual mutation, ever-changing in its collisions and repairs, always being spruced up: "Tati [as Hulot] happens upon all these scenarios that are then played out for the camera and we become voyeurs in this city of glass, witnessing technocratic bureaucracy rapidly overtaking a radical poetics of transparency" (Powell, 2005, p. 211). Throughout the film, Hulot appears from time to time, sometimes portrayed by Tati, sometimes as a double. We also witness Barbara being pulled along through various scenes on a tourist excursion through the glass city. But neither of them can fairly be said to be the film's protagonists. Tati intended for them to share the same significance as the other hundreds of characters and extras that crowded his cinematic frame. In this manner, Tati sought a kind of "democratic" filmmaking that would generate differing responses from individual viewers.

As such, *Play Time* defies easy categorization. It is a comedy, a romance, a farce, and a social commentary. The film also defies easy viewing. Tati shot his urban comedy in 70-millimeter format and refused to employ close-ups to fix his audience's attention. Instead, the film presents a broad and largely undifferentiated canvas in which each portion of the frame contains humorous interactions, structural details, and site gags.[3] Laurent Marie (2001) writes:

> Thanks to his use of the 70mm format and extreme depth of field, Tati creates a kind of dynamic maze through which the spectator must wander. His or her gaze must acquire a nomadic quality so as to err freely in Tativille in search of new discoveries. The spectator's gaze is therefore no longer controlled by the film's narrative. On the contrary, s/he has acquired a high degree of freedom: the spectator who watches *Play Time* circulates through the screen and each new viewing is therefore a new experience. Each new visit to Tativille leads to new pleasures. (p. 265)[4]

Contributing to *Play Time*'s disorienting tableau, Tati weaves together a soundscape of multilingual dialogue and sound effects that both comments on the film's imagery and confounds the audience's desire for orientation. The film's dialogue offers some degree of narrative direction, but is largely superfluous. Like a Chaplin film, *Play Time* possesses charms similar to those found in a silent film, even as students of aural landscapes would decry that notion.

Despite its occasionally frustrating construction, Tati's film offers a lighthearted lens on modernity that, despite its initial gloom, reveals an optimistic potential for urbanity to transform itself into a playground. In this manner, *Play Time* inspired a later film that also affirms humanity's ability to overcome the banality of bureaucracy, *The Terminal*, even as Spielberg's vision differs from Tati's in some important ways.

Steven Spielberg's *The Terminal* depicts the misadventures of Viktor Navorski, who waits in an international airport terminal for almost a year after his home country, Krakozhia, undergoes a coup. Not defined by the United States as a citizen of any country, Navorski must find lodging, food, and other essentials in a place defined around movement, not permanence. *The Terminal* borrows somewhat from the true story of Merhan Karimi Nasseri, who lived in France's Charles de Gaulle Airport from 1988 to 2006. However, unlike Nasseri's real-life terminal domestication, *The Terminal* fills its plot with a contrived romance and a sentimental pilgrimage that allows Navorski to leave the airport with some degree of triumph. Here, Spielberg abandon's Tati's inspiration by focusing on one protagonist. Whereas Tati's film wove Hulot's adventures among those of hundreds of other characters, often removing him from the frame for long periods of time, Spielberg's hero occupies a much more traditional film, complete with close-up shots to shape the audience's emotions. Even so, Spielberg mirrored Tati's construction of an airport-like city by building his own.

To create *The Terminal*, Steven Spielberg drew inspiration from Jacques Tati and his Tativille by constructing his own giant airport terminal. Designed by Alex McDowell, this film set offers more than a "sweet metaphor for all of America" (Thomson, 2004, p. 13). Instead, its steel frame and branching columns are based on airports found in Paris, London, Montreal, and Osaka (Iovine, 2004). In Spielberg/McDowell's hypermodern space, we witness a location that both reflects the world and resides beyond the world. Writing about Spielberg's film in *New Republic*, Stanley Kauffmann (2004) describes these two overlapping narratives:

> For myself, two views of airports prevail. First, a major airport terminal is a commercially compressed caricature of the civilization around it . . . [Secondly,] there is an entirely different terminal nightmare. It has nothing at all to do with the world around it. The traffic outside is a clever illusion. Instead, the terminal is a space station far away from planet Earth. (p. 20)

Both visions—the airport as symbol for the world and the airport as a terminal away from the world—offer insight into omnitopia. Both illustrate the manner in which contemporary urbanity offers a shopping mall-like caricature of modern life that is free of the local constraints of geography, nationality, and culture. Similarly, both films, *Play Time* and *The Terminal*, offer a lens into the five components of omnitopia: dislocation, conflation, fragmentation, mobility, and mutability.

Dislocation

Dislocation detaches a site from its surrounding locale. A dislocated place might be compared to a computer terminal through which one enters the "consensual hallucination" of cyberspace.[5] Going online, one does not exit the site that contains the computer terminal. One may continue to mark the spatial associations of an office or similar venue. However, the terminal detaches the user from locale. Such dislocation exists in other kinds of terminals as well. For example, an airport terminal such as LAX, with its security cordons and glass shields, presents the appearance of an insurmountable boundary to the Los Angeles visitor. Certainly, one may enter the city from the airport, eventually. But we should not confuse the city for the airport, even as so many do. In a state of dislocation, one observes merely surface façades that represent the locale beyond its bounds. By way of further example, we observe dislocation in most shopping malls and casinos. Insulated from the outside, sometimes surrounded by moats of pavement, these places create illusions that, once inside, one occupies a different world from the outside. In all manner of omnitopian places—Web sites, airports, shopping malls, casinos—dislocation works to create the sense that "here" removes the need for "there." Ultimately, a necessary condition of dislocation occurs when a traveler ceases to notice the outside locale at all. In omnitopia, one enters a structural and perceptual interior that so perfectly shields people from the outside world as to render it invisible, even temporarily unimaginable. Both *Play Time* and *The Terminal* illustrate the design, technologies, and interactions of dislocation.

Play Time begins with Hulot and Barbara arriving separately at Orly Airport, itself being dislocated from the broader environs of Paris. Hulot sets off in search of a bureaucratic official, M. Giffard, in an office building; Barbara becomes swept into a tourist excursion. Both exit the airport, but never manage to depart the dislocated enclave of omnitopia. Throughout the first half of the film, Hulot wanders from one site to another and always appears to be detached from other people. One of *Play Time*'s most iconic images occurs after Hulot gets lost in a maze of office spaces, finding himself on a mezzanine level that rises above a grid of cubicles. Each cubicle presents its own individuated container, white on the outside and seaweed green on the inside. Descending an escalator, Hulot scrutinizes the cubicles once more, which appear this time as file cabinets: This is a world of containers within containers. Glass walls and doors further demonstrate the frustration and struggles of people trying to make sense of these containers in *Play Time*. Consistently, they confound both the characters and the audience, blurring the borders between interiors and exteriors. In one scene, a worker in blue coveralls asks a doorman for a light for his cigarette. From the vantage point of the audience and from the ambient noise of car engines and horns, both men appear to stand outside. But the camera pulls back to reveal a glass door; the doorman stands inside while the workingman stands outside. Within *Play Time*'s office spaces, dislocation represents a strategy of collection, surveillance, and detachment. One might also recall the film's exhibit for a door that is made of a special material, rendering it utterly silent. The company's motto is, "Slam Your Doors in Golden Silence."

Beyond the specific site of the omnitopian office space, various *Play Time* characters witness and illustrate this construction of "Paris' " ability to separate its inhabitants from the "real" Paris and transport them into a generic city marked by repetition and standardization. For example, both Barbara and Hulot visit a nearby travel agency whose attendant, responding to a cascade of queries, scoots left and right on a wheeled chair. Behind him is a world map whose continents are linked by straight lines denoting airline routes. On the opposite side of the map, Hulot and Barbara separately survey a grid with no geographic references, only nodes in a network of interconnections colored red and white. Unlike travel agencies that promise to transport their visitors to special locales, unique and exotic, this agency's travel posters for distinct locales such as London, Hawaii, Mexico, and Stockholm feature a nearly identical international-style building adorned with some regional variation: an English bobby, a tropical umbrella, an adobe mission, and a snow skier. When the group of American tourists passes by these advertisements, Barbara surveys the poster for London and its towering office building until her colleague calls her outside: "Barbara, come here! Let's see the sites." There, they study an identical building, confirming its identity with the aid of a guidebook.

As a gaggling sign system for globalized tourist exchange, the *Play Time* tourists never leave their enclave; they are continually shuffled from place to place until Paris resembles just another set of shopping excursions. Even the Eiffel Tower, that most iconic of tourist backdrops, becomes merely a symbol without substance. At one point, Barbara manages to catch a glimpse of the Tower, but only as a reflection on a glass door. Joan Ockman (2000) writes, "The film's big joke is that the tourists never arrive in the historic and symbolic center of French and world culture. Rather, they pass their compressed holiday in its hypermodern simulacrum, a fact they hardly seem to realize" (p. 179). To be sure, touristic dislocation presents some manner of comfort, especially when one American visitor assures her friends, "Well, I feel at home everywhere I go." Toward the end of the film, once Hulot and Barbara have met at last, they visit a drug store after a long night of partying at the local nightclub. Barbara, interested in securing some sense of genuine travel, asks, "How do you say drugstore in French?" Hulot replies: "*Le Drug Store.*" In *Play Time*, the "real" world of nuance becomes replaced by a sterilized theme park of American internationalism.

In a similar manner, *The Terminal* detaches its protagonists from the outside world. The setting for this film, New York's JFK International Airport, occupies a liminal space between countries. Within this enclave, Viktor Navorski is caught: He no longer resides in his home country of Krakozhia, but he cannot visit New York. With its panes of plate glass and its instruments of bureaucracy, the terminal buffers its inhabitants from the snowy weather, the droning engines, and the honking taxicabs outside. *The Terminal* is in New York, but is not New York. In some ways, Spielberg's airport space resembles a Crystal Palace, the kind found in world's fairs since London's 1851 Exposition, with an overarching spindly skeleton of supporting beams and plate glass, reminiscent of a shopping mall. Here, detached from the city outside, "New York" exists only as a video seen airing in an immigration office featuring iconic figures like Tony Randall and The Radio City Rockettes hocking the virtues of their metropolis. Always inside, always observed, the terminal city is brightly lit, filled with consumer opportunities, exquisitely safe. And the immigrant cannot leave.

Explaining Navorski's conundrum, the director who oversees the airport's customs and immigration program announces:

> You don't really have a home. Technically, it doesn't exist. It's like a Twilight Zone. . . . It seems that you've fallen through a small crack in the system. . . . So, until we get this sorted out, I have no choice but to allow you to enter the International Transit Lounge. Alright? So I'm going to sign a release form that is going to make you a free man. . . . Free to go anywhere you like within the confines of the International Transit Lounge . . . I'm sure that Uncle Sam will have this all sorted out by tomorrow, and welcome to the United States, almost.

This "zone" occupies a paradoxical location, neither here nor there. Instead, *The Terminal* locates its passengers in a world of waiting. For Spielberg, the International Transit Lounge offers a smaller version of America. With its atomized people, each flowing from one nation to another, *The Terminal* creates an elevator for the whole world where each floor, each stop, and each conversation becomes a moment defined by its consumerist potential:

> Officer Thurman: Beyond those doors is American soil. . . . You are not to enter through those doors. You are not to leave this building. America is closed.

> Viktor Navorski: America closed. America closed. Wha-wha-what what I do?

> Officer Thurman: There's only one thing you can do here, Mr. Navoski: Shop.

Eventually, Navorski leaves the airport. His journey to the United States offers the culmination of that most primeval of tourist impulses: the collection of souvenirs. He makes this pilgrimage to collect one last memento for a collection of Jazz singer signatures sought by his father who had recently died. Even as Navorski completes a sentimental journey, America offers only a little more than the airport terminal. It is a shopping mall. And, like Tati's Paris, we expect no locale to erupt into omnitopia. Indeed, our first view of the New York skyline is reflected off the office-building façade of the airport. For both Navorski and Hulot, visits to contemporary urbanity result in a paradoxical dislocation. Yet these trips into omnitopia also expose the manner in which ostensibly distinct locations (e.g., office space and terminal space) begin to blur as well. In this manner, we identify the surface-level cohesion to otherwise separate spaces. This strategy may be labeled *conflation*.

Conflation

Conflation merges disparate experiences into a singular whole. As such, conflation crafts a pastiche of functions, referents, and settings, enabling multiple place narratives in a single location. To illustrate, a shopping mall food court presents a panoply of cultural references, the sense that one enters a smaller version of the entire culinary world when visiting this place. Similarly, Disney's EPCOT Center in Florida features a World Showcase where visitors survey an Italian piazza, a Japanese pagoda, a German village, a Mexican Aztec pyramid, and other similarly distinct sites, all within walking distance of one another. George Miller's 1998 film *Babe: Pig in the City* provides a cinematic example of conflation with its convergence of architectural icons such as the Empire State Building, the Sydney Opera House, and the Golden Gate Bridge in one city, creating a charmingly paradoxical metropolis. More recently, Chinese director Jia Zhangke's 2004 film *Shijie* (*The World*) further illustrates conflation with its depiction of a shabby Beijing amusement park whose apparent convergence of overlapping icons such as the Twin Towers and the Egyptian pyramids, all in miniature, fail to elide the banality of backstage life witnessed by park workers.[6] In all examples of conflation, one sees a necessary extension of dislocation. Being removed from a specific locale, one may enter a perceptual synecdoche of the world. Within omnitopia, conflation enables passage through multiple places that seem indistinct: Each flows into the other. Within this enclave, either in *Play Time* or *The Terminal*, one struggles to imagine a world "outside."

We first revisit *Play Time* and its architecture of multiple narratives. We see this from the first shot, as the camera pans down from a cloudy sky to a gray office building. The structure is nondescript: steel and glass in ordered rows. It is an organized grid of angles and edges. Inside, a long polished hallway divides

Eames-style chairs on the left and silvery cubicles on the right. The scene suggests the sterile ennui of a corporate waiting room. In the foreground, a woman asks her husband about his appointment and marvels when a uniformed official walks by. But she also asks about his vitamins and assures him that she has packed his pajamas. Nearby, another woman walks by, pushing a wheeled device. From behind, she appears to navigate a wheelchair down the hallway.

This must be a hospital. However, once more the angle shifts, and we hear an announcement chime signaling: an airplane is arriving. The woman formerly seen pushing a wheelchair enters the scene again. Now we can see that her "chair" is actually a baggage cart. The couple previously spotted conversing about vitamins and pajamas walk into the frame, now looking for gate information while an airplane's tailfin passes behind them. An office building, a hospital, and an airport, this site conflates three narratives of modernity: bureaucracy, sterility, and mobility. Writing about *Play Time*, Joan Ockman (2000) adds: "Office spaces, convention hall, hotel, housing block, supermarket, drugstore/snackbar, and a new restaurant metamorphose into each other as oneiric elements of an unmappable pedestrian and vehicular milieu" (p. 180). This dreamscape contains multiple stories that drift into one another, converging into a complete synecdoche for all of contemporary life.

The Terminal also portrays a version of modern life that crafts the illusion of completeness by conflating multiple sites into one location. As Navorski wanders through the International Transit Lounge, he discovers the whole world in a food court filled with "places" such as Dean & Deluca, Burger King, Sbarro, Nathan's Hot Dogs, Baja Fresh, Starbucks Coffee, Panda Express, Yoshinoya, and Au Bon Pan. Anticipating the premier of *The Terminal*, Gail Schiller (2004) described how 40 national chains built replicas of their businesses in Spielberg's set in hopes that they might make brief appearances in his film:

> Although brands saved DreamWorks millions of dollars in production costs, the retailers have no idea to what extent their stores and restaurants will appear, but the chance to have some level of exposure in a Spielberg-Hanks film made the investments worth the risk. (¶ 16)

A cinematic EPCOT Center, a celluloid world's fair, the gathering of cultural façades (an iconic panda, a French bistro, even a taste of "real" Coney Island hot dog minus the hassle of catching a subway to Brooklyn), *The Terminal* conveys its inhabitants to a world city whose local geographies reflect a corporate purpose.

Despite its resemblance to a shopping mall food court, *The Terminal* illustrates conflation most directly when Navorski leaves the lounge for that presumably private locale of a restroom where he can wash up and shave. One day he meets a pinstriped road warrior who is also shaving. Both men look into the mirror and the pinstriped man asks: "You ever feel like you're just living in an airport?" The businessman returns to shaving after a moment of reflection, leaving Viktor staring dumfounded into the mirror. We are meant to laugh at the irony of the question: Viktor Navorski does live in the airport. However, in a broader way, occupants of the terminal find that all places become conflated into a single place. Passing through from Krakozhia to New York, or anywhere in between or beyond, all the myriad narratives of persons and places become conflated. This omnitopian city invokes multiple narratives while affirming only one, that of the architects. Nevertheless, we cannot understand omnitopia from the standpoint of conflation alone. Instead, we find a confusing hodgepodge of partial texts with little context: fragmentation.

Fragmentation

Fragmentation splits a singular environment into multiple perceptions. As such, fragmentation reflects an essential counterpart to conflation; both work in tandem along differing levels of cognition. Although conflation gathers multiple sites into the same perceptual frame, fragmentation works simultaneously to fracture that omnitopian totality into isolated surface-level images, functions, and interactions. As a result, one can hardly discern a narrative or community within omnitopia. Aided by fragmentation, omnitopia does not reveal itself to be homogenous or totalizing as a prison or an office park. It rather appears as a loose assemblage of atomized interactions: accidental meetings, functional questions, and consumer purchases. More important, fragmentation also provides the means to posit genuine fissures within the omnitopian enclave even while these moments may be unforeseen and short-lived.

Although conflation enacts a complete perception, fragmentation destabilizes any coherent site of critique. In this manner, fragmentation works to splinter any sweeping historical narrative, crafting incongruent shards of the present, everywhere complete and distinct. We find fragmentation in the shopping mall food court mentioned in the earlier description of conflation when a patron chooses one vendor, imagining that "this" counter is somehow detached from the collection of counters. We also find fragmentation when we visit a fast-food restaurant and interact with workers speaking to people at the counter and in their cars via a headset, rendering both interactions automated and alienating. As a practice of late modern capitalism, fragmentation perfects the lessons of designers and planners who craft abrupt spaces of apparent novelty and variation that remove the coherent narrative.

Again, we find in *Play Time* several illustrations of omnitopian fragmentation, most predominantly in Barbara's role as a tourist. Although portrayed sympathetically by Tati as a young American in a tour group, Barbara nonetheless meets "locals" in a series of discrete functional exchanges in which Parisians become transformed into servants, sellers, and objects. Her photographic gaze, her use of technology to frame the world into a series of disconnected screens, results in a fragmented city of images. The blur and flow of omnitopian Paris becomes a personal slide show or TV channel to be switched at will. At one point, Barbara spots a woman selling flowers on the corner, dwarfed by the glass buildings that rise above. Her camera will transform the woman who interacts with others into a personal souvenir, but other people keep stepping into the frame. Barbara's struggle recalls the touristic frustration of trying to get the right shot, free from the flotsam of passersby who fail to coordinate with her narrative of Paris. Asking two other women to step outside of the frame, she explains, "That's really Paris!" To her consternation, however, locals (some looking decidedly unpicturesque) continue to intrude on her shot, some even posing with the flower-woman. Adding to her woes, another tourist (with an even more pronounced U.S. accent) asks if she will pose for *his* photo. In Barbara's Paris, each person is a fragmented *other* to be shot, discarded, or avoided. And she is not alone in being alone: Later on when two tour groups pass each other going in opposite directions on an escalator, one visitor says: "I wonder if there's anybody from Miami in *their* tour." In this phrase, and in Barbara's efforts to capture evocative images of the real Paris for friends back home, we consider the truism that tourists prefer to relive experiences rather than live them the first time.

Correspondingly, Hulot witnesses omnitopian fragmentation when he meets an Army buddy who insists that they visit his new apartment. The place resembles an office building, with broad plate-glass windows revealing each interior room to the outside. The apartment also suggests a grid of TV screens, each with individual images of domesticity. The scene that follows contains no dialogue; the audience remains outside with the street traffic. The only sounds come from passing cars and pedestrians. The frame contains two apartments separated by a wall. On the left, Hulot and his hosts watch TV for a while; on the right, a threesome watches its own TV. Both screens are built into the same wall, opposite each other, suggesting that both groups could just as easily be watching each other. But they are not. Each is isolated in its own chamber, viewable from the outside as a connected lattice of cells, but oblivious to each other. Tati further emphasizes his point about the bureaucratic atomization of people engendered by modern spaces when Hulot bumbles off. Alone in his apartment, his army buddy removes his jacket in an innocuous gesture. However, to the audience, this means something more. In the adjacent apartment cell, a lone woman stares at the wall separating her from the man, watching TV. To the audience, these two solitary selves stare at each other; the wall becomes a terminal through which they enter the same perceptual space, a communicating door. Theirs is an intimate exchange. As he slowly removes his jacket, the man performs a kind of striptease for her, and in return she adjusts her position back and forth, altering her view of the show that we can see but she cannot.

Yet their interaction is illusory. Each person is locked within a fragmented enclave, unaware of the other.

The Terminal also demonstrates the role of fragmentation in omnitopia. Initially, we spot obvious parallels as Navorski encounters the same kind of difficulties as the inhabitants of Tati's Paris: He finds that plates of plastic and glass create unexpected walls and windows. Travelers passing through the terminal may sense a perception of perpetual flow as discrete places blur. But Navorski learns that all places such as these invariably possess gaps and fissures; even in omnitopia, one may find locales. They tend to be atomized and temporary. Sometimes they are accidental; sometimes they are not. To be sure, accidental fragments, those unplanned by the authors, designers, and managers of omnitopia, must somehow be marked and surveyed. Navorski, a walking sign system for the failure of bureaucracy, represents an accidental fragment. At one point, the official in charge of JFK's immigration and customs system, Frank Dixon, tries to rid himself of this troublesome splinter:

> Frank Dixon: Airport's are tricky places, Mr. Navorski. . . . At twelve o'clock today, the guards at those doors are going to leave their posts, and their replacements are going to be five minutes late. . . . Just today. Just this once. No one is going to be watching those doors. And no one is going to be watching you.
>
> Viktor Navorski: So America not closed.
>
> Dixon: No. America, for 5 minutes, is open.

Even for an officious bureaucrat like Dixon, omnitopia must be capable of breaking itself into two or more contradictory narratives. But Navorski chooses to work within the bureaucratic process, to leave legally.

At first, Navorski searches for an exit by following the rules. Every day, he engages in a routine with Officer Torres, the administrator who regularly rejects his request for a visa. For her, at first, this custom follows a well-defined script. For him, each performance enacts a moment of potential fragmentation in which everything can change. Yet the line of fellow travelers grows behind him, and Navorski must soon abandon his efforts. The fragment dissipates before vanishing all together. But certainly Viktor Navorski comes to know Officer Torres, and gradually both transform this atomized exchange into a genuine interaction, speaking of their personal secrets and longings. This truth, happily a truth of all nodes of omnitopia, lies at the center of this kind of place. The fragmentation that crafts moments free of social or cultural context also works to create a potential for omnitopia to dissipate. When Navorski walks through the terminal in his bathrobe amid travelers in business attire, he is at home while they pass by. Navorski reveals how omnitopia requires both structure and perception. Without one or the other, omnitopia pops like a soap bubble. But few temporary residents of an airport will think carefully about such matters because of their perpetual mobility. When omnitopia works, we are detached from our critical sensibilities. For that reason, we should slow down a bit and concentrate on the practice of mobility.

Mobility

Mobility orients a place around movement rather than stasis, an inevitable component of any urban site when populations of people and places expand beyond the pedestrian sphere where one may walk comfortably. Even in a small town, one must practice some degree of mobility, even to visit the central park for an afternoon picnic. However, omnitopian mobility differs from traditional urban mobility. Within omnitopia, mobility becomes essential to transform disparate places into nodes of the same place. Unlike an international exposition in which all things may be imagined underneath one roof, omnitopia must connect literally distinct geographies while rendering them as being perceptually unified. To accomplish omnitopian mobility requires more than cars, walkways, trams, and the like. This manner of mobility calls for the perception of flow. One quickly discerns which gate to select, which exit ramp to take, and which shuttle to catch, anywhere in the world, without stopping for long at any site. In this flow, one senses a motive power that organizes an otherwise random shuffle into a directed march. To that end, the language and signs that assist omnitopian mobility must be simple or at least difficult to misinterpret. Only when mobile technology fails (e.g., the elevator breaks down, waiting for the airplane) does "this" place adopt meaning. Beyond its ability to connect the disparate nodes of omnitopia, mobility also reduces one's ability or even one's inclination to contemplate edges or foundations. The strategy of mobility reduces, even criminalizes, the possibility to reside in one omnitopian location for an unauthorized purpose or inordinate amount of time. Within omnitopia, we find it almost unthinkable to question this place when we endlessly move through it. Rather than moments of stasis, we perceive perpetual flow.

Play Time depicts urban flow as the process of waiting and movement, beginning and concluding with an airport. In this manner, Tati defines modern urbanity as built from the comings and goings of strangers. He demonstrates how mobility rather than permanence marks contemporary life in this city of planes, buses, and cars. The question remains—whether anyone actually goes anywhere. For example, we return to Hulot's journey through the glass and steel labyrinth of modern "Paris" and find him visiting an office building where he asks the doorman (sometimes called a porter by reviewers of the film) to help him find Giffard the bureaucrat.[7] The doorman obliges, announces Hulot's arrival, and asks the visitor to wait. The composition of this scene is telling: Tati composed the image so that half could contain the sitting Hulot and half would contain a lengthy hallway that stretches back toward infinity. Prior to seeing Giffard enter the hallway, the audience hears the sound of stiff heals slapping against the polished floor. Then, for an interminable period of time, the functionary advances toward the foreground. Hulot hears the footsteps and hastens to arise, but the doorman bids him to remain seated. The rhythmic patter of steps provides the only sound for a moment as Giffard walks smartly closer, growing larger. Again, Hulot begins to rise, but the doorman tuts once more. He knows how long this performance lasts, and he knows that there's no point in standing during this formality. For 47 seconds, Giffard and his slapping shoes draw nearer while Hulot sits and waits. Giffard arrives at last and asks Hulot for his papers. Upon receiving the documents, Giffard departs and Hulot is led into a glass antechamber and asked to wait once more. As he sits, the audience hears the alternating hum of some internal machine and the drone of external traffic. This scene demonstrates *Play Time*'s view toward mobility. It reflects power and agency, but it also reflects a certain futility. The bureaucrat walks and walks, but the gridiron lines and lights on the hallway, and the steady pace of his steps suggest no potential for progress. Similarly, Hulot waits and waits before being invited to walk at last, only to wait some more in another room.

Like Hulot, Barbara the tourist enters a place of perpetual movement. But she never really goes anywhere new. Even so, mobility is vital to her version of Paris. An unplanned pause invites the potential for disappointment, as if one might spot an empty pixel on a computer screen. Continual motion frees the planners and passersby from that risk. Consider the American tour group that flows from escalator to pedestrian walkway to bus. Outside of the airport, they ride a bus, its huge glass windows resembling the scenic compartment of a streamlined train. At one point, the tourists gawk at the small size of French cars while marveling at the comfort of the bus. The scenic windows transform a parking lot of immobile cars into an assembly line or a battalion of soldiers passing in review. The tourists have traveled, recently to Amsterdam, now to Paris, but their fetish is not the place, but the means of getting through. Their bus follows arrows that lead to Paris. *Play Time* is filled with arrows of both the painted and neon variety that direct and misdirect. When Barbara's bus stops momentarily, a small number of tourists step out and point at the buildings before their guide hustles them back into order. Looking through a plate-glass window of his own, Hulot sees some of this. Riding a tour bus or sitting in the waiting room, those anti-spectacles of modernity, Barbara and Hulot both represent the anti-*flâneur*. Instead of transforming the city into their own personal narratives, these characters' mobility is shaped for forces beyond their comprehension. Only in spite of themselves do Barbara and Hulot get anywhere at all. Such pessimism cannot last long in a Tati film, though, or in our inquiries for that matter. Even the most naive inhabitants of omnitopia manage to make mobility work for them.

Like *Play Time*, *The Terminal* begins in an airport, a waiting place amid a world of movement. The film's tagline, "Life is Waiting," becomes noteworthy here as mobility and waiting speak to a broader perception generated by airports within and beyond the cinematic apparatus. Consider dialogue between Viktor and Amelia the flight attendant who discuss the intersecting roles of location and technology that keep them in their place(s), that is keep them moving:

Amelia Warren: You heading for home?

Viktor Navorski: Uh, no, no . . . I am delayed a long time.

Amelia Warren: I hate it when they delay flights. What do you do?

Viktor Navorski: Oh, I go from one building to another building. I have beeper.

Amelia Warren: Oh, contractors. You guys travel as much as we do.

We might define the *contractor* as a character from contemporary life, a persona that adopts several guises: the road warrior, the frequent flyer, maybe even the freeway flyer who shuttles between loosely overlapping locales of the academic enclave. Moving and waiting, waiting to move: These are the alternating poles of the mobile self in omnitopia.

Later, Navorski confides with Warren, telling her that he is no contractor; he is not part of the upwardly mobile club (a glaring reality for the traveler unable to enter any of the various "clubs" that form a network of privilege uniting international airport terminals). Viktor Navorski is not mobile at all. But Amelia cannot fathom the meaning of Viktor's message:

Viktor Navorski: I live here.

Amelia Warren: What?

Viktor Navorski: I live here, in terminal. Gate 67.

Amelia Warren: You live in the airport?

Viktor Navorski: Yes. Day and night. This home, like you. They tell me to wait. So I wait.

Amelia Warren: All frequent flyers feel the same way you do, Viktor. Everybody's waiting. Everybody. For a flight, for a meeting . . .

Even so, for Viktor, waiting becomes a form of resistance (even as the prospect of a lengthy airport stay represents a kind of hell for most other travelers). Despite immigration and customs officer Frank Dixon's efforts to be rid of Navorski as a living embodiment of the fragments that frustrate bureaucrats everywhere (not just those in Paris and New York), the immigrant chooses to live in the airport for months. The nature of this choice calls to mind Shome's (2003) articulation of "the politics of mobility":

> Who moves, where, and under what conditions, and who does not move and stays in place, under what conditions, have to do with how individuals are differently situated in relation to structures that enable movement or the lack of movement. In the case of [many] immigrants, the politics of mobility in which they are caught is neither subversive nor oppositional. (p. 53)

Navorski intended to enter the United States, but, as an immigrant, his type of mobility could hardly parallel those of most U.S. tourists who might visit his (fictional) country. Movement by choice, movement by circumstance, movement by force: These cannot be confused for one another. What remains, however, is the ways in which the mobile (or mobilized) person transforms the site through which movement occurs. Simultaneously, we must also consider the manner in which places themselves move and mutate to accommodate (or frustrate) the actions of their inhabitants.

Mutability

Mutability enables the perpetual change of a place. As a practice of omnitopia, mutability reflects a range of potentials: It may be employed to destabilize a critical response by altering the foundation on which such an attack could be launched. It may also provide the means through which occupants of omnitopia may change the scene for their own purposes. Omnitopian mutability is best illustrated by its continual and apparently automatic adaptation to changing exigencies. Although the twisting, growing, and morphing buildings of Alex Proyas' *Dark City* provide an evocative illustration of mutability, we also find this practice in more banal sites. For example, we queue at the airport and study the evolving mazes of retractable line-control ribbons, wondering about the precise stimulus that commands a staffer to craft an opening or alter the flow of waiting flyers. An hour later, more people arrive, and the ribbon line has been altered to accommodate them. Sitting at our gate, we know that previous flyers used this same site to visit a different place; later, flyers will journey elsewhere from this site. Although some gates may be regularly associated with certain flights, the portal generally leads to one location in the morning, another in the afternoon, and yet another in the evening. Another day, perhaps at an amusement park, we visit a site that alters itself according to changing expectations, marketing campaigns, seasons, and even hourly weather patterns. Rides close, become revised, and even adapt to new purposes. Even Disney's Haunted Mansion transforms itself into a backdrop for *The Nightmare Before Christmas* at both the California and Japan amusement parks (as of this writing, at least). As such, these rides become a metaphor for more than mobility; they become a sign of constant change. Even so, we also find the mutability of omnitopia to contain the seeds for its transformation, even momentarily, into a locale. We learn the codes, study the practices, observe the habits, and sometimes alter the place to suit our own purposes.

Play Time depicts contemporary life as a site of continual change and surprising mutation. In its modern places, interiors become exteriors, and, enfolded by plate glass, all places become interiors. Moreover, all objects possess multiple purposes. Sometimes these mutations are joyous or at least humorous, as when the tourist group visits an office building featuring displays from an international exposition. Some stop to marvel at a display that features a faux-Greek marble column serving as a trash receptacle complete with a flip-top lid. Other times, these mutations confound us. For example, early in the film, Hulot wanders the hallway concourses of a gray building before passing a silvery alcove. Attached to the inner wall, a map draws his attention. In particular, a red box on the image contributes the only saturated color in the entire scene. Hulot steps into the recessed space to get a better look, his umbrella dangling from clasped hands at his back. Suddenly, an office worker clutching a green folder marches tidily into the alcove and presses an unseen button. Doors appear and quickly close while Hulot flails about in a panic, alarmed that the alcove is actually an elevator. An exterior view of the building aided by now-seen indicator lights next to the elevator reveals that Hulot moves up and down several floors. At last, he exits what appears to be an identical space, but, naturally, he has exited onto a different floor. Before long, searching for Giffard amid a room of cubicles, Hulot comes across a receptionist, positioned at an intersection of a grid. Her uniform resembles that of a flight attendant. Hulot crosses her path and stops to tip his hat to her. She nods to him and turns her swivel seat. When Hulot turns at a right angle and passes her compartment, she stares at him once more. As always, Hulot is astounded and confused.

Eventually, however, *Play Time* admits Tati's real aim: not to confound his audience, nor to mock his characters, but to propose that even the most oppressive locations may be mutated by those who would possess them. *Play Time*'s nightclub scene provides vivid illustration, gathering most of the characters spotted throughout the film in an upscale restaurant where, despite an architect's planning and owner's herding, people manage to transform a staid evening into a raucous carnival, nearly destroying the place in the process. One moment stands out, when a wealthy American patron (an obnoxious one, at least) seizes a section of the restaurant and transforms it into his own personal salon, using broken latticework that hangs from the ceiling as a makeshift door. In this moment, omnitopia becomes broken into a series of personalized locales: moments of improvisation, intoxication, and community. However, the film's most poignant moment of mutation occurs at its conclusion, in which the city becomes transformed into a carnival.

The scene begins when Barbara leaves with her tour group after spending a few moments at last with Hulot. Her bus enters a traffic roundabout, a circular queue. Then suddenly the roundabout assumes the identity of a carousel with colorful cars circling a red- and white-stripped pole. Even a girl on the back of a motorcycle rises and falls to the rhythm of the music, while red and blue cars rise and fall on mechanical lifts in the gas station. For a moment, the entire city is a gigantic whirling toy, and all of its inhabitants are players within it. Almost imperceptibly, the music ceases and the carousel stops. But soon a businessman puts a coin in the meter and new music starts the turn of cars once more. Even the tourists in their bus resemble riders of a roller coaster when seen from the view of the window cleaner whose every tilt of glass results in oohs and ahhs from the visitors to the Parisian carnival. In this fanciful moment, *Play Time* leaves its audience with a sense of optimism: Omnitopia is powerful; it is not immutable.

Although *The Terminal* does not provide such a sublime *dénouement*, Steven Spielberg's homage to Jacques Tati nevertheless manages to fill its airport with moments of mutation. In fact, the film's opening credits appear on a marquee sign whose words are composed of flipping characters. This sign provides a recurring image and sound throughout the film. With this device, we are reminded how the airport functions as a place of movement, yes, but also change. The place simply cannot accommodate the overlapping and criss-crossing flows of traffic from so many directions with a fixed identity, so each gate possesses only a momentary meaning to those who pass through them without reflection. Later in the film, lost luggage becomes high stakes in the card games played by the community of workers who go beyond the doors locked to most of us who travel. *The Terminal* is an airport only to those flyers who pass from gate to gate. To its long-term occupants—the officials, the guards, and the low-wage workers who possess the keys and know the maps—the airport is much more.

Viktor Navorski must learn the art of mutation to make a temporary home in JFK International Airport. Accomplishing this task requires a large degree of work, both cognitive and physical. First, he must learn the codes of this place; most literally, he must learn the language. Fortunately, he has TV programs with their news scrolls to augment his use of travel guides borrowed from the bookstore that he uses as a library. Second, he must make money to afford sustenance from the array of fast-food restaurants throughout the airport. Again, fortune appears in the form of a baggage cart dispenser, which he converts into a source of income. Finally, Navorski needs shelter. His response to this exigency is most telling. Navorski finds a gate scheduled for refurbishment and constructs his living space there, moving chairs, adjusting lights, and making repairs. Even the soda machine becomes a refrigerator for him. Amid the detritus of 1970s-era design, most notably the mustard-yellow and eggplant-colored chairs, Navorski alters this site into a tolerable habitat, his temporary home. In this way, we find that mutation within omnitopia works both ways. It constantly reconstructs the world, lest its occupants become too comfortable. Yet, it also admits the possibility that even the least powerful among us may find ways to make do, creating locales that others cannot see.

Conclusion

The strategies of dislocation, conflation, fragmentation, mobility, and mutability reveal essential practices of omnitopia. Dislocation detaches a place and its people from the larger world, constructing an isolating chamber whose membranes may be relatively permeable but are nonetheless difficult to transgress without authorization. Conflation works to collapse varied spatial and temporal narratives into one arcade: crafting an illusion of completeness. Fragmentation works simultaneously to craft abrupt moments of disjuncture in a manner that releases the tension of the impossibly grand narrative. Mobility enables, even requires, movement through distinct locales, leaving us unable to pause long enough to study the structures through which we pass. Mutation draws from each of these strategies to enact places and perceptions of constant change, removing the physical or temporal coherence necessary to mount a meaningful response. Yet as we have seen, this strategy may become a tactic of resistance, or at least of pleasure, if craftily deployed.

What remains is for us to investigate omnitopia beyond its cinematic exemplars, and even beyond the framework we have already considered. In this way, we exit the theater and enter the modern world once more. Here, we see a world that has learned the lessons of previous utopian visions ranging from 19th-century expositions to 20th-century "urban renewal" in the United States. Amid such spectacles and grand boulevards, individuals bump against each other like billiard balls, alienated from one another. Objects of the modern world become abstract. As both a consequence to this condition and as a reaction to its failures, omnitopia enacts the totalizing gaze and ubiquitous place that cannot be as easily dismissed as its utopian progenitors, creating a global enclave beyond the colorful façades of the shopping mall and the whoosh of electric trams. To demark its practices, and to demonstrate eventually how folks appropriate its powers, we must first look more deeply at omnitopian places.

Notes

1. I borrow this phrase from Mike Davis' (1992) essay, "Fortress Los Angeles." In that chapter, Davis also writes, "The new Downtown is designed to ensure a seamless continuum of middle-class work, consumption, and recreation, insulated from the city's 'unsavory' streets. Ramparts and battlements, reflective glass and elevated pedways, are tropes in an architectural language warding off the underclass Other" (p. 159).

2. Tati's *New York Times* obituary notes how the director spent $800,000 to construct Tativille, a hypermodern version of Paris, which resulted in massive overruns on the *Play Time*'s budget. Tati once remarked that the film put him "rather deeply in the red" (Lawson, 1982, p. 15).

3. Labeling *Play Time* as one of the "Great Movies," Roger Ebert (2004) notes that Tati's film "is a peculiar, mysterious, magical film. Perhaps you should see it as a preparation for seeing it; the first time won't quite work" (p. 3)

4. Jonathan Rosenbaum's (1973) fascinating interview with Tati reveals that viewers of *Play Time* must learn to avoid the right angles followed by the film's characters, to let their gaze wander in arcs upon the screen. Rosenbaum writes that, otherwise, "[p]ursuing the action in straight lines, we become victimized, imprisoned by the [film's] architecture" (p. 37).

5. In *Neuromancer* (1984), William Gibson defines *cyberspace* as: "A consensual hallucination. . . . A graphic representation of data abstracted from the banks of every computer in the human system" (p. 51).

6. With their frequent convergence of distant geographies, "tiny towns" provide still another example of conflation. Examples around the United States include Ave Maria Grotto in Cullman, Alabama; Tiny Town U.S.A. in Hot Springs, Arkansas; Tiny Town, south of Denver, Colorado; and Roadside America in Shartlesville, Pennsylvania. A delightful international example may be found at Cockington Green in Canberra, Australia.

7. Although we never discover precisely why Hulot searches for Giffard, if we view *Play Time* as a sort of sequel to Tati's 1958 film *Mon Oncle*, we may speculate that Hulot wishes to deliver a letter of recommendation (Chion, 1997).

References

Chion, M. (1997). *The films of Jacques Tati* (M. Viñas, P. Williamson & A. D'Alfonso, Trans.). Toronto: Guernica.

Davis, M. (1999). Fortress Los Angeles: The militarization of urban space. In M. Sorkin (Ed.), *Variations on a theme park* (pp. 154–180). New York: Hill and Wang.

Ebert, R. (2004, August 29). A magical mystery tour de force. *Chicago Sun-Times* (Sunday Showcase), p. 3.

Gibson, W. (1984). *Neuromancer*. New York: Ace Books.

Iovine, J. V. (2004). Hi, honey, I'm at the airport. *The New York Times*, p. 36.

Kauffmann, S. (2004, July 26). Time suspended. *The New Republic*, p. 20.

Lawson, C. (1982, November 6). Jacques Tati, actor and director who created Mr. Hulot, is dead. *The New York Times*, p. 15.

Marie, L. (2001). Jacques Tati's *Play Time* as New Babylon. In M. Shiel & T. Fitzmaurice (Eds.), *Cinema and the city: Film and urban societies in a global context* (pp. 258–269). Oxford: Blackwell.

Ockman, J. (2000). Architecture in a mode of distraction: Eight takes on Jacques Tati's *Playtime*. In M. Lamster (Ed.), *Architecture and film* (pp. 171–196). Princeton: Princeton Architectural Press.

Powell, H. (2005). Recycling Junkspace: Finding space for "Playtime" in the city. *The Journal of Architecture, 10*(2), 201–221.

Pratchett, T. (2004). We build worlds, we don't just terraform planets. In G. Fuller & R. Harley (Eds.), *Aviopolis: A book about airports* (pp. 105–109). London: Black Dog Publishing.

Rosenbaum, J. (1973). Tati's democracy. *Film Comment, 9*(3), 36–41.

Schiller, G. (2004, May 5). Retailers book space on "terminal" set. *The Hollywood Reporter.* Retrieved on January 31, 2006, from http://www.hollywoodreporter.com/thr/marketing/article_display.jsp?vnu_content_id=1000502765

Shome, R. (2003). Space matters: The power and practice of space. *Communication Theory, 13*(1), 39–56.

Thomson, D. (2004, July 4). Film studies: As bright as a shopping mall, as resonant as a cemetery. *Independent (London)* (Features), p. 13.

Wood, A. (2008). "Small world": Alex Proyas' Dark City as omnitopia. In J. Perlich & D. Whitt (Eds.), *Sith, slayers, stargates and cyborgs: Modern mythology in the new millennium* (pp. 121–142). New York: Peter Lang.

II

—————— Overview ——————

One age boasts coliseums, another erects cathedrals, and another builds sky-scrapers. We know much of the dominant narrative of human society by studying its grand places. Yet contemporary life, its sweeping vistas and globe-girdling ambitions, its purgatorious bureaucracies and petty tyrannies, may be best understood when we attend closely to the far more banal places found in airports, hotels, and malls, sites that reflect the colonizing trajectory of omnito-pia from sharply detached places of pure mobility through temporary abodes of domesticity to everyday pedestrian sites of labor, commerce, and entertainment. Each of these sites demonstrates aspects of dislocation, conflation, fragmenta-tion, mobility, and mutability, and we might be tempted to strictly analyze these sites according to that framework. However, although these terms provide an adequate lens for the description of omnitopia, they offer an insufficient stance for its analysis. As a result, the question remains: How can one best analyze omnitopia? Respecting the impossibility of finding one universal answer to that question, anticipating the emergence of varied approaches, each drawing from the personal and professional inclinations of their practitioners, I offer an approach that has already yielded fruitful results.

I propose that omnitopia may be fruitfully revealed through a process of *localization*. To localize means more than to identify, confine, or transfer from a central point. Localization also may be said to transform a borderless con-tinuum into a meaningful place. From this perspective, localization reconfigures omnitopia, converting the ubiquitous enclave into a specific site imbued with time and character. From this stance, one may argue that localization reverses omnitopian practices. In place of dislocation, one reconnects an omnitopian node to its surrounding environment. In place of conflation, one reveals edges and borders. In place of fragmentation, one connects individual facades to deeper, sometimes hidden, structures. In place of mobility, one stops and surveys a site over time. In place of mutability, one studies how omnitopian nodes fix certain types of behavior and discourse as incontestable. These reversals inspired by localization offer a way to decode omnitopia, although not necessarily in a "critical" way. In fact, localization may be more accurately viewed as a study and practice of performance.

This performance of localization works to *act on* omnitopia, offering an interpretation that both explains and confounds omnitopian practices through engaged observation. This type of performance, based on the observation of signs, images, referents, and utterances, may recall, if only fleetingly, Clifford Geertz's (1973) notion of *thick description*. Certainly one hopes to offer a deep structure of truth when writing about omnitopia, not imposing meaning from above, but revealing meaning from the ground. Thus, "[r]ather than beginning with a set of observations and attempting to subsume them under a governing law, [one] begins with a set of (presumptive) signifiers and attempts to place them within an intelligible frame" (p. 26).[1] However, we are wisely reminded of Néstor García Canclini's pithy statement that "the anthropologist arrives in the city on foot, the sociologist by car and via the main highway, the communications specialist by plane" (cited in Tomlinson, 1999, p. 6), and I am therefore compelled to emphasize that localization should not be confused with ethnography, at least not in its traditional sense. One does not localize omnitopia by trying to interpret a place as "the locals" see it; for in omnitopia, there are few locals. Most of us are just passing through (indeed, with all due respect to Canclini, one should *strive* to enter omnitopia by plane). When localizing omnitopia, one should desire to move, flow, and drift through its corridors while stopping and reflecting at unauthorized and unscheduled times and places, creating a locale where others might only see homogeneity. Such is the nature of localization: not an objective recounting and description of observable phenomena, but rather a purposefully subjective articulation of a place precisely designed not to be taken personally.

An ideal tactic of localization arises when one practices *flâneur* gaze, the construction of a mobile narrative that is both intoxicated by and detached from the built environment. This notion of *flâneur* arises from the writings of Walter Benjamin, whose fragments of 19th-century Paris inspired the method for those chapters that follow. Benjamin's *flâneur* studies the city as a performance, entering the urban world in a manner both detached and personal.[2] For this figure, "[t]he city splits . . . into its dialectical poles. It opens . . . as a landscape, even as it closes . . . as a room" [M1,4/417].[3] Entering this space, transforming exterior designs into an interior monologue (a long "passage," in at least two senses of the word), the *flâneur* reads supposedly separate locales as a grand continuum even while unpacking the totalizing enclave into distinct spaces. Walking about, the *flâneur* enacts a series of movements and glances, simultaneously gazing on the entire scene and becoming lost in the labyrinth of details. Turning this way and that, photographing a faux-rusty sign, reporting overheard snatches of conversation, and gazing intently on objects meant to be unconsciously processed, the *flâneur* weaves multiple times and places into a coherent scene, reflecting (in this case) the operationalization and unraveling of omnitopia.

The *flâneur* avoids abstractions, whether they are maps or organization charts. The goal is not to reify the strategy of a place, "making invisible the operation that made it possible" (de Certeau, 1984, p. 97). Instead, the *flâneur* transforms place into performance. Such a performance reads places as scripts, but also writes on them the scripts of memory and desire, composing meaning from apparently random and disconnected referents. Certainly, Tim Edensor (2001) reminds us that this performance, similar to that of the contemporary tourist, "can be conceived in more ambivalent and contradictory terms, can be understood as intentional and unintentional, concerned with both being and becoming, strategically and unreflexively embodied" (p. 78). Yet these qualities of ambivalence and contradiction are necessary to the *flâneur* gaze, not antithetical to its pleasures. The researcher becomes a tourist, simultaneously forgetting and remembering the borders required by detached observation. Of specific interest to this process is how the *flâneur*'s performance crafts a dynamic and paradoxical interaction between the lone observer and the crowd. Wandering the streets, the *flâneur* is both at home and rootless, alone and surrounded, ambivalent and intoxicated. From this standpoint, the *flâneur* need not be imagined as some specialized observer, but rather viewed as a choice available to anyone who wishes to see what other people ignore.

In the next three chapters, I offer an illustration of my efforts to perform the localizing view of the *flâneur* gaze. My studies of airports, hotels, and malls have relied on days and nights of wandering through these places, both in the United States and elsewhere, studying the permeability of borders, noting authorized and unauthorized behaviors, and observing traffic flows within and around them. During these observations and afterward, I tried to accomplish three goals: identify historical processes that have led to an omnitopian sensibility, describe rich examples of omnitopian practice, and evaluate potentials (intentional or accidental, strategic or tactical) to invoke a sense of locale within these omnitopian nodes. From field notes, voice recordings, photographs, and souvenirs, I paid close attention to places that most folks dismiss as being devoid of meaning, studying the ways these sites communicate something about people and values. These places, after all, increasingly reflect and affect values of what may be said. Part II summarizes the results of my inquiries into omnitopia as being more than a concept, but rather as enacting a network of places.

Notes

1. I also drew inspiration from Michael Leff's (1980) extension of this framework to the practice of rhetorical criticism, such that, "The interpreter keeps his or her atten-

tion focused close to the ground, and while the explanation of what is seen often has potential implications that extend beyond the particular case, the potential is not realized in terms of a disembodied abstraction" (p. 347).

2. I am not the first communication scholar to propose that Walter Benjamin's *flâneur* can be usefully articulated from the perspective of performance. For example, Michael Bowman (1988) notes how the *flâneur's* strolls "register all the 'shocks' of modern life, against which our psychological and cultural apparati have inoculated us, in order to recombine them into a new product" (p. 8).

3. My choice of ellipses [obscuring the phrases "for him," "to him," and "around him"] cannot elide the debate waged by feminist-identified readers to define the *flâneur's* role within the structure of patriarchy. Janet Wolff (1985) has described the impossibility of the *flâneuse*, while Wearing and Wearing (1996) have sought to replace the *flâneur* with the *choraster*. Other scholars have compared the *flâneur* to the prostitute (Buck-Morss, 1986) and to the paparazzi (Jokinen & Veijola, 1997). This being said, feminist readings of the *flâneur* are no more homogenous than feminist theorists. For example, Anne Friedberg (1993), Anke Gleber (1999), Mica Nava (1997), and Elizabeth Wilson (2001) have argued that 19th-century and early 20th-century women employed comparable tactics to those of the *flâneur*.

References

Benjamin, W. (2004). *The arcades project* (H. Eiland & K. McLaughlin, Trans.). Cambridge, MA: Harvard University Press.

Bowman, M. S. (1988). Cultural critique as performance: The example of Walter Benjamin. *Literature in Performance, 8*(1), 4–11.

Buck-Morss, S. (1986). The flaneur, the sandwichman and the whore: The politics of loitering. *New German Critique, 39,* 99–140.

de Certeau, M. (1984). *The practice of everyday life* (S. Rendall, Trans.). Berkeley: University of California Press.

Edensor, T. (2001). Performing tourism, staging tourism: (Re)producing tourist space and practice. *Tourist Studies, 1*(1), 59–81.

Friedberg, A. (1993). *Window shopping: Cinema and the postmodern.* Berkeley: University of California Press.

Geertz, C. (1973). *The interpretation of cultures: Selected essays by Clifford Geertz.* New York: Basic Books.

Gleber, A. (1999). *The art of taking a walk: Flanerie, literature, and film in Weimar culture.* Princeton: Princeton University Press.

Jokinen, E., & Veijola, S. (1997). The disoriented tourist: The figuration of the tourist in contemporary cultural critique. In C. Rojek & J. Urry (Eds.), *Touring cultures: Transformations of travel and theory* (pp. 23–51). London: Routledge.

Leff, M. (1980). Interpretation and the art of the rhetorical critic. *Western Journal of Speech Communication, 44,* 337–349.

Nava, M. (1997). Women, the city and the department store. In P. Falk & C. Campbell (Eds.), *The shopping experience* (pp. 56–91). London: Sage.

Tomlinson, J. (1999). *Globalization and culture*. Chicago: University of Chicago Press.

Wearing, B., & Wearing, S. (1996). Refocusing the tourist experience: The flâneur and the choraster. *Leisure Studies, 16*(4), 229–243.

Wilson, E. (2001). *The contradictions of culture: Cities, culture, women*. London: Sage.

Wolff, J. (1985). The invisible *flâneuse*: Women and the literature of modernity. *Theory Culture & Society, 2*, 37–46.

4

Airports

[T]he notion of the terminal as a passageway for travelers vies with the conception of it as a city on a hill, an enclave amid wastelands.

—Martha Rosler (1994, p. 69)

If you travel by airplane long enough, you will eventually label an airport as "yours," label and airport as "yours." Your home terminal is filled with familiar signs and pathways, even smells that convey a sense of place that cannot be duplicated. You may even get to know workers at the concessions on a first-name basis, or you may offer a knowing nod to the security person who smiles when you pass into the secured regime of "airside." My home airport is Mineta San José International Airport (SJC), named after former Secretary of Transportation Norman Y. Mineta. My first visit to San Jose deposited me to the "old terminal" where passengers descend onto tarmacs and walk to the terminal in a manner that reminds me of 1940s-era movies. Unlike many other international airports, SJC is so close to San José's urban core that it forces strict height limits on downtown buildings, lest they interfere with flight plans. In this way, I share with anyone who has spent some time in flight the sense that all airports are unique to someone.

Travel long enough and you will discover the quirks of other airports too. Just as your originating airport offers a conduit to home and hearth, other airports you may frequent become dependable for the frustrations they inspire or the otherworldly beauties they contain. Dallas becomes a massive tram system. Heathrow becomes an overcrowded mess. Singapore becomes a customer service mecca. Each airport becomes a place worthy of memory, a unique site worthy of stories and souvenirs, and, for many passengers, a miniature version of the places they represent. Although these airports will never be confused with your "home" airport, they offer a comforting familiarity despite the occasionally hellish memories they inspire. From this sense, one may fairly wonder how any airport could be bound within omnitopia because all of them are meaningful in some way, even if only in a bad way.

Even so, I propose that airports become omnitopian when they allow entrance into a convergence of connected spaces, each flowing smoothly from one to the other, allowing a momentary forgetting of geographic location. As nodes of omnitopia, airports further represent the refinement of public life and meaningful communication to functional and commercial exchanges. Finally, as more and more places appear to resemble airports, we begin to identify a colonization of an omnitopian sensibility that denigrates the value of place even as more varied sites are connected by shorter travel times. Careful study of these omnitopian nodes requires that we shift our attention from somewhat caricatured cinematic exemplars toward an analysis of the structures and perceptions that comprise the terminal. To that end, we concentrate our attention on the terminal as all-place, the terminal in motion, and the terminal's aura of atomized interaction before concluding with an application of this perspective to the post-9/11 airport.

The Terminal as All-Place

When we speak of "the" terminal, we refer to a manifestation of omnitopia, that continuum of ubiquity that relies on many factors to exist, beginning with a desire, even if inchoate, to inhabit an enclave of dislocation. The nature of this enclave offers a starting point of analysis. Marc Augé (1995) offers an exceptionally fecund point of departure with his articulation of non-places:

> [N]on-places are the real measure of our time; one that could be quantified—with the aid of a few conversations between area, volume and distance—by totaling all the air, rail and motorway routes, the mobile cabins called "means of transport" (aircraft, trains and road vehicles), the airports and railway stations, hotel chains, leisure parks, large retail outlets, and finally the complex skein of cable and wireless networks that mobilize extraterrestrial space for the purposes of communication so peculiar that it often puts the individual in contact only with another image of himself. (p. 79)

Although airports remain connected to a range of ecologies, some natural, some human made, they reside within abstractions. Augé's description of airports follows from this line, suggesting discrete waiting places of empty and meaningless exchanges, punctuated by signs that signify only other constellations of signs. Following Augé, even if rejecting his conclusions, a number of scholars have sought to study the ways in which meaning manages to erupt amid these isolated and isolating places. Murphy (2002) offers one illustrative direction in this regard, proposing that performances of normality and impromptu acts of resistance demonstrate the impossibility of non-places. I, too, presume such a possibility. But I think that both Augé and his critics should focus less on individual (and individuating) locations and concentrate more on how separate places converge, at least in perception, into one. I believe the global complex of airport terminals offers an exemplary starting point for this analysis.

When the terminal functions according to design (avoiding the editorial implications of additional descriptors such as "best" or "insidiously"), distinct spaces of reflection or even resistance blur into a seamless whole. As a result, when describing airports as nodes of omnitopia, we should not refer to one terminal except as an example reflecting omnitopian terminals. In other words, the terminal is the domain where all gates lead, a secure synecdoche of the world. To provide further insight to this notion, we should consider the etymology of the word *terminal*. The word stems from the Latin *terminus*, referring to a marker that designates a border. That border, difficult to the privileged among us to see, remains powerful indeed for many people, especially those stateless people shuttling from immigration office to immigration office within a disciplined conveyer belt.

Nonetheless, the concept of terminal eventually becomes associated with lines of transportation ending in certain locations. Intriguingly, the meaning evolved from border to center (of sorts) when terminals began to represent junctions between multiple transportation lines. One may still end a journey at the terminal, but one more frequently passes through terminals on the way to the end. More important, the collective dream of places within this passage becomes a place unto itself, an enclave most notable for its promise (even if tragically unfilled) of security. Within the hub-airport terminal, one need never step outside into the dangerous environs of urban cores. Here, we might differentiate between hub airports, the focus of this inquiry, and regional or municipal airports whose gateways and passenger spaces fail to offer the tools of connectivity typically found in the terminal (Rutner & Mundy, 1996). When one surveys the terminal, one discovers an interconnected matrix of transportation devices that connect passengers as fluidly as possible to automated teller machines, hotel shuttles, atrium lobbies, elevated walkways, food courts, theme restaurants, and enclosed malls that permit one to read the world as a coherent narrative, unperturbed by local politics or characters.

As an ideal, if not as a reality, the terminal promises consistency, a terrain that allows almost no topography, only a series of smooth, unstriated transitions. This ubiquitous, placeless city represents a rhetoric of ubiquity wherein, as the aphorism reminds us, "Wherever you go, there you are." A reasonable response to this rather gloomy assessment of terminal life is to celebrate recent attempts to make airports more than a series of shuttles, gates, and chairs, efficient in their simultaneous elegance and lack of comfort. For example, one might propose that recently built or renovated airports such as those found in Denver and Hong

Kong offer bold architectural challenges to this notion of anonymous architecture. Hong Kong's International's airy spaces and Reagan National's historical playfulness provoke visions of a truly new kind of airport design, places worth visiting in their own right.[1] Gottdiener (2001) writes,

> [A] new aesthetic specific to airline terminals has emerged. It deemphasizes ticketing areas and the elements of the 19th-century railroad terminal in favor of a direct, visible connection between passengers and their jets. High domed structures using natural light create a large scale that helps minimize the intrusive aspects of airport commercialization. Their airy feel, helped along by large plate glass walls, seems an antidote to the kind of oppressive enclosure of the older airports that have grown by adding on. The spectacular structure of the new terminal spaces seems to float in the air or to be poised to take wing. (p. 70)

However, the ideal mode of movement, defined by brief moments of consumption rather than reflection, ultimately serves to affirm this notion of omnitopia, such that failure of the airport to flow into the larger grid of human conveyance (e.g., the well-publicized difficulties of the Denver baggage system in its early years) reflects a much more serious problem than the design of pleasant interiors. Here, the generic quality of the terminal, its familiarity and consistency so aptly described in Anne Tyler's *The Accidental Tourist*, serves a practical function (Walters, 1993). The terminal reduces the need or even the validity of specialized locales by offering a calm respite from the frenzied challenges of contemporary life. To enter a strange airport and navigate its complexity is to embrace the hope that one place is pretty much like another.

This is not to presume that the terminals of individual airports are literally alike, any more than must individual computer terminals be homogenized to transport their users to the consensual hallucination of cyberspace. Omnitopia does not denote literal interchangeability. Although commercial globalization may be illustrated by the efficient exchange of standardized shipping containers, omnitopia thrives in fragmentation, the appearance of distinct locales.

> Cairo Airport may look nothing like Singapore's Changi Airport, but its information is the same—it is designed to process mobility. It is a self-renewing machine that "refreshes" after each take-off and landing. Planes download passengers, baggage, cargo, excreta, and rubbish, and, then, upload passengers, baggage, cargo, fuel, food and packaged gadgets. The airport propels and regulates direction and flow. The sky is turned into bandwidth as planes move along specified air corridors. (Fuller & Harley, 2004, p. 43)

Certainly, terminal loudspeakers may announce local or state ordinances ("Florida is an indoor clean air state. Smoking is prohibited in the terminal . . ."), and one may find an MSP pin in Minneapolis, some Silicon Valley t-shirts in San

Jose, or a miniature Eiffel Tower in Paris, but the authors of these cultural totems rarely claim any connection to their wares; these are trinkets extolling the virtues of logos, not locales. Moreover, the various port authorities, management consortiums, and company shareholders responsible for the construction of the terminal are generally invisible to those who inhabit these locales. The airport terminal may be named for a famous local citizen; its architecture may be loosely inspired by regional décor; and even its shape may suggest idiosyncratic whimsy, but its ideal form is organized around consistent signage, uniform package styles, and unchanging expectations. The terminal is a process as much as a place.

In this process resides a question: When you visit an airport, do you visit the city in which that port is located? Here, one might recall a headline of the satirical newspaper, *The Onion*: "Woman who 'loves Brazil' has only seen four square miles of it." Writing in *Proceedings of the Institution of Civil Engineers (Transport)*, De Neufville (1995) supports the claim that airport terminals invoke a separate identity from the cities that surround them:

> The notion that the passenger building is a terminal implies that the loads on the building are independent of its design. If passengers want to see Paris, they are unlikely to let the design of a building influence their travel plans. (p. 98)

Patke (2000) adds that the airport may be compared to the mall, both mediating between inside and outside, offering an illusion in place of the real place. Gazing out the windows of a terminal at LAX, you are rewarded with a postcard view of the city's towers shrouded by a thin layer of haze, but the view is no more LA than a mural or painting. One is not "in" LA while passing through LAX any more than one gets wet while "surfing" the Internet. In a major airport like LAX, you never get the sense that "at last, I see what Los Angelinos are like." There are no real Angelinos in LAX. No Californians or Americans, either. In fact, omnitopia as a series of waiting rooms becomes *most* pronounced to the international traveler who is otherwise unable to read the signs and nuances of a place. For me, this notion becomes most vivid when I look back on a recent tour of airports in Japan, Hong Kong, and Singapore. Reflecting on that intense burst of *flânerie*, I find it most accurate somehow to write in the present tense. The perceived timelessness of omnitopia demands such prose, I think.

Departing San Jose on a Tuesday afternoon, I arrive in Narita Airport at about 4 p.m. on Wednesday, 11 hours later. Residing in a temporal space that bends and crosses reality like a tesseract reminds me of Pico Iyer's account of flight:

> [Not] knowing whether I was facing east or west, not knowing whether it was night or day, I slipped into that peculiar state of mind—or no-mind—that belongs to the no-time, no-place of the airport, that out-of-body state in

> which one's not quite there, but certainly not elsewhere. My words didn't
> quite connect, and the world came to me through panes of soundproof
> glass. I felt myself in a state of suspended animation, five miles above the
> sea—sleepy, light-headed, unsure of how much pressure to put on things. I
> had entered the stateless state of jet lag. (2000, p. 59)

Arrival means shifting from one way station to another. Narita serves as the
standard transition point for international travelers visiting or passing through
Tokyo. Well designed for long-term stays, Narita includes plenty of amenities
for travelers planning to spend more than an hour within its confines: meeting
rooms, dayrooms, Internet cafes, massage chairs, and "media rooms" for watching
movies. The terminal is kept scrupulously clean and is well guarded by patrolling
security personnel. As I depart the plane, I am buzzed with excitement. I have
no clue where I'll sleep this evening.

Narita resides far from the heart of Japan's capital city, in a different prefecture,
in fact. Although Tokyo International Airport lies nearer to the city, it concentrates
on domestic and cargo traffic more than international traffic. I note this with some
amusement and annoyance. Train lines run directly from Narita to mammoth
(and astoundingly complex) Tokyo Station, departing directly from the airport.
Yet the fastest of these takes about an hour and costs a bundle. Oddly enough,
this is an improvement over the previous era, when visitors were forced to take

Image 8: Tokyo Train. *Photograph by Andrew Wood*

shuttle buses to more distant train stations connecting to downtown Tokyo. The airport awaits the opening of the Narita Rapid Railway in 2010. In the meantime, most visitors bypass more pricy trains (with their reserved seating and more direct routes) and take the Kaisoku Airport Narita Train instead. During rush hour, this means up to an hour and a half of strap-hanging if you don't snag a seat early or if you choose to abandon yours for elderly or infirmed travelers. I give up my seat going both directions. The feeling of a good deed lasts a while, but I must admit that the trips stretch quite a bit beyond that point.

I exit onto one of the many, many platforms of Tokyo Station. Immediately, I learn that this city's interconnecting trains, subways, and buses create a tangle of routes. Not knowing the language, I must learn quickly the meanings of various icons placed to guide me. One symbol, a man racing through a door, looks positively ominous, particularly with the green shadow extending from his leg. Before long, I reason (before reading the tiny English script) that this sign means "exit." More than any other sign, knowing where to exit marks freedom within omnitopia. Here I recall wandering the floors and walkways and passages of interconnected Las Vegas hotels, sensing that I may never escape this enclosure. The dearth of windows and the lack of natural light create a claustrophobia that may be compared to residents of a maximum-security prison. But seeing the running man, his green shadow reminding me of a mid-century detective book, offers me the path outside. Only at this moment, departing a subway station set at a far distance from the airport, do I feel that I've departed omnitopia.

The Terminal and Movement

Movement—from airport to plane to airport to subway to station to exit—illustrates a central objective of omnitopian design, the goal (if not the practice) of constant flow. Unless conducting research on airports, most inhabitants hope merely to pass through each threshold with an aim of departure. One can hardly wonder. Apart from quirky cinematic figures, few people would wish to live in an airport. This is not to ignore the temporary cessation of movement that may be found in all airports. Lloyd (2003) reminds us of the principle of "dwelltime" being built into the designs of contemporary airports, the assumption and even desire for passengers to depart the moving pathway from time to time, to chat, to shop, to rest:

> The modernist spatial strategies of the functionalist "city of circulation" advocated by architects such as Le Corbusier have been radically reconfigured by new economic formations such as the airport mall. The opposition of habituation and circulation in the modernist urban model is overridden by new spaces that offer "pleasurable waiting." (p. 107)

Adey (2007) advances this line of reasoning with an analysis of how spectacle and commerce have been intertwined in the terminal to inspire more than mere movement, but rather to blur the airport and other components of contemporary life, most notably, malls:

> From the airline's point of view it is advantageous for passengers to move through the terminal as quickly as possible, so that they may avoid delays waiting for lost or late passengers. Yet the airport wants passengers to dwell for as long as possible in the shopping and catering facilities provided. The result is a balance between mobility and immobility. (p. 522)

In these moments of immobility, one may stand under a screen to search for a connecting gate, one may sit near a panoramic window to watch the planes land and depart, one may stroll through shops in search of souvenirs, and one will certainly wait in a security queue. Like the casino, the mall, and even the penitentiary, motion and stasis are complexly intertwined in the terminal. As Salter (2007) emphasizes, "The trick of the modern airport is to present immobility as mobility, stagnancy as efficiency, and incarceration as freedom" (p. 53). One gathers from these sorts of analyses a desire to complicate mobility, to reveal its polysemic nature, and to point out its limitations. Such is a worthy project. The terminals known by deported immigrants cannot be confused with the "transports of delight" built for "first-class" passengers (Urry, 2001). Some people can't wait to get out of an airport, whereas some can't manage to get in. Yet one must not forget that airports, ultimately, are about movement. One may wait in an airport. One may shop in an airport. One may be delayed in an airport. One may be arrested in an airport. But one eventually must depart an airport. This is the indisputable goal of mobility. Despite stories of homeless occupants of the terminal, virtually every traveler you meet in the terminal is simply passing through.

For many of these mobile inhabitants of the terminal, movement becomes more than a structural necessity; it becomes a form of pleasure. Consider the odd comfort of a discarded *USA Today* you might pick up while sitting in a terminal. The "hometown" paper for most mobile Americans, *USA Today* reveals little detail about a specific locale, even where it is found, leaving news about regional festivals, byzantine city hall politics, and local arrests for petty crimes to the local papers. Like fast-food restaurants near a busy interstate highway and national cable channels in an impersonal hotel room, however, *USA Today* promises consistency. One may pick up a *USA Today* in one airport terminal, read the paper on an airplane, and leave it in another terminal, confident that the paper can circulate around the country from anonymous reader to anonymous reader, at least for a day.

A similar example of how airport terminals become nodes of mobile
media may be found in the InMotion portable entertainment services that are
available in airports stretching from Anchorage, Alaska, to Tampa, Florida. The
InMotion service, by its name alone, indicates the company's mission: to provide
mobile passengers mobile entertainment without regard for place. Paradoxically,
InMotion promises to accomplish their purpose, not through the annihilation of
place, but through the conflation of place. With this service, travelers can rent
DVD players and films at one location and return them elsewhere. The stag-
geringly complex infrastructure that makes possible this transformation from
traditional point-of-sale relationships between consumers and merchants is made
possible by computer networks, overnight mail, and a network of pick-up/drop-
off terminals. This distributed economy reflects the larger practice of ubiquitous
merchant presence of brands that promise to offer (in the argot of new media
companies) more immersive content-rich, higher bandwidth user experiences.
The ubiquitous presence and fluid transmission of these media illustrate a growing desire for mobile identity and homogenized culture that allows us to bypass
locales in place of an endless "here."

Within this flow, individual character may be found, but it is either fleeting
or suspect. In the terminal, distinctions between individual nationalities, racial
categories, and ethnic groups diminish within the homogenous community
of movement except, as we find herein, at security screening points. Even in
international terminals, one finds few moments in which cultural differences
assert themselves in ways that transcend superficial, mass-produced fashion.
Once more, Pico Iyer (2000) reminds us:

> A modern airport is based on the assumption that everyone's from some-
> where else, and so in need of something he can recognize to make him feel
> at home; it becomes, therefore, an anthology of generic spaces—the shopping
> mall, the food court, the hotel lobby—which bear the same relation to life,
> perhaps, that Muzak does to music. (p. 43)

Initially, an inbound plane may disgorge hundreds of folks from a unique location,
each sharing the same language and styles of attire. But soon, this momentary
explosion of difference quickly becomes homogenized. The purpose of the terminal is to minimize these moments of locality as quickly as possible, to drop
people like a sluice into the urban core. This is not to suggest that such "sluicing"
occurs without difficulty. Writing in *Transportation Research*, Odoni (1992) states,
"Implicit in the formula is the idea that occupants of a space somehow disperse
to make use of an entire area. People are not gasses, however, and unfortunately
no such physical law exists for them" (p. 29). In the absence of physical laws,
made firm through structure, the terminal relies on a discourse of utterances,
rules, and practices, all reminding us: keep moving.

Image 9: Keep Moving. *Photograph by Andrew Wood*

To manage this flow of human and machine traffic, the terminal expands outward in a complex of entrances, passageways, holding areas, turnabouts, and exits, all designed to facilitate movement. Writing in *International Civil Aviation Organization Journal*, Fentress (2000) comments on the contemporary goal of terminal design:

> A terminal must be designed so that the architecture of the building aids in leading the passenger from curbside to aircraft, and from aircraft to baggage claim, in the most direct way. The lighting design complements the architecture while providing comfortable, ambient natural light to assist passenger orientation throughout the building. . . . Concern with humanism is becoming integrally expressed in airport terminal architecture. Comfort is paramount: spaces soaring, not constricting; edges and surfaces softened; services easy to locate; feelings of tunneling of burrowing through the "machine" of the building minimized; circulation paths determined as much as possible to reduce the appearance and feeling of herding. (pp. 13–14)

Despite the appearance of an open and airy venue, repetition and modularity become even more deeply woven into the terminal aesthetic. As airlines emerge, merge, and collapse, gates and even terminals require a fundamental mutability in order to function. Consider the wide-body passenger jet that must be able to employ any number of gates depending on the needs of maintenance crews and the alteration of security procedures. Veteran fliers learn to memorize certain gates for certain departures, but they also prepare for unexpected changes. Even terminal signs must be modular. One does not travel to Miami from a certain gate. Rather, one travels to any number of locations from a gate whose name is temporary, a shell to be quickly cast off. Only the moment defines the destination. Given the ceaseless flow of mode and media, it is easy to get lost. In response, one finds overhead "you are here" views at various nodes of the network. These signs do work to provide orientation to an airport, but they do not create spaces that might be described as meaningful or unique. Traveling from city to city, terminal to terminal, and gate to gate, one imagines the overhead views to be manifestations of the same matrix: different angles of the same homogenous structure.

The quintessential example of how the terminal invokes fluidity may be found in its moving pathways. Designed to facilitate rapid transfer of travelers from gate to gate, these devices make plain the distinction, even the antipathy, between mobile and less mobile occupants of the terminal. Typically, one finds static travelers weighed down by luggage or, perhaps, in no hurry, lining the right side of the platform. For fast-moving terminal dwellers, these baggage-laden folks become obstacles. Streaming along the left, the more rapid traveler demonstrates mastery of the central lesson of the terminal: pack light because anything you need may be purchased in small quantities at an airport concession. Once the moving walkway becomes a place, a location, or something worth remembering, it fails in its central task. Further, one might imagine standing next to a walkway as travelers stream past, standing or walking. A person failing even to walk alongside the moving path, choosing instead to become an immobile pedestrian, becomes suspect. Why would someone stand in an airport unless they're planning to move once more?

Beyond the moving walkway, one finds the growth of trams (popularized in 1971 at Tampa International Airport). These people movers transform individual buildings into passenger through-stations defined by decentralization and decreased walking distance (Mumayiz, 1989). Trams are even used within large linear spaces such as Detroit's Edward H. McNamara Terminal ("New Hub," 2002). Through the aid of moving walkways and trams, the first-generation grand terminal of pre-World War II, and even the second-generation airports of the late 1950s and early 1960s, become replaced by third-generation midfield airports that can accommodate wide-bodied jets (Mumayiz, 1989). Again, they work when they cannot be noticed. Noticed, they do not work.

One might find a counterpoint to this notion of fluidity in the form of those uncomfortable chairs found in airport gates. However, those who have spent hours in one of these chairs recognize a profound irony. Racing through an airport, scooting past static figures lining the right-hand side of the pathway, one discovers the destination of the harried denizens of the terminal: a gate, a conduit, a portal to yet more travel. No one really wants to sit in an airport; the practice represents defeat of the purpose of travel. The place of delay, often packed with crying infants, lounging teenagers, stressed parents, and mobile phone-engaged business travelers, has no meaning except as a location from which anyone with any sense wishes to depart. The network of media nodes—wireless faxing, global telephone connections, and Internet access—makes the terminal an annex, a temporary appendix, a "branch office" between other presumably more meaningful places. Perhaps this sense of mobility is perhaps best seen in a place such as Hong Kong, whose airport personnel are well practiced in moving large groups of people. Once more, I select the present tense to recall a recent visit.

It is late when I arrive, but Hong Kong's International Airport is bustling with fast-moving passengers and strictly efficient experts in crowd control. I am engulfed in a crowd of deplaning travelers, submitting to its direction and pre-suming that it will take me where I must go. Collectively, we flow along moving walkways and escalators through customs and toward the departure space. I spot a hotel check-in desk and find myself selecting a room without much conscious effort. The attendant shows me the cost, notes the currency exchange, and books my room. I'm not really in Hong Kong, and I'm no longer on the airplane, but rather somewhere that is not quite physical, a site of transfer that is not quite here and not quite there.

After arranging my room, I am pointed to the airport bus desk. I state my name and hotel, and a uniformed fellow slaps a sticker on my shirt. I hear something about "orange," and I am pointed down an escalator. I have no idea where I'm going, but I trust the system. Descending, I see orange vests. I make eye contact with the wearer of one, and she points to a seat. Within a minute, a bus arrives, and the driver calls my last name. Soon we depart the airport and head for the mainland. Onboard, we streak along a long bridge that connects us to our destination, Tsim Sha Tsui on the Kowloon Peninsula. To the left, I spot another bridge lined with a red strip that resembles a laser under the moonlight. Our drive reveals an increasingly impressive array of buildings, each appearing as a clone of its neighbor, as if local urban designers decreed that if one build-ing works pretty well a dozen clones work even better. But Hong Kong harbor is special. With its size, height, and animated color, this city boasts one of the most impressive skylines in the world.

The next day, I return to the airport, where I plan to sleep for the night. It has been a few years since I've slept in an airport, a couple nights in Wash-ington, DC's Reagan National Airport, and I figure my research would benefit from the lousy night's sleep. Unfortunately, I am unable to get "airside" and am stuck in the terminal's cold, immense enclosure. An advertisement proclaims the airport's design: "Uplifting architecture, bathed in natural light. . . ." After midnight, however, there's nothing natural about the harsh white light that fills the cavernous terminal. It's like living under a giant parachute. Most frustratingly, the terminal seating includes dividers that render it impossible to stretch out for sleep. Some folks who, like me, are anticipating a morning flight manage to contort their bodies into some sort of sleeping position, but I cannot. So I put my belongings in a cart and shuffle from place to place. Heavy-lidded, I offer a wan smile at fellow airport zombies who glide past. By 2 a.m., I decide to search for a wireless hotspot. A couple of coffee shops offer desktop Internet access, but I'd rather not worry about folks lining up for their turn. Ostensibly, there is no free wireless in the terminal, but a little patience and some hunting reveals a few tiny spots where I can get passable reception. So I surf and write and wait for Singapore Airlines to open their desk. Even while stationary, I search for ways to move through cyberspace. Taken together, the moving walkway, the tram, the terminal seat, and even the computer terminal enact a paradoxical practice of movement best described by the lyric of a 1987 song by the Irish band, U2: "running to stand still." With this omnitopia of movement, one struggles for moments of genuine human contact. One finds, instead, a world of atomized interactions.

The Terminal and Atomized Interactions

Standing in line to board a Southwest Airlines flight in San Jose, a 50-something woman rushes up behind me in a panic. "Are you Las Vegas?" she asks. "Vegas," I reply. "Group A?" she confirms. "Yep," I reply. There really is nothing else to say. Moments such as these illustrate how the terminal reduces human relationships to a series of anonymous interactions. To the harried woman, I am merely a conduit to information, which is a conduit to a place. I am marked by my utility, and I am quickly discarded thereafter. One might recall dialogue from the 1999 film, *Fight Club*: "Everywhere I travel. . . . Single-serving sugar, single-serving cream, single pat of butter. The microwave Cordon bleu hobby-kit. Shampoo-conditioner combos. Sample-packaged mouthwash. The people I meet on flights? They're single-serving friends."

A visit to SJC provides further illustration. Bobbing forward in the grinding queue as passengers lingered in the liminal space between grounded movement and airborne docility, a woman speaks energetically to no one. Only after the tiny microphone that hung under her chin reveals itself do her words make a little bit of sense: "This piece of paper supports a *dialogue* that facilitates our interface with the creative *team* [emphasis hers]." One cannot help but wonder at the role of performance in this locale. Does the nearby man with brand-new DVD player/computer absolutely need to pace the terrazzo floor, his new toy perched precariously on one hand, a mobile phone jutted in front of his face with the other? For many inhabitants of the terminal, the conspicuous display of media use provides a clear indication of the atomized state of human relationships: I am not really here. Dickinson (1997) described this sensibility aptly, noting, "the emphasis on stylized, performative identities within modern consumer culture; the ways transnational culture at once atomizes and abstracts place-based communities" (p. 4). The rhetoric of the terminal is the speech of anonymous authors whose words receive no response and suffer no consequence, the construction of the atomized individual. The text may be judged effectively by its ability to appear utterly corporate and imminently anonymous.

Reading the terminal demands close attention to the methods by which individuals employ wireless connections to hybrids of home, office, and entertainment to maintain that anonymity, even with persons sharing the same location. After all, the airport hub is also a network hub. That is to say, the terminal offers an increasingly wireless interchange of data conduits through which individuals zealously maintain their connections with workspaces and loved ones who are not there. The odd sensation of observing intimate strangers in the terminal, persons in close proximity walking from gate to gate together but talking with persons not there, reflects a larger contest of meanings between immanent place and omnitopia. In fast-food pit stops, it is difficult to determine whether people sitting at the same table are together when each person is caught up in animated conversation on his or her individual phone. Portable MP3 players, with no moving parts to skip the beat while jostled, allow individuals to craft atomized aural spaces. Terminal inhabitants bop to their own personal concert halls as a blur of strangers rushes by. Here, we are wise to consider how the terminal works to blur alienation and intimacy.

Like the mobile phone user in places of public transit who is unable or unwilling to modulate her or his volume to reflect the personal nature of the interaction, the terminal dweller imagines the locale to be private when it is quite public. Perhaps it might best be termed *pseudoprivate* by the invocation of an illusory sense that one's interactions are located somehow in another space than that shared by fellow travelers. Random interpersonal connections, like those sought by various airport peddlers of religion, must be metered to the rapidity of the fast trot. Otherwise how would you inspire spiritual reflection (and maybe a small donation) from someone lugging his or her temporary load of worldly possessions from one gate to the next? I reflect back to a LAX visit, observing well-scrubbed 20-somethings who engage in a delicate dance with the law as they gently accost passersby. Passengers standing in line to get a plastic boarding pass are generally safe, but mobile folks in between the islands of lines are fair game. A crew of college jocks find themselves joined by a friendly kid in a suit and spats. Saving souls with time-tested lines, he is brushed off, but turns quickly to a passing woman. "Shake a hand and make a friend," he coos: "I like your smile." The unsmiling woman keeps walking, her gaze communicating disgust as if she is stuck in flypaper. Overhead, hidden speakers blare: "You are not required to give money to solicitors. This airport does not sponsor their activities." The person who occupies the terminal moves through a series of locales designed to allow both the mass conveyance of large groups and the individual freedom of solitary travelers. In this way, the terminal enclave offers a permeable membrane of perceptual distinctions.

That being said, the membrane may be pierced in a myriad of ways. Eruptions of locality, most notably in those unplanned and unauthorized moments in which people use and manipulate places to their own ends, occur frequently, and they can easily transform even the most banal places into meaningful spaces. Some of these moments may be meaningful and affirming. Others are simply odd. Consider the example of one airport men's room in Minneapolis–St. Paul International Airport, which has become (at the time of this writing) a tourist attraction. Initially, we might reflect on the typical design of a terminal restroom. For understandable reasons, this kind of site is designed entirely for fluid movement and aided by curved pathways that guide users to entrances and exits, often without the potential delay of crossed paths. One enters the terminal restroom with no desire to remember one's actions therein. Success is smooth departure. Yet airport travelers have transformed one otherwise forgettable site at MSP into a meaningful place (Capecchi, 2007). This is the site where Idaho Senator Larry Craig was arrested for allegedly soliciting sex from an undercover police officer. Beyond Craig's own supposed transformation of this place into a space for illicit sex, one cannot help but marvel at the ways in which tourists queued up to photograph a place that they'd otherwise walk past (or through) as quickly as possible:

> Since Aug. 27, when the arrest of Mr. Craig became known publicly, the restroom has become a source of amusement for travelers and employees at Minneapolis-St. Paul International Airport. Some pose for pictures before the outer door. Others enter to zoom in on the light-blue stall the senator used, the eighth of nine in a row. The undercover officer who arrested Mr. Craig was in the stall to his right, the seventh stall. . . .
>
> Jeff Lehman of Saugatuck, Mich., used his cellphone to capture a close-up of the stall Mr. Craig used, and attached a caption: "We call that 'The Minneapolis-St. Paul Recreation Center.' " . . .
>
> Back from a trip to Lincoln, Neb., Robert Kelen went into the men's room to change his 15-month-old daughter's diaper for "historic reasons." When he reappeared, he patted the baby's stomach. "Eloise," he said, "now you can say you've been there." (p. 20)

The potential for an interchangeable restroom to become a "here" or a "there"—a place worthy of time, a place representative of a time—in other words, a *locale*, illustrates the tenuous borders of the omnitopian enclave.

These constructions of locality need not be so sordid. I recall another visit to LAX in which I sought to photograph the rows of uncomfortable chairs filling a forgotten gate. Nearby, a fellow strummed a guitar. For no identifiable reason, a flight attendant ambled by and then paused, asking if she could play. For a few moments, she gamely struggled through a few chords. No musician myself, I could tell she was still learning, but for some reason a small crowd gathered, drawn to the music and its own growing sense of community. For 5 minutes or so, she played while an ad hoc chorus sang along. I don't remember the song, but I do remember the longing to join them. Just then, a gate change announcement sounded, and the group quickly disbanded. Within seconds, I could find no trace of this community, not even an abandoned newspaper. Moments such as these demonstrate the ease at which omnitopia may become a locale; they reveal the ease at which "the" terminal becomes "a" terminal, at least for a time.

We must emphasize the possibility, even the inevitability, of puncture to the omnitopian enclave. A consensual hallucination, again employing William Gibson's brilliant phrase, omnitopia resides in the choice to reside within omnitopia. One may easily choose not to live there, to transform ubiquitous place into local space. Such is the moment known by all of us who have attempted to navigate a fluid pathway through urban streets only to confront a panhandler whose request for spare change creates a site of contention, a locale where needs and motives assume a deeply personal meaning. Anyone who has talked with a panhandler, or has been one, knows how easy, and sometimes how necessary, it is to pierce the omnitopian bubble. Such a moment may be filled with potential, the joy of human contact, or it may be fraught with fear and anxiety, because just as the terminals of omnitopia may contain transcendence, they may also contain terror. In those explosive seconds that fracture "before" and "after," boundaries and borders reveal themselves suddenly in sharp relief.

Airports in the Post-9/11 Era

Although most people recall the September 11, 2001 attacks for their burning images of collapsing buildings, horrifying moments of pluming smoke that tumbled through the streets of lower Manhattan, an almost similarly frightening moment was the announcement that all commercial air travel anywhere in the United States had been shut down. There was something almost existentially unsettling about the reality that every plane flying across the nation had been forced to land, a sense that the entire country had been called to halt. Along with the televised violence of 9/11, the temporary collapse of U.S. air travel blew apart the promise of placeless, frictionless, anonymous flight. Prior to the terrorist attacks, the breathless accounts of survivors, the solemn mutterings of enhanced security measures, air travel had become a nonevent for most travelers. The notion that one might sit for hours in a cramped and uncomfortable series of rooms (even one that moved) became a blank spot within one's itinerary. Air travel was reduced to merely a series of times and gates, departures and landings. The potential for community, the shared narratives of air travel, had lapsed like forgotten stories told by one's elder relatives. At once, lithe visions of the Age of Mobility, a fanciful notion that certain populations have become unencumbered by geographical and even temporal limitations, lost their validity. In many ways, we therefore consider a rhetoric of space and travel that suffers from the destabilizing assault of current events. After all, can the fantasy of motionless travel ever reassert itself in the public unconsciousness now that no traveler may be anonymous, now that we have all become New Yorkers?

In the aftermath of the attacks, airport security that served to protect the omnitopian promise of perpetual movement fell under scrutiny. A system that allowed terrorists to bring box cutters and other low-tech weapons onto passenger planes was revealed to be grossly ineffectual. In this fearful era, we become increasingly deliberative of the words we might say within a terminal. Even prior to the attacks, few people would be stupid enough to talk about bombs in an airport. But now the word *bomb*, even the thought that one might accidentally utter the word, leads us to a miasma of self-discipline and self-doubt. In this context, the airport steadily ceases to be a fluid locale. Can one imagine an airline advertising itself as "ready when you are" on these days when we are warned to arrive hours before our departure time? We are now trained to view our selves and each other as potential threats, and we must contemplate our responsibilities in these places. What would you do if someone acted suspiciously in the terminal? What if that person stood up and announced that he'd blow up the plane? Few can imagine any ending to this event short of the total destruction witnessed on September 11th. Few can then imagine any response other than one that is similarly total. All of us must consider ourselves as potential killers, ready to do whatever must be done to stop a terrorist. Assuming that experts alone will save us simply doesn't make sense anymore. Air travel has become literally a scene of life or death.

Now, the *spectacle of the frisk* has assumed its place among the performances that define contemporary air travel. Well known to international travelers who pass through dangerous locations around the world, to Americans the random frisk represents a striking blur of public and private interactions. In a public site, we grow accustomed to viewing individuals pulled from queues, their possessions opened and studied, their bodies turned into maps of hidden threats. The gloved hands of the inspector traverse the shoulder blades, down an invisible axis toward the hips, then toward the feet. Often accompanied by a metal detecting wand, the ordeal is mediated by questions and unspoken rules of decorum: "Will you unbuckle your belt? May I open this bag?" Invisible lines of demarcation separate the inspected passenger from others who wait nearby. Yet all may observe the spectacle. Does he fold his underwear? What's in that zipped bag? Why did she pack so many sweaters? At once in the terminal, this interpersonal dance

Image 10: Airport Corridor. *Photograph by Andrew Wood*

of touch and display reveals a network of surveillance practices that remains otherwise unnoted in public life. Beyond the local spectacle, moreover, we find ourselves tied within a web of individuation and deindividuation marked by ubiquitous surveillance.

In a place where every act must be subject to institutional gaze, secret locations are almost always illegal. Certainly, the dreary and institutional style of endless corridors and lines of chairs has begun to give way to broad sunny expanses and towering glass. One imagines the inspiration to come from convention hotels in large cities. However, even this generic spectacle must be balanced by the construction of smaller, more human-scale spaces, if only to enable surveillance practices. Each corner and every alcove must be monitored, lest private activities take place in public forums. This function extends beyond the panoptic surveillance practices of the prison city imagined by dystopian authors from George Orwell to Mike Davis. Even the most personal practices in the fluid terminal—meeting a loved one, talking to a distant friend, sleeping along a wall—assume a curious public quality. We observe the displays of affection, hear a melancholy voice, and hope that some stranger will awaken the traveler before his plane's departure. In short, we are witnesses to intimate moments as detached observers walking past. Viewing and surveying the choices made by strangers, we become accomplices in the construction and maintenance of a security apparatus designed anonymously. The rhetoric of the terminal communicates loudly that all inhabitants perform private dramas for a public audience. Structurally, the stage, however, is composed of interconnected spaces, those momentary, tactical, incomplete, and isolated choices made by strangers. More than an invisible theatre, the terminal is a mobile drama whose actors and spectators are interchangeable, unknowable. Writing in *Jane's Airport Review*, Carr (1997) adds: "Technology is nearing a point where security will be the only necessary human contact a passenger need make en route to the gate, freeing airplane employees for other activities airside" (p. 11). In a place in which all other unplanned human interaction represents a threat, we find troubling implications for public life.

Conclusion

The airport terminal illustrates a rhetorical struggle between the universal metaphrase and the local utterance, an omnitopian node in which strategic design and tactical response compete for influence. Visualize the wired globe hopper on cross-continental trips, e-mailing the home office, chatting with loved ones thousands of miles away, and entering the disposable space of a video battleground on her or his laptop. An observation of the ways in which contemporary public life reforms our conception of place and an appraisal of its implications, omnitopia invites us to rearticulate place as a central axis of meaning production, a conflation of possibilities through which we might respond to the exigencies of public life. Such an inquiry demands close attention to human landscapes such as terminal space. In response, I have argued that terminal space creates a sense of all-place, invokes perpetual movement, and enacts atomized interactions.

Through this process, we recognize ourselves as passengers who construct meaning on the run, meeting an endless procession of props, tropes, and referents whose meanings blur through constant motion. Each fragment is necessarily incomplete, we know, and few of us truly wish to confront the complexities and contradictions of the places through which we pass. Yet we see something in the airport's connection to other peripatetic places—hospitality space, entertainment space, labor space, and domestic space—a new kind of polis, perhaps, alien to our conceptions of public life, but one we dare not ignore. After all, we now begin to see how the conceptual and ethical maps written on formerly distinct geographies become less and less sure in their foundations, and we struggle to recall how a response may be mounted or even imagined.

Note

1. One may be tempted to compare these glass enclosures to a world's fair Crystal Palace. But Rosler (1994) rightly calls to mind the more banal reality of terminal life: "Huge aimless spaces are marked off by rope-and-stanchion arrays to keep order among those lined up at ticket counters. Away from the central hall, acoustic tile in grim tracks, self-effaced flooring, fluorescent-lit low-ceilinged corridors are ubiquitous. The accountant and the crowd-control manager are the gods supplicated within" (p. 69).

References

Adey, P. (2007). "May I have your attention": Airport geographies of spectatorship, position, and (im)mobility. *Environment and Planning D: Society and Space, 25*(3), 515–536.

Augé, M. (1995). *Non-places: Introduction to an anthropology of supermodernity* (J. Howe, Trans.). New York: Verso.

Capecchi, C. (2007, September 18). Fateful bathroom draws crowds of the curious. *New York Times*, p. A20.

Carr, D. (1997). The 21st century terminal. *Jane's Airport Review, 9*(5), 9–11.

De Neufville, R. (1995). Designing airport passenger buildings for the 21st century. *Proceedings of the Institution of Civil Engineers. Transport, 111*, 97–104.

Dickinson, G. (1997). Memories for sale: Nostalgia and the construction of identity in old Pasadena. *Quarterly Journal of Speech, 83*(1), 1–27.

Fentress, C. W. (2000, November–December). Modern passenger terminals are more than buildings that facilitate air travel. *ICAO Journal*, pp. 12–14, 28.

Fuller, G., & Harley, R. (2004). *Aviopolis: A book about airports*. London: Black Dog Publishing Limited.

Gottdiener, M. (2001). *Life in the air: Surviving the new culture of air travel*. Lanham, MD: Rowman & Littlefield.

Iyer, P. (2000). *The global soul: Jet lag, shopping malls, and the search for home*. New York: Alfred A. Knopf.

Lloyd, J. (2003). Airport technology, travel, and consumption. *Space and Culture, 6*(2), 93–109.

Mumayiz, S. A. (1989). Development of airport terminal design concepts: A new perspective. *Transportation Planning and Technology, 13*(4), 303–320.

Murphy, A. (2002). Organizational policies of place and space: The perpetual liminoid performance of commercial flight. *Text and Performance Quarterly, 22*(4), 297–316.

New hub, no hubcaps. (2002, March 13). *Architecture week*. Retrieved September 11, 2007, from http://www.architectureweek.com/2002/0313/news_1-1.html

Odoni, A. R. (1992). Passenger terminal design. *Transportation Research (Part A)*, pp. 27–35.

Patke, R. S. (2000). Benjamin's Arcades Project and the postcolonial city. *Diacritics*, *30*(4), 3–13.

Rosler, M. (1994). In the place of the public: Observations of a frequent flyer. *Assemblage*, *25*, 44–79.

Rutner, S. M., & Mundy, R. A. (1996). Hubs versus hub-nots: A comparison of various U.S. airports. *Journal of Air Transportation Worldwide*, *1*(1), 81–90.

Salter, M. B. (2007). Governmentalities of an airport: Heterotopia and confession. *International Political Sociology*, *1*, 49–66.

Urry, J. (2001). Transports of delight. *Leisure Studies*, *20*(4), 237–245.

Walters, B. (1993, December). Grandiose ideas fade in an era of practicality. *Airport Forum*, pp. 43–46.

5

———————————— Hotels ————————————

The city manifests itself as twenty stories of continuous guest-room balconies bounding the pyramid of space. Their effect is to stripe the space
and to swell it as it climbs gloriously toward the pinnacle, which is faintly
luminous with natural light. You sense space, then enclosure, the feeling of
glass walls rushing toward you as they rush toward the top. . . . [E]veryone
wants to hush, respecting the interiority of this space, lending it the semblance of a cathedral.

—Todd Gitlin (1979, pp. 293–294)

Another convention hotel linked to modular food courts, commercial displays,
and covered walkways: an enclosed space with leafy plants and milling strangers wearing business suits and pleasant scents. An ethereal instrumental tune
drifts under the skylights, unobtrusive and somewhat predictable, a mixture of
"cool jazz" and 1970s-era "music of the future," something you might imagine
from EPCOT Center. The sun streams through glass doors that muffle the traffic
noise, borders that shut with a whispered thud. Overhead, a plaque announces
"Public Space." It is simple, direct, and utterly lacking in irony. Undoubtedly,
the people *look* like a public, thronging, laughing, and mingling from various
parts of the world. This mixture of persons could be visiting a conference or
a trade show or a reunion or just another weekend convergence of weddings,
receptions, collectable shows, and holiday opportunities anywhere. But they are
obviously not from around here.

Klatches of folks stare intently at downtown maps that list nearby tourist-
friendly (and tourist-priced) entertainment venues and restaurants. People queue
at the desks of concierges who offer the promise of theater tickets and reserva-
tions. Track-suited guests powerwalk their way toward the exercise room, where
they will watch cable TV and make miles on a treadmill. The public inside
doesn't remotely resemble the public outside. Moreover, the place marked by this
public is far removed from the place beyond its borders. The location could be

Vancouver or Chicago or Shanghai, but the location doesn't really matter. "Here," one inhabits merely a space of transit connecting more meaningful places that are hardly worth much reflection at all. However, these places of transit reflect the lived experience of mobile people whose wealth and privilege insulate them from another world marked by provincialism and dead ends. Abandoning urban life or, more appropriately, replacing public life, an insulated vision of the world colonizes outward.

At this point, we focus our attention on temporary enclaves along the highway and within the downtown core wherein omnitopia begins to infiltrate everyday life. In contrast to the airport, which remains for most people an extraordinary threshold to the unfamiliar, a conduit to impossible speeds, strange procedures, and frightening possibilities—the genuine potential for death—we anticipate some degree of familiarity when we pass through the threshold of a lodge. The roadside motel, the downtown hotel, and the sprawling convention center, despite their differences of style, design, and scale, produce some transient version of home, complete with bed, bathroom, and TV.

These places promise a personal refuge no matter how fleeting. However, these sites of temporary domesticity, individuating as they are, convey their inhabitants to a place set apart from the world around them. In a number of ways, these sites are communication devices to an omnitopian sensibility, training grounds for working and management classes alike. To enter that mindset, we begin in an unlikely place, the independent roadside motel. We read this place as a progenitor to omnitopia for motorists in the early 20th century. Through the motel, we may trace the divergence of omnitopia from its heterotopian pre-decessor. We then proceed by way of the motor hotel, illustrated by the Holiday Inn chain, in which values of safety and consistency were woven into peripatetic life, before concluding with an analysis of convention hotels that culminate the omnitopian integration of distinct locales into a familiar continuum.

Motels

Older U.S. motels, those built between the 1930s and the 1950s, provide a nec-essary starting point for our analysis of omnitopia, illustrating that practice's point of transition from its predecessor, heterotopia. One may even suggest that omnitopia collapses distinct heterotopias into a solid state. At this point, we should clarify our terms. Within a heterotopia, impulse of deviance or devi-ance may be safely managed (Foucault, 1986). From this perspective, we may term heterotopia a social safety valve (a term more frequently associated with the frontier). A heterotopia works primarily through its practice of dislocation. To enter a heterotopia, one passes through a permeable threshold between here and there, between youth and maturity, between disorder and order, blurring both poles and yet also offering a "third place" that is not entirely the place from which one exits. The act of entering a heterotopia offers potential emancipation from roles and expectations, along with the potential to calm the stresses that might otherwise erupt in some manifestation of antisocial behavior.

New York's Central Park provides an apt example. Amid a city that rumbles with race and class tensions, a complex amalgamation of people manages to coexist in the park. Writing of the place he helped design, Frederick Law Olmsted boasted of the socializing influence of this green space between the concrete canyons:

> No one who has closely observed the conduct of the people who visit the Park, can doubt that it exercises a distinctly harmonizing and refining influence upon the most unfortunate and most lawless classes of the city,—an influence favorable to courtesy, self-control, and temperance. (cited in Sutton, 2001, p. 96)

As a heterotopia, Central Park is a place set apart from the city, accessible but detached in both structure and perception. Entering its domain, persons of different social privilege can interact in a manner that is largely free from surrounding tensions. Heterotopia enables the perpetuation of social norms by allowing their temporary abatement. Here, one must emphasize the transitory nature of heterotopia. Despite its undoubtedly large homeless population, Central Park is a place built for visitation, not habitation. Like an amusement park or movie theatre, Central Park offers a *temporary* reframing of social order. In this manner, we may view the traditional independent motel[1] as an exemplar of heterotopia, at first. Eventually, however, we find the inklings of an omnitopian potential.

With their ancient sheets, Pepto Bismol-colored bathroom tiles, and pieces of yard sale-quality furniture, Mom and Pop motels preserve an almost forgotten component of American public life, the heterotopian enclave that allows travelers to detach themselves from the strictures of ordinary life and imagine fleetingly that they can shed their identities. The anonymity of the motel allows us to contemplate the freedom to deviate from social norms. Yes, such deviance is popularly portrayed as sexual. However, the freedom afforded by a motel need not be illicit. In a much more pedestrian way, the motel offers a chance to be less strictly oneself, to try out the persona of the lonely motorist who peers outward toward the horizon, far from narrow sidewalks, to be far from home—or simply to sleep with the same fellow traveler in a different bed. As a scholar and a traveler, I have come to love motels that cling to the highway even as they struggle to remain solvent in the face of national and international chains. However, motels also contributed to a colonization of omnitopian practice, dislocation through vernacular architecture and image fragmentation, reflecting a larger process through which they (and other peripatetic places) began to naturalize omnitopia.

For this reason, early to mid-century motels, with their promises of anonymity, their endless repetition of names like "Sunset," "Starlight," "Capri," and "Western," and their orientation around the comings and goings of automobiles, provide a useful case study for the growth of omnitopia in the United States.[2]

The motel appeared to serve the increasing numbers of motorists who drove farther and farther away from urban cores and began to discover a certain freedom that comes from avoiding the hotel register. The motel may be known by its location, adjacent or near a highway; its design, rooms with doors facing outward to accommodate parked cars; and its relative ease of entry. Unlike the urban hotel whose lobby affirmed the discipline of surveillance and display, not to mention rigid gender roles, the motel reflected a modern age of mobility whose architecture and practices helped craft a genuinely anonymous mode of lodging (Belasco, 1997). So important was the automobile to early 20th-century designers, many motel designers made room for cars between rooms, allowing occupants to slip directly from their cars into their lodgings, resulting in the infamous tradition of "no-tell motels."[3]

This phenomenon illustrates the motel's overlap of strategic purpose and tactical use. As envisioned by its architects and overseers, a motel offers a functional site to rent a room and perhaps consume a meal. The motel's strategies, although changing and evolving, affirm the perpetual purpose of place. However, the motel also provides a tactical locale, a site that may be adapted for temporary and (occasionally) unauthorized purposes. Bored couples may employ the motel for sexual experimentation. Drug dealers may transform the room into a meth lab. Historians of roadside Americana may photograph a closed relic as a site of pilgrimage. To these and other groups, the meaning of the motel is pliable, its meanings and uses sometimes being impossible for others to discern.

The overlap of meanings, although indicative of heterotopia, also reveals the seeds of omnitopia. As heterotopia, the motel is neither here nor there. Morris (1988) illustrates such a mentality when she describes an Australian variant of the American motor lodge:[4]

> A motel is a good place in which to consider the question of traffic, precisely because it is consecrated to proximity and circulation. It is neither the car nor the highway nor the house nor the voyage nor the home, but a space of movements between all of them. (p. 41)

Yet we also begin to discover traces of an omnitopian sensibility arising from motel design, portending a rhetoric of ubiquity in which the traveler may be home "everywhere." This notion of home rests on a vernacular discourse that illustrates the omnitopian principle of fragmentation: The motorist inhabits the same place wherever she or he visits. From this perspective, I find the motel to provide a sort of training ground for omnitopia that set itself deeper in the public consciousness than more distinct modes of travel, such as the airport.

To the motoring public for whom highway travel seemed to resemble a camping expedition, early motels sought to reproduce mementos of "home," or at least a home away from home (Margolies, 1995). Some of these sites of temporary domesticity harkened back to a permanence of stone and ancient techniques, illustrated by the soft primitive style of various stone cottages that began to dot the early 20th-century highways. In these cases, imagery of the primitive past and exaggerated icons of domestic bliss offered a comforting respite from the highway. Even in a dusty and distant town, the automobilist would not be threatened or transformed. This domestic fantasy, with lace curtains and the occasional white picket fence, attracted the early century motoring public (Liebs, 1985). But domesticity would soon be replaced by more exotic themes.

Despite initially being overshadowed by domestic theming, southwestern vernacular appeared early with the introduction of the first "motel" onto the American landscape. In 1925, Arthur Heineman built the Milestone Mo-Tel (now called the Motel Inn, but long closed) in San Luis Obispo, California. Collabo-rating with James Vail, Heineman envisioned his "Mo-Tel" as part of a chain of Spanish-mission style inns, each providing standardized accommodations along the Pacific coast. The word *motel* resulted from an amalgamation of *motor* and *hotel*, emphasizing the autocentric nature of this new style of roadside lodging. The mission theme represented a belief that motels could satisfy functional needs even as they fulfilled the fantasy of actually *going* somewhere. In her extraordinary analysis of Route 66 imagery, Lisa Mahar (2002) quotes an article from *Tourist Court Journal* to illustrate the power of these themed fantasies:

> If there are Indians around, or if it is in the Spanish section, or in the wild and wooly West, the guests expect the motif to be in keeping with the locale and with that for which the state is noted. Don't disappoint them. Make their dreams come true. (p. 77)

Other mission-themed motels (and their Pueblo cousins) arose throughout the country, supplanting the previously dominant domestic theme. Most notable uses of the rounded parapets and wooden beams of the mission style can still be found in some of the remaining Alamo Plaza Courts motels. Along with its various "branches" like the Alabama-based St. Francis Courts, these mission-style sites drew from cinema-fed fantasies of John Wayne movies. The southwestern vernacular fantasy also includes the small chain of "Wigwam Villages" across the southern United States, with fanciful façades that hid fairly typical motel rooms complete with tiny showers, coin-operated radios, and beds covered in native-looking spreads. A visitor to a "Wigwam Village" might have purchased a penny postcard displaying a U-shaped arc of teepees (not wigwams, it should be noted), each adjacent to an empty space fit for a neighboring car. With its highway border separating the "village" from the surrounding orange groves, the motorist might be tempted to contemplate the notion of a teepee as a partially

WIGWAM VILLAGE No. 4 — ORLANDO, FLORIDA

ORANGE BLOSSOM TRAIL, U. S. 441 AND U. S. 17; U. S. 92

Image 11: Wigwam Village Postcard. *Author's Collection*

permanent home, but would likely not consider the tragic irony of this pose. Selecting these vernacular fantasies, and others that included log cabins, colonial homes, and even trains transformed into motels, one does not expect to meet genuinely different people imagined to occupy these tourist locales. Instead, one settles for a pleasant fake and fleeting sense of being *someplace* different, a locale whose architectural designs, motifs, and referents point to a possible history, a potential truth that travel may broaden one's horizons, even if only until morning.

Visits to independently owned motels that were themed according to various vernacular fantasies provide a chance to view America as a kind of proto-omnitopia prior to the mid-20th-century rise of globalization and its attendant international-style architecture. As Daniel Boorstin (1992) wrote in 1961, "One thing motels everywhere have in common is the effort of their managers to fabricate an inoffensive bit of 'local atmosphere'" (p. 113). With the aid of these vernacular fantasies, motorists grew accustomed to the practice of dislocation and came to expect some sort of fragmentation among the smooth running of two-lane and mid-century interstate highways. It is useful to recall that dislocation removes a site from its surrounding geography. The motel demonstrates dislocation by becoming an interchangeable node that is adjacent to (but disconnected from) the highway. The motorist exits the automobile and nightly enters the *same place*, one marked by a bed, a closet, a bathroom, and a TV. One may be located along a specific numbered highway. But within the motel's vernacular façade, the motorist is *someplace else*. Over sufficient time, the motorist traverses geological boundaries, time zones, weather patterns, and cultural variants. The automobile frame dislocates the motorist from each of these.

For a number of observers, the motel room has become a synecdoche for modernity. I consider Iyer's (2000) "unideological vision of a city as a kind of motel room writ large" as apt illustration (p. 145). However, I would emphasize that these motel rooms ultimately serve to illustrate the incomplete project of the independent motel. Chains, beginning with Alamo Plaza and culminating with Holiday Inn, along with the rise of limited access interstate highways, would begin the slow decline of the Mom and Pop motel as a destination for either the tourist family or business traveler by the mid-1950s. Many of today's motels, somewhat ironically, have become locales in a real sense, places filled with time and character that are indisputably unique, places worth seeing in their own rights if only because they have survived the onslaught of the chains. But despite the persistence of these independent motels, they have been supplanted in the minds of most travelers by the likes of Holiday Inn. Although this chain would face competitive pressures that would lead it to experiment with creating its own rhetoric of locality, Holiday Inn began as a motel killer through its diffusion of the motor hotel concept.

Holiday Inn

In many ways, Holiday Inn may be called the Wal-Mart of the hospitality world because of its founder's desire to mass produce a safe, pleasant, and reasonably priced alternative to Mom and Pop businesses whose idiosyncrasies often proved to be frustrating. Holiday Inn began in 1952 when Charles Kemmons Wilson built a prototype in Memphis, Tennessee.[5] This new motor hotel proved so successful that Wilson soon built three more. Twenty years later, *Time Magazine* featured "America's Host from Coast to Coast" on their cover, celebrating a corporation that had franchised almost 1,500 inns in the United States and around the world (Anderson & Tompkins, 1972). Wilson imagined a chain of hotels that would offer low prices, consistent quality, and convenient locations to a generation of Americans heading out for the highway, modeling an international aesthetic that would reproduce itself throughout the world. Ibelings (1998) identifies examples of this international style in big hotels "which may have belonged to different companies but which nevertheless could be seen as part of one big—American—chain" (p. 34). This uniformity became associated with an American fantasy of freedom to travel widely without ever feeling distant from a domestic enclosure:

> [Holiday Inn] brought a new, modern look to the commercial landscape.
> Whereas many motels in the late 1950s and early 1960s were low-slung,
> neon-clad affairs stretched along the roadside, new Holiday Inns were glass-
> bright two-story structures poised by Interstate highway interchanges. The
> focus of the facility was inward, toward a public yet private recreational
> courtyard. (Jakle, Sculle, & Rogers, 1996, p. 284)

This inward focus and orientation around interstates, rather than small towns,
illustrates the role of Holiday Inn within a larger narrative of public life. Holiday
Inn created a safe place of dependable sameness. Yet like many of the themed
fantasies of contemporary omnitopia, Holiday Inn managed to employ a degree
of whimsy and an illusion of locality.

To ensure that his motor hotel would be instantly recognizable anywhere in
the world, Wilson mandated the placement of a "Great Sign" near each Holiday
Inn.[6] To ensure that it would also be viewable from miles away, the Great Sign
glowed garishly in green and yellow. Nelson (2002) offers a description of the
Great Sign's technological narrative and local allusion:

> Their marquees sported an emerald green curvilinear field with a big white
> neon "HOLIDAY INN" done in casual script. This was affixed to a red pylon
> atop which a yellow star exploded its energy into the night. Meanwhile a
> winking Vegas-style arrow pointed tired travelers to the office while an
> illuminated window box below advertised rates and local gatherings such as
> "Opaloosa Elks Fish Fry" or "Welcome Burlington High Senior Prom." The
> kinetic radiance turned the Great Sign into a symbol of American razzle-
> dazzle, for-sure-buddy-can-do optimism. (online, ¶ 6)

Anchored by the Great Sign and a proven business model, Wilson's Holiday Inn
far outdistanced his nearest competitor in the 1970s. Companies like Quality
Inn, Howard Johnson, and Ramada Inn found that keeping up with Holiday
Inn required matching the company step by step. The results are apparent even
today, with each room in most motor hotels looking pretty much the same as
any other room.

Holiday Inn perfected the roadside motor hotel, a reproduction of Wilson's
original innovation, until it eventually dispensed with the original. A most obvious example occurred in 1979 when board members pushed Wilson from his
leadership position. Three years later, the chain that once advertised "the best
surprise is no surprise" began to demolish its thousands of Great Signs, replacing
them with backlit plastic box signs and a professionally low-key symbol of the
star that once glowed so tackily.[7] To understand this transformation, we must
review the role of mutability in the construction of omnitopia. Holiday Inn's
apparently perpetual alteration of motifs demonstrates the power of corporations
and other entities to respond to changing exigencies by transforming the built
environment (Brand, 1994). After the attacks of September 11, 2001, air travel-

ers quickly reexamined their willingness to endure the time and confinement of highway travel. In response, Holiday Inn saw an opportunity to bolster its brand, most notably with its 2003 "Relax. It's Holiday Inn" advertising campaign and revival of its Great Sign. The campaign featured a simulation of the sign that once stood for the evocation of adventure on the road.

Holiday Inn also built a number of properties that would integrate imagery from the company's past into office park-style hotels, starting with a prototype built in 2004 in the Atlanta suburb of Duluth. The prototype employs traditional Holiday Inn imagery in a number of ways, including the outside marquee, internal artwork, and directional sign design. The outside marquee represents a compromise between municipal restrictions regarding the size and lighting of outdoor signs and the strategy employed by Holiday Inn to revive a beloved icon. The new sign presents a much smaller silhouette oriented around the horizontal axis, as opposed to the gigantic marquee that stood alongside Holiday Inns until 1982. The new sign is backlit, a contrast to the glaring neon and blinking light bulbs of the old version. Despite these differences, the new sign manages to convey much of the spirit of the original. The swooping arrow remains, along with the star that is now transformed into a stylized rendition behind the lettering. Inside the hotel, visitors find paintings that depict semi-abstract renditions of the "great sign." Some rooms include photographs of the great sign that have been pixilated and color-manipulated in a manner that transforms documentary images into art. Even some directional signs used to note floor numbers and escape routes are shaped to resemble the great sign that includes a stylized star. Newer properties also opened restaurants called "Kem's Café," featuring homestyle comfort food that enacted a nostalgic sign system for those who remember the name of Holiday Inn's founder.

With this experiment, one finds a strategy through which one chain hotel, and the many others it inspired, borrowed from motels, their autocentric placement, and their balance of locality and ubiquity. With Holiday Inn, we also see efforts to eschew the supposed bland, personality-free personae offered by the chains, choosing instead versions of a corporate past that fragments the most interchangeable hotel room into a place containing at least two temporal narratives, generic present and precise past. We now leave Holiday Inn in search of the most recent demonstration of the hotel's weaving of omnitopian sensibility into contemporary life, the atrium and convention hotel. In this final turn, we discover both how hotels blur into massively complex assemblages of discrete locations and how their users make themselves "home" in city ubiquitous.

Convention Hotels

A number of these large and complex cores found in central business districts located near mass transit hubs (a phrase bordering on redundancy given the cross-pollination of these functions) have entered the convention market, providing one-stop sites for a growing range of worldwide organizations whose members require face-to-face communication. Zelinsky (1994) proposes that the "conventioneer" reflects a new kind of traveler, one enabled by a sophisticated intersection of 20th-century era advances in communications, transportation, and organizational technologies: "Whereas pilgrims, season labor migrants, vagrants, itinerant scholars, mercenaries, affluent tourists, merchant adventurers, and other wanderers may have been among us for ages, the conventioneer is truly something new under the sun" (p. 68). The conventioneer, residing "near the core of our new social order" in Zelinsky's estimation, expects fluid motion through an integrated and enclavic mall. Fearing the dangers of the urban street, the conventioneer views the city through the carefully crafted prism of the conference hotel, searching for tourist-friendly chain restaurants and connected shopping opportunities to supply the sense of being somewhere. In many ways, the convention continues the tradition of world's fairs and expositions of the 19th and early 20th centuries, while presuming to offer much less of the "world" than could be found in its predecessors. Entering a convention hotel, gazing on the chatting, suited residents who sit in grand spaces, natural light pouring on them in a manner both cheerful and defused, one may imagine an interconnected conflation of conventions—Atlanta now, Vancouver next, Shanghai thereafter—and perceive in practice and in behavior one endless circuit.

Across and between each of these locations resides a nodal network that conveys inhabitants to omnitopia. While not anticipating the terminology espoused by this project, Judd (1999) describes this type of node as a tourist bubble, a referent that is well known to scholars of the modern leisure class:

> Where crime, poverty, and urban decay make parts of a city inhospitable to visitors, specialized areas are established as virtual tourist reservations. These become the public parts of town, leaving visitors shielded from and unaware of the private spaces where people live and work. (p. 36)

The tourist bubble enacts an enclave through regulation of entrances and departures, the deployment of uniformed police and private security, and the construction of physical borders and obstructions aimed at ensuring the fluid movement and consumer activity of visitors to the urban space. To understand this bubble, we should explore its history.

As large cities confronted the withering of their industrial economies in the postwar years, they increasingly jockeyed for prominence as tourist destinations, revamping their environs to accommodate a mobile and transient population that saw danger within the urban cores. Tourists of these nodes would find purchasable goods (from pricy meals to cheap souvenirs) that were unattainable or simply useless to the local population. The tourist bubble then expanded beyond the United States to enact a "Little America" wherever a large chain hotel was built, a magnetic force, a gravity well that bent local economies and cultural practices toward their well-apportioned lobbies (Boorstin, 1992). Sudjic (2006) recalls this trend from a geopolitical standpoint:

> During the Cold War, the modern hotel from Hilton or Holiday Inn in hand-me-down white Bauhaus concrete was as much the sign of an ambitious Third World capital as a national airline permanently on the edge of bankruptcy. You could find them in every contested city on the fault line between east and west. Hotels like these were ocean liners, marooned in a sea of medieval night, where expatriates could gather to construct a little bubble of western life in the midst of another world. (p. 1)

One could enter this international-style enclave and expect consistency: a decent bar, potable water, clean sheets, and a door that locked behind the passport-carrying "citizen of the world." What one could seldom find, however, was an interior that would be preferable to the touristic exoticism of the outside. The hotel lobby offered leather seats and a concierge who knew the local dialect, but the interior usually meant row upon row of dreary corridors leading to interchangeable and forgettable rooms. Inside this "Little America," one found no place to go but outside again.

Entering this era, an Atlanta-based architect named John Portman transformed the conventional design of the big box hotel. Portman differed from most of his peers because of his choice to learn both the science of architecture and the art of real estate development, choosing not to accept the conventional wisdom that designers should not be concerned with the market forces that shape their creations. Starting with small-scale projects, Portman gathered the corporate funding, municipal support, and popular affirmation to virtually rebuild downtown Atlanta. Thereafter, Portman and his associates exported a vision of massively integrated and coordinated structures all over the United States and throughout the world. Although he has designed a number of exposition halls, shopping malls, and related sites, this analysis concentrates on the Portman-style atrium hotel as a primary node within those larger networked enclaves.

Opened in 1967, Portman's Atlanta Hyatt marked the architect/developer's first illustration of how the hotel could serve as a node to the omnitopian enclave through its integration of an atrium to what had previously been a bureaucratic box of business offices, which just happened to include beds. To this tradition, the Portman atrium, an innovation he appropriated from a number of extant models of low-cost and efficiently designed places, ordered hotel rooms on the outer edges of a mammoth enclosure, drawing public interactions inside while constructing links to the city beyond:

> I wanted to explode the hotel; to open it up; to create a grandeur of space, almost a resort, in the center of the city. The whole idea was to open

everything up; take the hotel from its closed, tight position, and explode
it; take the elevators and literally pull them out of the walls and let them
become an experience within themselves, let them become a giant kinetic
sculpture. (Portman & Barnett, 1976, p. 28)

Portman imagined his atriums as liberating, as sites of community. Undoubtedly, he learned much from mall designers such as Victor Gruen, who, a decade
earlier, had designed an enclosed mall that was also built around an atrium.
Craig (1988) recalls the Portman atrium as a populist architectural form, an
inviting respite for adults freed from the drudgeries of their workaday lives.[8]
However, a number of other respondents found the first Atlanta Hyatt, and the
Portman projects that followed thereafter, to demonstrate the internalization of
public life, and the walling off of those who could no longer be viewed as parts
of that public.

Soon after that opening of the Atlanta Hyatt, one observer foresaw a challenge to locality. Describing the post-civil rights-era integration of the American
South into the broader national fabric—a region from whom writers such as T.
S. Stribling, Thomas Wolfe, Erskine Caldwell, and Flannery O'Connor had constructed trenchant depictions and castigations—Holman (1969) selects a Portman
atrium hotel to consider the South's tenuous identity. Although he concludes,
correctly, that locale can never be banished entirely from an urbanizing (even
globalizing) world, his question continues to contain the seeds of doubt:

> As tobacco roads give way to interstate highways, as country stores become
> shopping centers, as small towns become the suburban areas of booming
> cities, is the South as social subject any longer relevant? Can one take the
> glass-enclosed elevator to the twenty-second floor of the Regency-Hyatt
> in Atlanta and look out upon a world distinctively different from what
> he might see in New York, Chicago, or Los Angeles, even if he doesn't
> glance at the nationally televised game being played in the Falcons' and
> Braves' splendid new stadium, or listen to the homogenized accents of its
> announcer? (p. 31)

This home away from home, however, could not be located specifically in one
place. Rather, the Atlanta Hyatt stretched, reached, and connected to other
properties designed, built, financed, or otherwise blessed by Portman, resulting
in a coordination of hotels, showcase centers, restaurants, and office spaces,
building an omnitopian Atlanta within a downtown core. Portman and Barnett
(1976) recall:

> A system of bridges over streets and buildings will allow you to walk in
> a protected environment from Davison's [department store] to the Hyatt
> Regency or to the [other shopping opportunities] several blocks away.... It

is a little world of design and forethought with oases of space and of water, trees, and flowers in the aggregation of separate buildings that makes up most of downtown Atlanta. (p. 14)

This "little world," by definition and intention, excluded much. Although Portman was closely identified with efforts to harmonize racial communities in the "city too busy to hate," his integrated structures seemed to exacerbate Atlanta race and class distinctions, rather than ameliorate them. Newman (2002) recalls how African Americans mocked the skywalks as "honkey tubes" (p. 309), whereas Chen (2006) points out that even the supposedly privileged inhabitants of these walkways find themselves easily lost within the 14-block Peachtree Center that grew up around the Hyatt: "It is a sprawling complex linked with enclosed bridges that can make an uninitiated visitor feel like a hamster lost in a Habitrail" (p. 26). Even so, the Atlanta Hyatt inspired a number of similar and increasingly grander projects, including the Hyatt Regency in San Francisco's Embarcadero Center and the Westin Bonaventure in Los Angeles.

Today, no analysis of hotels can avoid quoting from Jameson's (1991) analysis of Portman's Bonaventure, which, by his reckoning, "aspires to being a total space, a complete world, a kind of miniature city" (p. 40). While offering merely a brief gloss on the Bonaventure, Jameson illustrates a common response to these sorts of powerful places, bold and brilliant as they are. To Jameson and those inspired by his writings, these structures threaten to overwhelm us with scale beyond human comprehension.[9] In contrast, Portman and his partisans report that the atrium expands the spaces of public life, conflating disparate spheres of human interaction, and reflects scientific and humane coordination of urbanity that had heretofore been marked by inefficiently designed and poorly executed silos. Although his earlier innovations are sometimes dismissed as dated, Portman's architectural firm continues to reshape skylines all over the world. Entering one of his atrium hotels today, one can easily understand why. To illustrate, I would reflect on two San Francisco Hyatts—one located downtown and one near the city's international airport—that illustrate the way in which contemporary hotels are both enclavic and borderless.

The downtown Hyatt, located in San Francisco's Embarcadero Center, boasts views of the city's iconic Transamerica Building and Coit Tower, while a pedestrian visitor confronts a towering concrete structure, gray and foreboding. On the sidewalks, buskers and hawkers appeal to visiting tourists who amble toward the nearby Ferry Building. Entering the Hyatt from street level, one must ascend an escalator to enter the atrium, a towering three-sided space that climbs toward a cleft of natural light. The interior is oriented around a spherical sculpture (entitled "Eclipse" by Charles O. Perry), which offers counterpoint to the sharp angles of the enclosure. Near the dim lobby, elevators carry aloft glass cars upward toward the light. Each of the Hyatt's 22 floors is bounded by a balcony that drips with artificial plant life. Doors leading to guest rooms lie hidden within deep alcoves. Walking the corridor, being unable to see more than one door ahead, one assumes that the living space is a flat and empty wall. Only when one looks across the chasm can the visitor see the structure of equidistant rooms. Exiting the atrium, the stroller enters Embarcadero Center by way of a concrete promenade that flows over the street level. An urban renewal site, the Center stretches along a spine of office towers and shopping venues, connected by skyway tubes and concrete walkways. Entering Embarcadero Center, passing over the streets of the city below, one imagines never having to leave.

I spent much more time at the San Francisco International Airport Hyatt (SFO-Hyatt), a structure inspired by Portman's atriums but created by another architect, Mark R. Hornberger. The SFO-Hyatt is a fortress alongside Highway 101, a concrete bunker set among glass-box buildings that seem lifted from Tativille. The SFO-Hyatt, like the others that gather near the airport, privileges its interior. The external face is composed of ribbed-concrete squares and double-insulated windows, the property bounded by fences, orange plastic webbing, and a narrow wall of plant life. Along with a frontage that serves as the hotel's backside, one finds shipping containers and construction work at the border of highway and hotel. Visitors arrive by interstate highway or airport shuttle, shunted inward to a protective enclosure away from the road.

The square inside rests on a sort of pedestal mounted by stairs and escalators, supporting a split-level dining area. On the periphery, a sports bar, a high-end Italian-style eatery, and conference meeting spaces bound the enclosure. Rising above this space and its clusters of chairs and alcoves, squared floors climb toward the roof. Above the eighth level, glass panels admit a sizable sliver of natural light on all four sides; the roof consists of 36 white tents supported by tubes that call to mind Denver's international airport. The light that flows through this fabric room is diffused enough to protect the interior from overly temperate afternoons, while festive lights strung from trees and wooden gazebos, complemented with bamboo trees, ensure sufficient brightness and organic color even when the skies outside darken. The gift shop sells postcards, t-shirts, and other souvenirs recalling the City by the Bay, Golden Gates, and Alcatraz prisoners for travelers too busy to see the real thing or those hoping to avoid the hassles of navigating the dense and hilly downtown for real. Walking by the gift shop, a guest points confidently to a counterpart, "You ever go to the Hyatt in town? They're all the same," in a tone that is a mixture of marvel and practiced indifference. Here, one finds an odd sense of safety, even in the elevators. A sign reads: "Should the elevator fail to open or the elevator not work: 1. Please do not become alarmed. 2. Please use red button marked "Alarm" to summon assistance. . . ." But one can hardly get too alarmed in a place like this.

Even more than the Embarcadero Hyatt, this place gathers an eclectic group of patrons. One morning, I spot workers setting up a $40 brunch, complete with chef-prepared omelets and hand-carved roast beef. A few customers lay down their credit cards to enter the pricy brunch section, but most folks settle for the cheaper breakfast buffet that is subtly separated from the expensive goods. The place is filled with families, SFO airport-delay detainees, and even a few baggy pants teens bedecked in slanty ball caps. A band belts out a bluesy rendition of the song "Route 66," followed by an upbeat version of "On Broadway" and a cover of "I Left My Heart in San Francisco" (intermixed with 1960s- and 1970s-era love songs), and I begin to spot regulars: patrons who chat knowingly with servers or even trade complements with the singer during her break. From the nearby sports bar, I hear cheers as football teams deliver for their fans. At once I remember the numbers of sports jerseys I've spotted on visitors to the atrium, and I reflect back on signs I saw praising the "Knuckles" sports bar as the most popular place to watch the game throughout the county.

At this point, I realize that omnitopia is increasingly connected to the quotidian structures and perceptions of public life. With the hotel as a gathering place for parties, dances, receptions, business meetings, get-rich-quick seminars, and even the occasional spiritual congregation, we witness the colonization of omnitopia into everyday life. Reflecting on this, I recall on the signs that I often see in convention hotels that do not sport their own enclosed Starbucks coffee bars, "We Proudly Brew Starbucks Coffee," and I observe a common strategy. Just as a coffee chain doesn't need to open an actual branch in a location to expand its brand, just as an architect is not required to personally reproduce a style for that design to be replicated elsewhere, omnitopia grows and integrates itself into the fabric of the world when its inhabitants accept its facsimiles as real, choosing simulacra of public life over the real thing.

Still, the tourist who sits long enough in an atrium hotel becomes a potential threat. Employees offer curt head nods, usually smiling, but eventually, inevitably, someone will amble along, maybe wearing an earpiece reminiscent of a secret service agent, and make inquiries. During a recent visit to the SFO-Hyatt, one such moment of surveillance occurred when a fellow approached me and asked, "Sir, are you with a group?" Recalling a number of similar questions, I've come to interpret this inquiry as a sort of code. He's not asking whether I'm with a wedding party or a local convention, but whether I'm a representative of an outside, potentially rival, organization. My interlocutor reminds me that the atrium is for registered guests only, and I remind him that I carry a plastic keycard that signifies my right to sit here.

Our conversation becomes much more pleasant when I openly share my reasons for visiting this property, a desire to visit Portman-inspired atrium hotels. He smiles broadly and remarks that he has never visited Embarcadero Center downtown, but that he has seen a similar style in Seoul, one that makes this place look tiny by comparison. In my travels, visiting the front and back stages of airports, hotels, and casinos, I've found that employees of most omnitopian enclaves are usually fascinated by the machinations of these places, keen to share their own tips to navigating them and spotting the peculiar nodes of omnitopian design that more passive tourists may miss. Although few will risk unemployment by opening locked doors or revealing corporate secrets, and a small number forget that the rhetorical edifice of "private property" becomes just as restrictive to them once they remove their nametags, most employees take an almost insubordinate pleasure in unveiling how their places work. They do not employ theoretical terminology, nor should they. But they quickly connect with the ideas I explore.

    Another evening, I open glass doors to stare out from my room onto the atrium enclosure. Standing on the sixth-floor balcony, I hear the rushing of a waterfall beneath me and gaze on a tiny forest of trees lit from above. The space creates an almost perfect square, so that I see levels of equally spaced rooms directly opposite my location. I lean over the balcony a bit and listen to the soundtrack of vaguely familiar tunes. In other rooms, people are watching TV or walking about in their bathrobes, drawing curtains and creating a seductive mystery. I then spot a man standing at his own balcony on the eighth floor. He too is staring outward. For a moment, I feel embarrassed at the prospect that he has caught me looking at him. But on closer inspection, it becomes clear that he is talking on a mobile phone and is probably oblivious to my gaze. Even if he isn't, I can easily disguise my attention by shifting my head slightly downward, craning my eyes on him. We stand there as strangers, emptiness between us, free to stare at each other or to ignore each other without consequence. At that moment, I am reminded of Siegfried Kracauer's notes of early 20th-century hotel lobbies:

> [The hotel lobby] reduces to the level of the nothing—out of which it wants to produce the world—even those pseudo-individuals it has deprived of individuality, since their anonymity no longer serves any purpose other than meaningless movement along the paths of convention. (p. 183)

We two, the man across the atrium and I, have become pseudo-individuals who just happen to have passed through the same lobby. In contrast, many of today's lobbies have lost their preeminence as sites of public display. They are dim and generic, holding places for kiosks that assist in automated check-in. Although the Kracauer hotel lobby was an ornamental church for an anonymous modernity, the contemporary atrium that encloses the stranger and I rises above the city, linking us both to the world all our own.

Conclusion

We have surveyed a range of 20th- and 21st-century sites of temporary domesticity, admitting a necessarily selective frame. Our goal has been to assess strategies through which an omnitopian sensibility stretches beyond the isolated and distinct nodes of mobility found in airports. From motels we found, despite efforts to craft fragments of locality through clever design or signage, a commonality to the roadside lodge, the assurance that one may traverse the country from room to anonymous room. From early chain hotels, we traced efforts to globalize the motel, editing away any remaining local character and assuring motorists the ability to enter their rooms without turning on the lights and to find private highway enclosures along almost every interchange. Again, efforts to instill some sense of place and time, illustrated by the "comfort food" of Kem's Café, offer only a fragmentary diversion from the coherent matrix of corporate-minded places. Finally, entering the grand atriums of Portman (and Portman-inspired) convention hotels, we view a culmination of the omnitopian integration of disparate functionalities into a coherent structure and perception. From the interstate and airport hotel, we now turn to places of pleasure, shopping malls, which have shared the lessons of the arcade, the atrium, and the world's fair. In the mall, we conclude our site visits to omnitopian sites that appear, but only appear, to be totalizing in their power.

Notes

1. For the sake of convenience, I use the word *motel* in reference to a wide range of lodges built along or near a highway and designed to accommodate guests who arrived by way of automobile. Prior to the Second World War, those properties that would now be called motels were more typically labeled *auto camps* or *tourist courts*. Unlike its pre-war predecessors, the motel is most remarkable for its line of rooms covered with one roof, often in an I shape, but sometimes in an L or U shape. In contrast, auto camps and tourist courts were generally composed of detached cabins or cottages, sometimes offering little more than farmer-built shacks.

2. In his study of Best Western, Yakhlef (2004) offers an intriguing analysis of the "spaces" created by brand names as motel and hotel owners attempt to balance local and global interests: "Generic spaces do not provide disembodied experiences. . . . Rather, they are embodied, being attendant on the specific representations of space of users and inhabitants of such spaces. Generic spaces are lived spaces" (p. 245).

3. The *streamline-moderne* Coral Court Motel, south of St. Louis, Missouri, was a most beloved and demonized example of the "no-tell motel" (Graham, 2000). The motel, an architectural delight, was bulldozed in 1995. Incidentally, one may visit an actual "no tell" in the form of the No-Tel Motel in Tucson, Arizona, although I don't recommend a long stay.

4. Morris' (1988) frequently cited essay more accurately may be said to analyze a motor hotel than an independent motel. The complex of spaces found in her Henry Parkes would hardly be recognizable to the aficionado of the American Mom and Pop motel. I would also share her admission toward the end of that piece that relatively little of her analysis attends closely to that property: "I can drive away still thinking about Henry Parkes, of whom I've had very little to say" (p. 43).

5. Eddie Bluestein, designer of the first Holiday Inn built in Memphis, proposed the "Holiday Inn" moniker after seeing the Bing Crosby film of the same name (Jakle, Sculle, & Rogers, 1996).

6. Although 43 feet is a commonly cited height of the Great Sign, the actual size varied considerably among Holiday Inn properties.

7. Traveling the United States in search of a Great Sign that somehow survived demolition, I discovered one in 2003 in Mount Airy, North Carolina. Like its Holiday Inn predecessor, the Mount Airy site had abandoned its original identity, but kept its "Great Sign," painted over to present a new identity of a Mom and Pop motel.

8. Craig (1988) reminds his academic readers of the playful attitude that Portman atriums inspired within convention-goers, asking, "Do adults act any more like children than when 'on convention'?" (p. 27).

9. Zukin (1991) astutely reminds us that Henry James' complaints about the plasticity of the Waldorf Astoria foreshadowed much of Jameson's reading of the Bonaventure.

References

Anderson, A., & Tompkins, J. (1972, June 12). Rapid rise of the host with the most. *Time Magazine*, pp. 77–82.

Belasco, W. J. (1997). *Americans on the road: From autocamp to motel, 1910–1945.* Baltimore: Johns Hopkins University Press.

Boorstin, D. J. (1992). *The image: A guide to pseudo-events in America.* New York: Vintage.

Brand, S. (1994). *How buildings learn: What happens after they're built.* New York: Penguin.

Chen, A. (2006, June 23). Fountains, glass and the enduring dazzle of atrium hotels. *The International Herald Tribune*, p. 26.

Craig, R. M. (1988). Making modern architecture palatable in Atlanta: POPular Modern architecture from deco to Portman to deco revival. *Journal of American Culture*, *11*(3), 19–33.

Foucault, M. (1986). Of other spaces. *Diacritics, 16*, 22–27.

Gitlin, T. (1979). Domesticating nature. *Theory and Society, 8*(2), 291–297.

Graham, S. (2000). *Tales from the Coral Court: Photos and stories from a lost Route 66 landmark.* St. Louis, MO: Virginia Publishing.

Holman, C. H. (1969). The view from the Regency-Hyatt: Southern social issues and the outer world. In G. Core (Ed.), *Southern fiction today: Renascence and beyond* (pp. 16–32). Athens: University of Georgia Press.

Ibelings, H. (1998). *Supermodernism: Architecture in the age of globalization.* Amsterdam: Nai.

Iyer, P. (2000). *The global soul: Jet lag, shopping malls, and the search for home.* New York: Vintage.

Jakle, J. A., Sculle, K. A., & Rogers, J. S. (1996). *The motel in America.* Baltimore: The Johns Hopkins University Press.

Jameson, F. (1991). *Postmodernism: Or, the cultural logic of Late Capitalism*. Durham, NC: Duke University Press.

Judd, D. R. (1999). Constructing the tourist bubble. In D. R. Judd & S. S. Fainstein (Eds.), *The tourist city* (pp. 35–53). New Haven, CT: Yale University Press.

Kracauer, S. (1995). *The mass ornament: Weimer essays* (T. Y. Levin, Trans.). Cambridge, MA: Harvard University Press.

Liebs, C. H. (1985). *Main street to miracle mile: American roadside architecture*. Baltimore: Johns Hopkins University Press.

Mahar, L. (2002). *American signs: Form and meaning on Route 66*. New York: Monacelli.

Margolies, J. (1995). *Home away from home: Motels in America*. Boston, MA: Bulfinch Press.

Morris, M. (1988). At Henry Parkes Motel. *Cultural Studies, 2*(1), 1–47.

Nelson, A. (2002). The Holiday Inn sign. *Salon*. Retrieved October 16, 2007, from http://www.salon.com/ent/masterpiece/2002/04/29/holiday_inn/

Newman, H. K. (2002). Race and the tourist bubble in downtown Atlanta. *Urban Affairs Review, 37*(3), 301–321.

Portman, J., & Barnett, J. (1976). *The architect as developer*. New York: McGraw-Hill.

Sudjic, D. (2006). The hotel wonders of the world. *The Observer*, Escape 1.

Sutton, S. B. (Ed.). (2001). *Civilizing American cities: Writings on city landscapes*. New York: Da Capo.

Yakhlef, A. (2004). Global brands as embodied "generic spaces": The example of branded chain hotels. *Space and Culture, 7*(2), 237–248.

Zelinsky, W. (1994). Conventionland USA: The geography of a latterday phenomenon. *Annals of the Association of American Geographers, 84*(1), 68–86.

Zukin, S. (1991). *Landscapes of power: From Detroit to Disney World*. Berkeley: University of California Press.

6

──────────────────── Malls ────────────────────

Malls and themed shopping-leisure environments are making downtowns
into places of specialized consumption segregated from the rest of the city.
In these environments, out-of-town visitors do mingle with local residents,
but both groups are prompted to act as if they are, in effect, in a dreamscape
far removed from the city that surrounds them.

—Dennis R. Judd (1999, p. 49)

The mall *is* modernity: so say its lovers and its critics. Shopping malls have
provided students of popular culture, design, and social interaction a potent
metaphor for soulless consumer excess as conveniently homogenous as the
place it represents. As an opportunity to feed our inner movie reviewer, that
adjective, *soulless*, has long offered a warrant for countless zombie references
that have animated essays about shopping mall behavior. Partially as homage, partially because I too enjoy a good zombie movie, I therefore fulfill that
unwritten rule about mall scholarship with my own obligatory reference to
George Romero's 1978 satire of mindless consumerism, *Dawn of the Dead*.
In fact, I won't conclude the present analysis without shooting zombies in a
place that bills itself the largest mall in the world. But you'll have to wait a
while to learn more about that feat. In the meantime, I hope to revisit the mall
as an entirely different place than the one found in decades of popular and
scholarly critique. I hope to reveal how the mall is increasingly integrated
into a network of related consumer, commercial, entertainment, domestic, and
travel spaces that reveal both the death of the heterotopian enclosure and the
colonization of the omnitopian enclave into contemporary life. This analysis
requires close attention to a fascinating structural and perceptual phenomenon
whose changes in design and practice signify important transformations in
public life.

Initially, one might wonder whether the mall continues to earn its spot as exemplar architecture for contemporary life. Having replicated itself so abundantly throughout the United States and around the world, the mall is so banal, so commonplace, that it slips from consciousness. Moreover, the quintessential suburban shopping mall—enclosed and climate controlled, two floors of long concourses, mirrored escalators and splashing fountains, acres of parking moats, and a food court or two—is being replaced by new categories of shopping center, most notably lifestyle centers. Yet the mall continues to command scholarly attention. At the mall, we find more than a place to shop. The mall has become a version of society, a community of shoppers, and a marketplace for identities. Since its inception, the mall has always represented something alien, mildly frightening. Yet within its glass doors, the omnitopian project neared completion as the perfect enclave:

> [The mall could] break so many rules and preconceptions because it was completely separated from the rest of the world. It was its own world, pulled out of time and space, but not only by windowless walls and a roof, or by the neutral zone of the parking lot between it and the highway, the asphalt moat around the magic castle. It was *enclosed* in an even more profound sense—and certainly more than other mere buildings—because all these elements, and others, psychologically separated it from the outside and created the special domain within its embrace. It *meant* to be its own special world with its own rules and reality. That was the first and most essential secret of the shopping mall. Its space is also special because it is *protected*.... (Kowinski, 1985, p. 60; italics original)

Safety, distance from the urban ruin, a new city of comfort and commerce: The mall has failed in some senses, fallen into disregard by many of us. Yet its promise of protection has already mutated into more complex kinds of enclave, especially those whose walls cannot be seen.

I have chosen to revisit the mall to study ways in which the detached enclosure gives way to the enclavic node. I first outline a brief history of the shopping mall, focusing on Minnesota's Southdale Center. Then I describe efforts by one traditional mall, Alberta's West Edmonton Mall, to craft an entirely interior world that offers references to the exterior without providing connections to the outside. Finally, I describe the post-mall movement of lifestyle centers that claim to reconnect commercial spaces to the flows of contemporary urban life, visiting California's Santana Row. From this effort, I hope to reaffirm a larger goal—to rethink the enclave as more than a segregated community of like-minded people or things located in a knowable (and assailable) geography.[1] I see the post-mall movement is reflecting a new enclavic sensibility that resides both within and beyond "local" geographies. But the only path from here to there runs through the mall.

Image 12: 1907 Postcard of Central Park Mall. *Author's Collection*

The First Mall

As will shortly become apparent, writing even a brief history of malls is a risky proposition; the distinctions between "firsts" so frequently rest on selective interpretations of various boosters. At least the etymology of mall remains relatively uncontroversial, even as the word's meaning has changed substantially over the centuries. The word *mall* stems from the 17th-century English *Pall-Mall*, a hybrid between croquet and golf that borrowed from French, Italian, and Scottish predecessors. Pall-Mall referred to the game, along with the mallet and pitch where the game was played. With the game's declining popularity in the 18th century, Pall-Malls became transformed into tree-lined promenade paths, the walk in London's St. James' Park providing the most commonly cited example. The word *mall* thereafter grew to reflect a pedestrian walking space—one that might be lined with fashionable shops. For that reason, the Washington, DC grassy walkway between the Lincoln Memorial and the Capital Building is called a *mall*, only one that lacks adjacent shops. By the mid-20th-century, designers of pedestrian-only shopping sites adapted the word *mall* for their purposes, particularly in North America. The mall would thereafter refer to a shopping corridor, which may or may not be enclosed.

Shopping center historians heap credit (and blame) for this innovation on Victor Gruen, a Viennese commercial architect who fled his home in 1938 to escape the Nazi regime. Inspired by the open, modern, and democratic spaces of post-1848 Vienna, Gruen viewed architecture as a means to reflect his socialist ideals. Soon after his arrival in New York, Gruen developed a reputation as a visionary who transformed tiny storefronts into immersive spectacles. He also designed a handful of exhibits for the 1939–1940 New York World's Fair, where he found time to gaze on Norman Bel Geddes' Futurama exhibit.[2] At the Fair, Gruen intensified his belief that careful design could replace the undisciplined hodge-podge of urban life with efficient, humane, pedestrian-oriented communities. He perfected that goal by designing properties on both coasts of the United States. But Gruen is best known for his design of Southdale Center, which opened in the Minneapolis suburb of Edina in 1956. Although Southdale would hardly appear to merit scholarly attention (it's just a shopping center, after all), this site provided the template for almost every mall built over the next 30 years.

Commissioned by the Dayton Company, Victor Gruen Associates designed Southdale in a "double-pull" design, including two department stores connected by a multilevel concourse of arcades.[3] Placing two competing anchor stores in one shopping center was considered a radical notion at the time, but Gruen knew that both properties could reinforce each other so long as they were separated by a sufficiently developed concourse of shops and dining opportunities, as well as plant life, bird enclosures, art exhibits, and a three-story central garden court. A press release from Southdale's opening offers a vivid description of that space:

Image 13: Southdale Center Postcard. *Author's Collection*

> A modern interpretation of traditional market squares, the Garden Court is
> the center's showplace, its magnet. A block long and three stories high, it is
> partly covered by a louvered skylight. Colorful shopping lanes lead into it;
> stores and shops are clustered around it. Gaiety is injected into the court
> through color, lighting and other means. Whether sitting on a rest bench
> or at a table off the sidewalk café, the shopper finds pleasant eye-catching
> features all about him [sic]; brightly plumed song birds, art objects, decora-
> tive lighting, fountains, tropical plants, trees and flowers. They quicken the
> human impulse to mingle, and create an atmosphere of leisure, excitement
> and intimacy similar to the one which can be found in some European city
> market squares. (Ruder & Finn, 1956a, p. 1)[4]

Although the Garden Court offered a respite from walking, Southdale was also
designed to keep people moving. Escalators and stairways were employed for
customers to visit both floors according to a figure-8 loop, a potentially endless
(yet pleasant) progression of shopping mobility.

Most important, Gruen enclosed all of Southdale in a climate-controlled
interior to ensure that shoppers would visit regardless of the outside weather.
Constantly maintained temperatures would protect against the Minnesota's noto-
riously brutal winters and surprisingly warm summers. Rejecting the outside
arcade "mall" that had dominated shopping center design to that time, Gruen
oriented Southdale's amenities away from the streets, offering few windows to
pique the interests of outside strollers. Another press release marking Southdale's
opening illustrates the interior focus of this mall:

> Southdale shopping center could be called in psychological terms "an introvert
> center." On the outside it presents a quiet and dignified appearance, inviting
> the shopper to enter through one of ten huge all-glass entrances into the
> interior. Once having passed through these doors, the shopper is drawn
> through broad lanes with store fronts of great variety on both sides to the
> real heart of the center a block long. . . . (Ruder & Finn, 1956b, p. 2)

Although Gruen hoped that Southdale would boost the vitality of public life,
that it would contribute a sense of community to the entire Minneapolis region,
Southdale was viewed by most of its users as a safe and inviting enclave from
the perceived and real risks of urban life.[5]

One might further illustrate this enclave by the surrounding parking lots,
a model of the moats that would appear in virtually every suburban mall built
thereafter. Gruen would eventually bemoan the manner in which these moats
separated his shopping centers from the surrounding cities, but at first he enthu-
siastically compared them to the models provided by Ebenezer Howard's garden
cities. Gruen intended that the shopping center would be pedestrian-centered,
and yet he knew that that would have to be connected to rapid transit systems.

To ameliorate the resulting dangers of human–auto interaction, Southdale was surrounded by a ring road (similar to the *ringstrasse* of his home city of Vienna), where cars would slow down before depositing drivers to parking lots. As Gruen and Smith (1960) wrote in their manual for shopping center design, the ideal center would separate driver from car as quickly as possible:

> The separation of pedestrian areas from transportation areas is one of the cornerstones of good planning. Transportation areas require considerable space within which the movement of vehicles of various types can be accomplished as effectively as possible. It is inherent in the character of transportation areas that a certain amount of danger, noise, fumes, confusion and distraction is created within them. These characteristics result in tensions and feelings of anxiety in the shopper which distracts him [sic] from the task at hand: the business of shopping. (p. 81)

It need not be overstated that Gruen did not invent the shopping enclosure. Similar ideas could be found in 19th-century arcades and further backward toward the earliest covered bazaars. But Southdale's addition of climate control and internal focus to its other functional and design attributes promised something new, foreshadowing a transformation of suburban life. This is the key to understanding what the suburban shopping center was meant to be.

Gruen sought to reinvent urban life, not to merely build a mall. After all, in Gruen's parlance, a "mall" referred simply to an open public space situated between the shopping arcades. Gruen certainly hoped to create a massive shopping enclosure where consumers would circulate on two levels of shops and department stores. But Gruen wanted more. He dreamed of modern and functional urban spaces that avoided the mistakes of the big cities—places organized around sustainable and complex communities like the one he left behind in Vienna, a city with a "nearly perfect plan" (Gruen, 1964, p. 38). Southdale would form the heart of a vital city that contained administrative, medical, educational, and social resources. One would not simply shop at Southdale; one could live there. This model of total planning, he proposed, signified a means to avoid the short-term developments that bedeviled so much of urban life as he saw it:

> The construction of a parking garage here and there, spot rehabilitation of slums, the building of freeways and attempts in any of the other directions, when undertaken without guidance of an over-all master plan, have generally proven costly and worthless in the long run. The real need is for an improvement of the entire environmental quality of the urban core and an integrated attack on all problems. (Gruen & Smith, 1960, p. 271)

No doubt, this kind of total planning inspired Walt Disney's vision of EPCOT Center, a prototype community marked by the efficient distribution of pedestrian and wheeled traffic almost as much as its distinction as a rigidly regulated enclave.

As is typical of these sorts of dreams, the practice failed to meet the promise. Surrounding itself with a sea of parking spaces, Southdale soon abandoned the rhetoric of community building. But mall historians can hardly dismiss Southdale as a failed experiment. As Gladwell (2004) notes:

> Victor Gruen designed a fully enclosed, introverted, multitiered, double-anchor-tenant shopping complex with a garden court under a skylight—and today virtually every regional shopping center in America is a fully enclosed, introverted, multitiered, double-anchor-tenant complex with a garden court under a skylight. Victor Gruen didn't design a building; he designed an archetype. (p. 122)

Over the next three decades, developers borrowed from that archetype, employing community language in their mall names,[6] even as they gradually abandoned the community-design concepts that Gruen envisioned. These developers, increasingly financed by publicly traded Real Estate Investment Trusts, exploited changes in the tax code such as telescoped depreciation allowances to build malls quickly and cheaply on inexpensive farmland that sprawled farther and farther away from population centers (Gladwell, 2004). The malls that flowed from their spreadsheets offered no pretense to the revitalization of life through suburban innovation as Gruen had hoped, and they quickly grew to symbolize the kind of banal sprawl that he detested.[7] Rejecting the offspring that sprung from his imagination, Gruen famously announced, "I refuse to pay alimony for those bastard developments" and returned to his native Vienna ("A pall," 1978, p. 116). The mall failed and yet it thrived, producing grander and more compelling places, each competing for recognition as the largest. Such ambition leads us to investigate the mall as a climate-controlled spectacle. It's hardly an original stop along our journey; many scholars have tramped its concourses over the years, but we must visit Canada's West Edmonton Mall for ourselves.

The (Once) Biggest Mall

West Edmonton Mall (WEM)[8] was once labeled the largest mall in the world, larger even than Minneapolis' Mall of America.[9] Located in Alberta, WEM sits on a prairie about 5 miles from downtown Edmonton. Opened in 1981 and growing in four phases since then, WEM now encloses about 5.3 million square feet (3.8 million square feet of Gross Leasable Area), covering the equivalent of 48 city blocks and providing 20,000 parking spaces ("The official"). The mall advertises 800 stores, shops, and services; 110 restaurants, cafes, and fast-food outlets; and

Image 14: West Edmonton Mall. *Photograph by Andrew Wood, Used by Permission*

59 entrances.[10] Indoor attractions include an amusement park, a waterpark, an ice skating rink, two miniature golf courses, and even an enclosed lagoon that contains a replica of the Santa Maria. Some of the mall's other properties would surprise U.S. readers: a casino, a tattoo and piercing shop, a check cashing and money lending store, a liquor store, an adult "boutique," a head shop, and even a chapel. Once labeling itself the Eighth Wonder of the World (more recently, "The Greatest Indoor Show on Earth"), WEM now must settle for also-ran status in the competition for world's largest mall, having been surpassed by even larger properties in China and Dubai (Boswell, 2004). Nonetheless, this mall represents a quintessential example of total enclosure.

I visited WEM in early 2007 to survey its design and practices. When I told colleagues about my impending visit to WEM, I conflated my day and night plans into the grand announcement, "I plan to live at the mall." It seemed a reasonable enough convergence of plans. I recall passing through customs at Edmonton International Airport and earning special treatment from the official who couldn't quite jibe my purpose. "College professor? Visiting West Edmonton Mall? You sure you don't work for the airline?" I could not figure how that clarification would make sense to the man. But I managed nonetheless to board my shuttle and traverse the lonely prairies before taking my exit at the Fantasyland Hotel, a 12-story complex that is fragmented into a range of theme spaces like Roman Room, Polynesian Room, African Room, and Truck Room (where, yes, you can sleep in the back of a pickup truck). Integrated into the mall, offering 24-hour access to its concourses, Fantasyland would be my home and refuge during 3 days of mall wandering.

I arrive at WEM wearing flimsy pants, an old college t-shirt, and a pair of flip-flops. It's cold and windy, but I plan to spend every minute indoors. This mall is built to accommodate that desire. Passing through the doors, one enters a protected and sophisticated interior that promises to contain the whole world, where every step away from the outside leads to a richer and more vivid version of reality.[11] Margaret Crawford (1999) states: "Exaggerating the differences between the world outside and the world inside [represents] a basic mall trope: an inverted space whose forbidding exteriors [hide] paradisiacal interiors" (p. 22). One may forget the "outside" entirely within an enclosed domain such as WEM. During my visit, Christmas trees are still standing to accommodate a movie being filmed in the mall. Days, even seasons, have no meaning inside. Aside from the occasional presence of some monumental clock in a central gathering area, the presence of human time told in hours and seconds can rarely be discerned at all. To keep people moving, top-40 music plays from speakers placed throughout WEM. Mercifully, the up-tempo tunes are much improved over the bland blanket of sound that once deadened public spaces.[12] The songs are universally peppy and toe-tapping, even if the playlist occasionally includes a few evocative and unexpected ironies such as the Eurythmics' "Here Comes the Rain Again," The Doobie Brothers' "Taking' it to the Streets," and Gary Numan's ode to the ultimate mobile enclave, "Cars." WEM reflects the enclavic impulse to dislocate oneself from unpredictable weather and unplanned interpersonal interactions.

Ultimately, WEM's world is far more complex than a mere shopping center. It may better be termed a facsimile of a world's fair. Recall that the Victorian origins of the modern world's fair offered a temporary convergence of nationalist propaganda, corporate shilling, low-brow amusement, and one other necessary ingredient: a semblance of educational appeal. The earliest fairs were sold as a means to social uplift, teaching their visitors about the handicrafts and social practices of varied cultures, the contributions of the host nation to human civilization, and the self-evident values of technological advancement (a word that would never be placed in quotation marks by their organizers). Purchasing a ticket to pass through the gates, one performed the identity of enlightenment. No one would claim such a position at today's malls, but they are otherwise generally similar in their offerings to those found at a world's fair. The presence of commodification need not be emphasized here; it is apparent enough. But malls often find room for cultural and educational displays: art exhibits, historical displays, local photographs, and the like. During my visit to WEM, I gaze on a flamingo enclosure that offers factoids about the creatures, I photograph a statue dedicated to oilers that helped grow the provincial economy, I look over cases containing Chinese vases, and I even spot a display dedicated to geology. Even the Segway spot, the place where folks pay to rent the personal mobility devices to cruise around an indoor course, is advertised as an educational exhibit: "Learn to ride a Segway!" WEM continues the world's fair tradition of commercializing prepackaged places as vehicles for self-improvement.

WEM expands on this premise by offering three theme streets: Bourbon Street, Chinatown, and Europa Boulevard (as well as a United Nations of fast-food eateries that includes China Walk, Sbarro, New York Fries, Tokyo Express, TacoTime, and, inevitably, KFC).[13] Bourbon Street and Chinatown exist as over-lapping worlds: the former on level 1, the latter on level 2. Bourbon Street is marked primarily by its placement of oversized harlequin figures, wrought-iron balconies, and the presence of glowing neon signs that advertise almost a dozen medium-range restaurants, including Boston Pizza, The Old Spaghetti Factory, and Jungle Jim's Eatery, where patrons are invited to "Eat Your Face Off!" In

Image 15: Europa Boulevard. *Image courtesy of West Edmonton Mall*

contrast, Chinatown features hanging dragons, ceremonial arches, koi ponds, and a number of shops whose advertisements and wares are generally geared toward Asian-speaking visitors. T&T Supermarket, a store belonging to Canada's largest chain of Asian supermarkets, anchors the zone. Europa Boulevard, however, fascinates me the most. Its arched glass roof shelters a European-style streetscape that includes *al fresco* dining and faux building facades. At last, I have returned to the arcade. In this mall, even the ostensibly distinct architecture becomes another node to the same place, one open 24 hours a day.

At 4:30 a.m., I leave my room for an early morning walk through the mall. Although the shops close at around 9 p.m., the mall's concourses are open all night long, and not just to hotel guests. Joggers, for example, use the mall as an indoor track. Its grand spaces and long vistas are also filled with the sounds of floor cleaners. In their nearby enclosure, the mall's flock of flamingos are asleep, each perched on one spindly leg, their heads coiled and burrowed backward into their wings. I commit to not waking them, but manage to roust them from their slumbers anyway, just standing there. Virtually all of the birds startle each other into alertness, and they begin to stretch and preen themselves before plunging their heads back among their feathers in what appears to be a rebellious effort to return to sleep despite my presence. There's something delightfully unauthorized about wandering a mall before the shops open, living a childhood fantasy of transforming a public place or, more accurately, a corporately owned place used by the public, into a private enclave.[14] When I was a kid, that fantasy manifested itself in the construction of "forts," the heady realization that these pillows owned by parents or some other authority figure (grandparents, in my case) could be transmogrified into something uniquely *mine*, a safe place.

Leaving WEM, I find myself reflecting on the extension of the total enclosure concept to cities like Calgary, Minneapolis, Montreal, and Osaka, which have borrowed from mall technologies to create interconnected spaces of domesticity, commerce, and entertainment through skyways and underground connections.[15] From these examples, one might presume that the mall would provide a foundation for urban life: a world of arcologies or even a global city. But this model would soon decline, a victim of a growing desire to reinvigorate public spaces. In its place, new types of shopping centers promised visions of small-town life—places to walk outdoors and meet friends near fountains that glisten in the sun. These post-malls offered an escape from the enclosure, even as they produced a far more potent enclave.

The Post-Mall

Enclosed malls suffered a slow decline from the 1970s through the end of the century. Perhaps the most vivid example of that decline may be found at the

Sherman Oaks Galleria, viewed worldwide as an archetype for the mall. Producers of *Fast Times at Ridgemont High* selected the Galleria as a prime filming site, and that mall became the mythical center of the 1980s-era Valley Girl subculture. By the 1990s, however, the Galleria had lost much of its pop culture cachet, and the 1994 Northridge Earthquake only served to hasten the mall's decline. In 1999, the mall's owners closed the Galleria and transformed the site over 3 years into an open-air center. No longer would motorists enter the mall through a parking garage, and no longer would the Galleria seem more like an aquarium than an arcade. Ripping the roof off the mall appeared to signify the rejection of Victor Gruen's total enclosures (after the architect had abandoned his progeny). In place of the enclosed mall, we witness the rise of the lifestyle center.

Lifestyle centers nearly complete the disintegration of the mall and the mutation of its commercial purpose into a larger and much more complex omnitopian network. Unlike the traditional mall, with its concourses of interior fantasy and its acres of exterior detachment, an enclosed city reminiscent of *Logan's Run*,[16] the lifestyle center colonizes typical commercial spaces to revitalize the city "outside." Doing so, the lifestyle center reflects a culmination of the omnitopian turn by creating a perceptual "interior" that is conceivably accessible to everyone but practically limited to those who follow the rules of its performance. The lifestyle center accomplishes this task by exploiting a nostalgia for human-scaled locales whose scripts for human interaction are knowable and consistent (Stewart & Dickinson, 2008). The common design of the lifestyle center promises a version of the small town or the provincial village that resides somewhere in media memory, the promise of home and hearth: nostalgia as temporal enclave.

This manner of nostalgia reflects a modern notion of the term that differs substantially from its origins. In 1688, a Swiss doctor named Johannes Hofer first proposed nostalgia—a neologism from the Greek *nostos* (homecoming) and *algos* (pain, grief, distress)—to account for a bodily disease that soldiers, students, and domestic workers suffered after being far from home. Gradually, the medical usage of nostalgia softened in the 19th century, until it assumed its current benign definition: a longing for the past, which is often (not always) connected to some fantasy of place. The transformation of enclosed mall cities into "tiny towns" reflects a peculiar nostalgia that has been artfully crafted for corporate purposes. This practice cannot be limited to the design of shopping centers.

Throughout the 20th century, various forms of popular culture responded to the feeling of unease associated with the rise of corporate centered urban life. This unease, often reported to afflict the economically privileged with notable frequency, responds to recollections of simpler places and "old times."[17] Henry Seidel Canby's *The Age of Confidence: Life in the Nineties*, published in the midst of the Great Depression, offers a vivid example of this kind of nostalgia, warmly recreating the author's hometown of Victorian-era Wilmington, Delaware:

It was a culture with mores, it was a Life in which one quickly knew one's place, and began that difficult weaving of emotions with experiences that is called growing up, in a set of circumstances which one could not and did not really wish to alter. Time moved slowly while your personality twisted and doubled on its course. The town waited for you. It was going to be there when you were ready for it. (1934, p. 31)[18]

Turning to TV, we might also recall *Twilight Zone* episodes that played on similar impulses. An episode entitled "A Stop at Willoughby" depicts the plight of an overworked media executive who dreams of escaping his harried life to live in an temporal enclave set in 1880, "where a man can slow down to a walk and live his life full measure." Similarly, an episode entitled "Walking Distance" portrays yet another media exec who slips back in time to the hometown of his childhood, a small world of carousels and cotton candy on a warm summer evening, before learning that he cannot remain in that temporal enclave from the frustrations of his present life. His only solace is hopeful advice offered by his father: "Maybe when you go back . . . you'll find that there are merry-go-rounds and band concerts where you are. Maybe you haven't been looking in the right place. You've been looking behind you . . . Try looking ahead."[19] Finally, we might relive our chuckles in the 1994 film *Pleasantville*, in which a teacher provides a sweetly paradoxical description of a town's geography:

Jennifer: What's outside of Pleasantville?

Miss Peters: I don't understand.

Jennifer: Outside of Pleasantville? Like, what's at the end of Main Street?

Miss Peters: Sue. You should know the answer to that! The end of Main Street is just the beginning again.

In these popular culture examples and in countless others, media-fed nostalgia reenacts that myth of eternal return, that ever-present hometown in our collective memory. This temporal enclave promotes a preferred version of the past as therapy against the present.

This nostalgic turn animates the trend toward the construction of lifestyle centers. Yet I believe we should contextualize these centers in the broader movement of new urbanism, a collection of people and practices working to redesign cities to be pedestrian-friendly, coherently themed, and community-centered. Generally, this form of architecture is designed to appeal to folks who are nostalgic for small-town life. A quintessential example of new urbanist development is a planned community built by the Disney Development Corporation in central Florida: Celebration. Built as a sort of anti-EPCOT, this community was designed to resemble a typical southern small town built in the 1930s. Yet its earliest amenities included a fiber-optic network, intranet, and a state-of-the-art hospital. As the community was first being advertised, a videotape playing at the Celebration Preview Center promised a "new American town of Fourth of July parades and school bake sales . . . spaghetti dinners and fireflies in a jar." During that same period, a promotional sign reinforced Celebration's heterotopian overlap of times and places: "Imagine how great it would have been . . . to live fifty years ago with all the neat gear you have today." As Celebration sought to create genuine community (even after Disney bowed out of the project), lifestyle centers advertise a sense of "place" beyond the price tags.

Lifestyle centers are relatively new, entering the lexicon in the 1980s and reflecting a fast-growing trend in shopping center design.[20] They may be identified by relatively compact collections of high-end shops, sit-down restaurants, and amenities such as fountains and chairs, all situated outdoors. Lifestyle centers also include other forms of mixed-use development, such as apartments and condos, to create a sense of vibrant urban life and, as McLinden (2005) notes, to spread the risk of investment. Attempting to create a "main street" vibe, lifestyle centers typically lack anchor stores, although they may be placed in close proximity to a big-box store or even a nearby mall.[21] Lifestyle centers promise short walking distances between car and store, often via curbside parking,[22] to enhance a sense of convenience and safety not often found in parking lots that surround older malls and more recent big-box-based "power centers."[23] Writing in *Slate*, Andrew Blum (2005) states somewhat pointedly, "The lifestyle center is a bizarre outgrowth of the suburban mentality: People want public space, even if making that space private is the only way to get it" (¶ 8). Although some observers debate the utility of the "lifestyle center" concept, even imagining post-lifestyle centers,[24] one can hardly debate the significance of this design.

Santana Row, located in San José, California, represents an exemplar lifestyle center in its efforts to re-create the vibe associated with a Parisian town. Opened in 2002, Santana Row features 70 shops such as Crate & Barrel, Borders, and Gucci, as well as five spas, a hotel, and restaurants like Left Bank, which labels itself "an authentic Parisian-style brasserie." Above many of the pedestrian-level properties reside apartment and condo spaces. King (2002) quotes one of Santana Row's developers as boasting "a world-class Main Street, perhaps a new urban paradigm for America" (p. A23). Santana Row also includes themed elements such as "weathered" doors, decorative balcony railings (on blank walls), and a vintage wine bar whose entrance resembles a gothic cathedral. As one would imagine, this urban fantasy is designed and marketed to appeal to wealthy shoppers. It provides a vivid setting for the performance of class that is physically accessible even while it is rhetorically restricted.

Image 16: Santana Row. *Photograph by Andrew Wood*

One day in spring, I visit Santana Row in mid-morning. The popular life-style center sits on the corner of Stevens Creek and Winchester Boulevard—two busy thoroughfares that hum with traffic pulsed by the adjacent freeway. Nearby, the Winchester Mystery House attracts tourists with its story of a widow who added room after room to her rambling house in a bid to appease the ghosts of people killed by Winchester rifles. But this morning I can hardly discern the noise of the outside world. The weather is drizzly, and it looks as if only a few condo dwellers are walking the pathways. One woman pushes her dog in a baby carriage. Smiling and nodding hello, I amble along, looking into windows and studying the varying surfaces of the walkways. The place resembles a nice little town with its fountains, chairs, and smiling folks. I even spot a hotdog vender advertising something called chicken apple sausage. For a while, I sit above a Borders bookstore, sipping coffee out of a paper cup and looking down on the scene. It's fun to seize a god's eye view, to gaze on it all. But eventually I yearn to leave; I want to see the edges of Santana Row. Past the fake doorways and ornamental climbing vines, I find myself back on Winchester Boulevard. I stand in a median across from the googie-style Flames Restaurant, looking at a tower-ing salmon-colored wall. Outside Santana Row, the walls are tall and flat. I snap a photograph of an empty wooden bench, light post, and a stairway leading to locked door. I flash back on Sarah Winchester and her twisting stairs that lead nowhere, her enclave against the ghosts of the modern age. I get hungry for one of those hotdogs. It's so much nicer "inside."

Places like Santana Row, along with hundreds of other lifestyle centers in the planning stages, represent more than a semantic abolition of mall terminology and more than the surface-level addition of Main Street form to commercial function. For many people, the lifestyle center *becomes* Main Street. As Reno (2006) notes, "The malling of America has taken a decidedly Disney-esque twist. Designed like elaborate outdoor movie sets, lifestyle centers are meant to look like real towns, with curbed streets, parking meters and themed architecture" (p. 60). This Disneyfication of urban life reflects fear of the city's unplanned interactions and real physical dangers. But it illustrates even more the contemporary nature of the omnitopian enclave. No longer placed within the arcade or the automobile or even the total interior that links its inhabitants from enclosure to enclosure, the omnitopian enclave is a synecdoche of the world that gathers even rhetorically bounded exteriors into a perceptually roofed interior. As the lifestyle center illustrates, one no longer must search out a heterotopian "other place." Omnitopia is ubiquitous, eventually so much that *places* eventually may become unnecessary.

Conclusion

I promised not to conclude without shooting some zombies, and I will deliver. I have always loved zombie movies, and my favorite one is *Dawn of the Dead*, George Romero's 1978 follow-up to *Night of the Living Dead*. Given a bit more of a budget than his first film, enough to shoot in color, at least, Romero selected Pittsburgh's Monroeville Mall as the site for his epic battle between a hardscrabble crew of survivors and the legions of carnivorous ghouls. The movie is a blood-splattering spectacle, but it also offers some degree of social comment. When one of the survivors explains the rush of zombies on this modern fortress, his explanation represents the bloody heart of Romero's satire of consumer unconsciousness:

> Francine: What are they doing? Why do they come here?

> Stephen: Some kind of instinct. Memory, of what they used to do. This was an important place in their lives.

Countless armchair sociologists who heard that line whispered to themselves, "I could write a *thesis* on this movie! A *dissertation*!" The owners of the Wild

West Shooting Centre in West Edmonton Mall thought something much more elemental: "It *would* be fun to shoot zombies at a mall." People like me would pay for the experience.

It's been almost 15 years since I fired a weapon of any sort. But the Wild West allows even unlicensed folks like me to select their fantasy, from a pee shooter to a hand cannon. I think about renting the 357 Magnum, but something about the H&K USC semi-automatic carbine speaks to me. Gun rental does not include the rack of shells, nor the souvenirs that I surely will buy, so the whole package comes dearly. But at least the paper targets are free, and the Wild West offers several; or you can bring your own as long as you don't shoot images considered "in poor taste" by the management (Taylor, 2006, p. A03). I think about the cost, as well as the silliness of this exercise, and consider turning around. But then I see the zombies, a paper target featuring creepy ghouls marked by target rings. At once I have no doubt. I will shoot zombies in a mall. Quickly, I am led around the corner to grab ear and eye protection. I then step toward the line. An old fellow, focused, patient, and aware, walks me through the proper handling of the HK and reminds me, gently, that he'll lay hands on me if I do anything to spook him. He then instructs me how to shift the paper target, closer or farther from me as I choose, and hands me the HK. I am unsure of myself, of how I look holding this thing, but years of TV and movie watching provide the script, and I know what to do. I gauge my distance from the target zombie and aim carefully; I hold my breath, squeeze gently, and fire.

Pumping round after round into paper zombies, pushing them farther and farther downrange, I look beyond West Edmonton Mall, squinting my eye to imagine cinematic cities filled with lurching zombies. Shell casings explode from the HK, clanging onto the floor, and I think about the popularity of *Dawn of the Dead* and its unspeakable fantasy of shooting regular people. In zombie movies, the hero inevitably has to gun down someone he knows, someone like him. The target is not evil; it is merely unlucky. There arises a certain justice in the shooting of a zombie, a cosmic calculus through which any one of us could become a target or a hero. To visualize such violence as somehow authorized and pleasurable becomes pornographic in the age of Columbine, Virginia Tech, and Northern Illinois University. But zombies remain fair game. Their embodiment of justifiable homicide still sells movie tickets. Fewer and fewer of us visit actual malls where George Romero saw consumers as walking undead, but we still catch zombies among us. They are the dupes of modern life, the victims of forces beyond their control, and in omnitopia, we imagine there is no escape for them. This tempting notion affirms the academic sharpshooter who throws literary bolts against mass culture. It reveals who the zombies are and who we are not. So I went to the (once) largest mall in the world and shot zombies, happy not to be one of them, and blithely ignoring how the dichotomy on which this privilege rests is not as secure as it once was.

Hereafter, we advance an argument that both culminates and dismantles the omnitopian project. The places that connect us to the one vast room have spread themselves and multiplied, stretching along elevated walkways and underground tunnels to create a vast interior that resembles the world. Inside, we are confident and yet somehow discontented. In a number of ways, we seek some kind of exit. From this point, we find two directions outside the omnitopian enclave—one through performance and the other through the dissolution of place. Eventually, we conclude that the locale, so artfully reproduced in phantasmagorias like Santana Row, has not been totally edited away from the landscape, that it waits for us still. Throughout this next turn, we affirm the ways in which people do more than "make do" inside omnitopia. In this way, we can abandon the nightmare of the mall zombie as a cinematic stand-in for the far more complex practices of public life.

Notes

1. Admittedly, my selection of exemplars is fairly typical of mall scholarship, and I appreciate Salcedo's (2003) invitation to study malls outside of the United States and Canada. However, this project does not address the dizzying array of malls to be found around the globe. Instead, my project analyzes a trend whose roots reside in North America.

2. Hardwick (2004) writes, "For Gruen, Futurama and the fair created an impressive vision. The Vienna he had left was a compact city of few cars, limited indoor plumbing, and no major highways. . . . The exhibition, on the other hand, heralded a new way of life in which planners and corporations could work [together] and improve the existing city" (p. 19).

3. Many histories of the mall refer to this practice as a "dumbbell design." Although the dumbbell description roughly approximates the reality of shoppers walking from one anchor store to another, the early layout of Southdale more closely resembled a lightening bolt than a dumbbell. The mall also contained a basement level, which included some shopping venues.

4. The connection to European structures was intentional, flowing from Gruen's admiration of Milan's Galleria Vittorio Emanuele II (Hardwick, 2004).

5. Not coincidentally, Gruen imagined that his shopping centers would also provide some protection against intercontinental ballistic missiles, which presumably would head for the big cities and bypass the interstate highway-adjacent malls. As Minnel (2004) describes, the resulting "cold war utopia" offered "the only container that could preserve all the good qualities of humanity through any sort of shock, whether rain, smog, traffic jam, or postnuclear snow. . . . The perfect bubble-world—the long-sought utopian refuge from the antisocial troubles of the world" (p. 124).

6. Bayley (2004) offers useful insight on mall-naming practices: "So far as the naming is concerned, all these American malls are evidence of the unquenchable thirst for the English picturesque. You get squares and fairs, forests, gates, dales, valleys, parks,

lands. You get Eastport and Westport. For all I know somewhere among America's 1,200 or so malls there may be a bothy or a gazebo too" (p. 5).

7. Despite their banality, malls were undoubtedly popular. Jackson (1996) cites reports from the 1970s, claiming "that the typical American was spending more time at the mall than at any other place other than home or work" (p. 1114).

8. Although locals generally call West Edmonton Mall "West Ed," I follow the practice of most scholars of this site and refer to the mall as WEM.

9. Since 2006, The Triple Five Group, a company representing the Ghermezian family who also own West Edmonton Mall, has run The Mall of America (Pristin, 2006).

10. These figures are provided for illustrative purposes only. Precise numbers fluctuate and are often subject to debate, especially given the role of boosterism found in many materials quoted by mall researchers and journalistic sources.

11. Underhill (2004) discusses the transition zone near the entrances where the less successful stores are. The assumption is that customers don't make their purchase decisions until they have gotten acclimated to the mall, which occurs later on in their stroll.

12. Muzak once served as an all-purpose capsule for distillations of pop music that were heard in waiting rooms, elevators, and on-hold telephone receivers. Jones and Schumacher (1992) offer a useful introduction to the company, explaining that Muzak was originally designed to improve efficiency and reduce stress in factories. Later on, this "functional music" was tailored to meet the needs of retail and service clients in the postwar era. Today, Muzak offers narrow "brands" of music drawn from its large collection of songs as originally recorded by their artists. Rarely will you hear "elevator music," even in an elevator. Despite the company's rebranding, however, Muzak struggles to compete with newer satellite-based music networks.

13. The artifice found in these venues reminds many mall observers of Disney's fantasy worlds. Shields (1989) describes how "the events of different epochs, cultures, and settings are . . . combined in a Disneyland-esque 'pastiche' of scenes" (p. 153). Hopkins (1990) adds that the mega-mall completes the temporary fantasy of amusement parks and worlds fairs, explaining, "The mega-mall is 'spectacle' integrated into the everyday and open year round" (p. 8). Finally, I should note that WEM contains some literal references to Disney too, as illustrated in its Kiddyland rides that feature Bob the Builder, Winnie the Pooh, Tigger, and Mickey Mouse, whose car plays a snippet of "It's a small world."

14. When I was a child, E. L. Konigsburg's *From the Mixed-Up Files of Mrs. Basil E. Frankweiler* provided my first glimpse of this fantasy.

15. Climate is both a practical justification for many of these projects and a euphemism for middle- to upper class excuses to avoid the urban cores. Boddy (1999) affirms: "[W]hen we talk of protecting our citizens from the extremes of climate with new downtown bridges and tunnels, what is actually being promoted is more social than meteorological" (pp. 138–139).

16. *Logan's Run* portrayed its futuristic home for youthful and hedonistic city dwellers as a utopian enclave amist a ruined outside world wrecked by war and ecological collapse: ". . . a great domed city, sealed away from the forgotten world outside. Here, in an ecologically balanced world, mankind lives only for pleasure. . . ." Beneath those (obviously) plastic domes lay a colorful city, a jeweled toy, whose complex artifice managed to match and surpass the famed urban landscapes of *Metropolis*, *Just Imagine*, and *Things to Come*. Seeing *Logan's Run* for the first time as a child, I was struck with the visual power

and sheer audacity of the film's opening scenes depicting the city as seen from above. *Logan's Run* was my first childhood encounter with the "god's eye view."

17. My use of "old times" is an homage to Larry McMurtry's book and Peter Bogdanovich's film *The Last Picture Show*, with special warmth for Ben Johnson's monologue about his character's youth.

18. New readers of Canby's recollections will be undoubtedly distressed by the author's blithely offensive language regarding the "Darkies" or "Micks" or "Plain People," who, like the patrician collective he calls "Us," learned their "place" in the hierarchy of Wilmington society. Nonetheless, I include this excerpt out of awareness that most temporal enclaves require troubling social divisions.

19. One cannot help but find some insight in both episodes' selections of their time travelers' employment. In both stories, we meet executives who suffer from corporate prisons and private lives marked by artificial achievement. In both episodes, the protagonists escape to a natural and organic world of timeless materiality, either in some Currier and Ives fantasy or in the equally fanciful recollections of childhood.

20. Developed by G. Dan Poag and Terry McEwen, The Shops of Saddle Creek represents the nation's first lifestyle center. The Shops opened in a Memphis, Tennessee, suburb in 1987, inspiring rapid growth of this design. Sarkar (2005) quotes International Council of Shopping Centers figures that compare a mere seven malls built between 2002 and 2005 to 101 lifestyle centers over the same 3 years. Moreover, Mitchell (2006) cites a developer claiming that only one enclosed mall opened in all of 2006, The Mall at Turtle Creek in Jonesboro, Arkansas. Even the Turtle Creek property includes 75,000 square feet of outdoor shopping space along with its 230,000 square feet of indoor retail.

21. Malls are increasingly integrating lifestyle components in colder climates. For example, Thorne (2005) quotes a real estate consultant who forecasts that at least half a dozen traditional enclosed malls in Canada will become indoor–outdoor hybrids by adding lifestyle "tails." Warner (2005) adds, however, that although lifestyle centers represent the contemporary trend in shopping center design, hot and humid locations will continue to demand enclosed malls. For example, indoor centers are in the design phase in areas of the southern United States where Mexican tourists are enjoying more freedom to visit the north and shop.

22. McKinley (2006) reports that storefront parking ranks higher than strolling ambience to patrons of lifestyle centers, which results in complex negotiations among planners and tenants to balance placement and percentage of parking spaces to various retail types.

23. Many communities are rethinking the value of traditional parking lots. For example, Groover (2006) describes plans to transform acres of mall parking lots into infill locations for hotels, office buildings, and condos.

24. Hazel (2005) proposes that "omnicenters" represent the next stage of shopping center design: a convergence of lifestyle and power center.

References

A pall over the suburban mall. (1978, November 13). *Time Magazine*, pp. 116–117.

Bayley, S. (2004, April 11). Notes & theories: How to celebrate the 50th birthday of the shopping mall? Try ripping off the roof . . . (London). *Independent*, Features, p. 5.

Blum, A. (2005, April 6). The mall goes undercover; it now looks like a city street. *Slate*. Retrieved March 29, 2007, from http://slate.msn.com/id/2116246/

Boddy, T. (1999). Underground and overhead: Building the analogous city. In M. Sorkin (Ed.), *Variations on a theme park: The new American city and the end of public space* (pp. 123–153). New York: Hill and Wang.

Boswell, R. (2004, November 3). Dubai megaproject would dwarf Canadian landmarks. *The Montreal Gazette*, p. A23.

Canby, H. S. (1934). *The age of confidence: Life in the nineties*. New York: Farrar & Rinehart.

Crawford, M. (1999). The world in a shopping mall. In M. Sorkin (Ed.), *Variations on a theme park: The new American city and the end of public space* (pp. 3–30). New York: Hill and Wang.

Gladwell, M. (2004, March 15). The terrazzo jungle. *The New Yorker*, pp. 120–127.

Groover, J. (2006, September). Mall parking lots are too valuable for landlords to waste on cars. *Shopping Centers Today*. Retrieved April 11, 2007, from http://www.icsc.org/srch/sct/sct0906/index.php

Gruen, V. (1964). *The heart of our cities: The urban crisis: Diagnosis and cure*. New York: Simon & Schuster.

Gruen, V., & Smith, L. (1960). *Shopping towns USA: The planning of shopping centers*. New York: Rheinhold.

Hardwick, M. J. (2004). *Mall maker: Victor Gruen, architect of an American dream*. Philadelphia: University of Pennsylvania Press.

Hazel, D. (2005, March). Three in one. *Shopping Centers Today*. Retrieved April 11, 2007, from http://www.icsc.org/srch/sct/sct0305/dev_lease_1.php

Hopkins, J. S. P. (1990). West Edmonton Mall: Landscape of myths and elsewhereness. *Canadian Geographer*, 34(1), 2–17.

Jackson, K. T. (1996). All the world's a mall: Reflections on the social and economic consequences of the American shopping center. *The American Historical Review*, 101(4), 1111–1121.

Jones, S. C., & Schumacher, T. C. (1992). Muzak: On functional music and power. *Critical Studies in Mass Communication*, 9(2), 156–169.

Judd, D.R. (1999). Constructing the tourist bubble. In D. R. Judd & S. S. Fainstein (Eds.), *The tourist city* (pp. 35–53). New Haven, CT: Yale University Press.

King, J. (2002, December 29). Main street mirage; retail complexes mimic quaint urban districts. *San Francisco Chronicle*, p. A23.

Kowinski, W. S. (1985). *The malling of America: An inside look at the great consumer paradise*. New York: William Morrow.

McKinley, E. (2006, February). These centers made for walkin', but not too far, please. *Shopping Centers Today*. Retrieved April 11, 2007, from http://www.icsc.org/srch/sct/sct0206/feat_lifestyle_walk_park.php

McLinden, S. (2005, January). More centers add homes to mix. *Shopping Centers Today*. Retrieved April 11, 2007, from http://www.icsc.org/srch/sct/sct0105/cover_2.php

Minnel, T. (2004). Victor Gruen and the construction of cold war utopias. *Journal of Planning History*, 3(2), 116–150.

Mitchell, D. (2006, February). Turtle Creek sole U.S. enclosed mall to open during '06. *Shopping Centers Today*. Retrieved April 11, 2007, from http://www.icsc.org/srch/sct/sct0206/feat_turtle_creek_mall.php

Pristin, T. (2006, November 8). Partners out, owner plans to expand giant Minnesota mall. *New York Times*, p. C2.

Reno, J. (2006, December 4). Scenes from a new mall. *Newsweek*, p. 60.

Ruder & Finn Inc. (1956a, October 7). *Press release: Garden court.*

Ruder & Finn Inc. (1956b, October 7). *Press release: Southdale Center.*

Salcedo, R. (2003). When the global meets the local at the mall. *The American Behavioral Scientist, 46*(8), 1084–1103.

Sarkar, P. (2005, May 3). The new face of retail; Mimicked Main Streets, mall makeovers seek to lure shoppers. *San Francisco Chronicle*, p. D1.

Shields, R. (1989). Social spatialisation and the built environment: The West Edmonton Mall. *Environment and Planning D: Society and Space, 7*(2), 147–164.

Stewart, J., & Dickinson, G. (2008). Enunciating locality in the postmodern suburb: FlatIron Crossing and the Colorado lifestyle. *Western Journal of Communication, 72*(3), 280–307.

Taylor, B. (2006, January 28). Real guns! Real bullets! The whole family will enjoy! *The Toronto Star*, p. A03.

The official West Edmonton Mall Souvenir book & visitor guide. (2003). Edmonton, Alberta: The Edmonton Marketing Shop.

Thorne, S. (2005, January). A tail for two malls. *Shopping Centers Today*. Retrieved April 11, 2007, from http://www.icsc.org/srch/sct/sct0105/focus_canada_1.php

Underhill, P. (2004). Inside the machine. *Wilson Quarterly, 28*(1), 30–41.

Warner, S. (2005, March). Enclosed mall? You bet, it's 120° out. *Shopping Centers Today*. Retrieved April 11, 2007, from http://www.icsc.org/srch/sct/sct0305/cover_3.php

III

───── Overview ─────

Contemporary life may be likened to a bead of mercury.[1] When at room temperature, mercury flows as silvery liquid, transforming natural and artificial terrains into reflections of its presence. Filling gaps and fissures, mercury might separate itself into distinct rivulets that glisten with elegant toxicity. Mercury shares its name with the Roman god of commerce, travel, cunning, and theft. It is a messenger too fleet to be touched. We see reflections of mercury in many places that may be termed *modern*. Here we encounter architectural design and human practices whose intersection results in a peculiar principle of contemporary life: Places and people become valuable when they reflect our wishes with the fidelity of a perfect mirror—in short, when they become invisible. Within these places, we become like beads of mercury also. We learn to flow through specific locales of the human and natural environment without friction. Localized, unscheduled interactions between ourselves and others carry the risk of harm or at least uncertainty. Commercial lives in transit, we need not dodge and weave, we need not steal ourselves away; we walk in public places as anonymous as unmarked graves.

Yet we err when assuming that omnitopia's toxicity is life threatening. Indeed, I advance a different argument—that people in the most omnitopian nodes, mercury-like in their mirroring of modernity, find myriad pleasures, if not the means of resistance, to their designs. They may even discover a sense of ownership of these places. As a longtime inhabitant of omnitopia, I know this for sure. Even as a teenager, when I waited tables in a Florida Steak 'n Shake, I grew accustomed to patrons regaling me with stories about how they used to frequent the *first* Steak 'n Shake—in Indianapolis, in Springfield, in Bloomington, and almost a half dozen other sites. A certain pride of place animated their stories. "My" restaurant in Clearwater, Florida, thousands of miles distant from the franchise home, was nice enough. But the original, the first, was a site worthy of pilgrimage. The first one, incidentally, was in Normal, Illinois, but I never corrected my customers. In many ways, this book was born in fast-food restaurants like Steak 'n Shake (whose slogan, "In Sight It Must Be Right," was meant to convey a sense of security and confidence). These places represented my

first encounter with the omnitopian sensibility before I could even imagine such
terminology. Although these places were repetitious and even dangerous—one
can hardly imagine a healthy lifestyle of fast-food consumption—they were also
meaningful to those people who claimed them.

Finding meaning within omnitopia foretells the means to moving beyond
its invisible frontiers. This effort begins at Las Vegas, which represents both the
epitome of omnitopian structure and perception and a potent place to mark its
transcendence through post-tourism. Beyond Las Vegas, we find no place, but
instead the performance of placeless enclaves with the aid of personal entertainment devices such as the Apple iPod. Conveying its users to peripatetic worlds
that converge disparate experiences into a coherent singularity, the iPod leads us
finally to imagine a postomnitopian world of renewed meaning in the power of
place. We therefore conclude our journey with a reverence for locales that are
sometimes enduring, sometimes temporary, and sometimes fleeting. Along the way,
we will make a stop at the Armpit of America, so bring your antiperspirant.

Notes

1. I thank my friend and colleague, Phil Wander, for offering this observation
during one of our many office chats.

7

—————— Performance ——————

The emerging order of the strip is a complex order. It is not the easy, rigid order of the urban renewal project or the fashionable "total design" of the megastructure. . . . It is not an order dominated by the expert and made easy for the eye. The moving eye in the moving body must work to pick out and interpret a variety of changing, juxtaposed orders.

— Venturi, Brown, and Izenour (1996, pp. 52–53)

I stand atop the Eiffel Tower, gazing over the Nevada desert. To reach this summit, I pay $9 to ride an escalator, cross a bridge, and enter a lift. Along the way, I pause by a poster reproduced from the 1889 Paris Exposition; a little boy peers upward through a looking glass. I imagine him staring at the tower before reading his exclamation: *"Je Peux Voir Le Sommet!"* Before I am permitted to climb to the top of this tower, I must cross a walkway that leads to the elevator. There, I am instructed to stop at a velvet robe before being admitted into a photography area. The photographer instructs me to place my bags on the floor and positions me in two poses, one standing arms outstretched. I am assured that this position conveys my excitement to be here. The photographer's assistant hands me one ticket for each photo and helpfully reminds me that I can purchase prints downstairs.

I enter the elevator, climb 460 feet, and exit onto the observation deck. Buffeted by the warm desert breeze, I hear the unzipping of camera bags and watch as fellow tourists reenact the discipline of the photography area. They busy themselves with technical details and position each other in poses that strike me as typical: looking out over the landscape or smiling directly at the photographer. Their digital cameras emit an electronic "shutter click" sound that reminds me of old SLR cameras. I circle the observation deck and spot the faux towers of New York–New York, imagining an invisible axis between these two places. I am a researcher contemplating what Roland Barthes (1997) called a "new sensibility of vision" (p. 9). I am also a tourist taking pictures in Las Vegas.

Before long, two young women walk past me, smiling at each other and
fiddling with their cameras. They are wearing good walking shoes and short
white socks. One leans on the railing to gaze at the awesome vista of tall buildings and streets that shimmer in the summer heat. Then, for just a moment, she
jerks her head back and forth with frenzied enthusiasm. Her friend laughs, and
I instantly recall the scene from *National Lampoon's Vacation*. With her manic
performance, the woman has become (at least for me) Clark Griswold hoping
to capture the majesty of the Grand Canyon in one hyperkinetic gaze. At once,
the Eiffel Tower is dragged from the desert and merged with the well-known
comedy before providing an example for this project. Detached at least four ways
from the Paris that is "real," I'm beginning to see that "what happens here" may
not be restricted entirely to Las Vegas.

Beginning with its advertising campaign, "what happens here, stays here,"
Las Vegas abandoned efforts to transform its "Sin City" reputation into a fam-
ily-friendly destination, one oriented around "gaming," of course.[1] Starting in
2003, TV spots began to depict titillating scenes from tourist fantasies that
revealed just enough plot (and sometimes just enough skin) to indicate that
consequence-free "adult play" and all-night debauchery awaited even the most
staid tourists. In one spot, a woman engages in steamy flirtation with a limo
driver, but after exiting the car, she adopts the guise of a business professional.
The advertisement conveys a simple and compelling message: In Las Vegas, she
(and you) can be both. However, I believe that the campaign works on another
level as well: The advertising complicates the totalizing power of Las Vegas to
contain and restrain performances of tourism. To be sure, the campaign employs
a certain enclavic rhetoric, given that Las Vegas contains a world of its own that
is a world apart, and yet I propose that such enclaves are much more permeable
than they might appear.

While we undertake an investigation of omnitopia as being more than the
artful management and manipulation of the built environment, we must begin
by considering the possibilities of *performance* within and beyond its walls. I
choose performance as a lens for this inquiry because of its convergence of
corporeal and perceptual dimensions. One performs oneself in a place, using
the props that are made available. But performance also allows the recasting of
those props and the rewriting of preset scripts in ways that can be surprising
and potentially emancipatory. With the aid of performance, we soften and make
transparent even the most rigidly erected structures, creating our own spaces
among the most powerful places. Moreover, with performance, we may imagine
roads that lead outside of omnitopia. Eventually we will continue on this path
as we consider the potential of an entirely perceptual universe, one devoid of
physical limitations, before concluding with efforts undertaken by strangers to
rediscover the locales that make public life meaningful. But getting there requires
a strange route, one that leads through Las Vegas.

I have chosen Las Vegas as a site to culminate our investigation of various omnitopian nodes such as airports, hotels, and malls because this city embodies the ways in which distinct locales blur into a continuum of fantasy and consumer desire. As the urban world appears to "learn . . . from Las Vegas," we are wise to study its complex spaces as a site that inspires increasingly ubiquitous performances (Venturi, Brown, & Izenour, 1996). Moreover, if one may visit the capital city of omnitopia, it would be Las Vegas. Of course, the potential of a "capital" to omnitopia reveals the means to its elimination, given that no omnitopian node may be more "central" than another. In Las Vegas, we find both the height of the omnitopian sensibility and the way to imagine a postomnitopian world. Our present effort therefore may be termed a tour of Sin City with the purpose of unpacking overlapping strategies and tactics of omnitopian tourism. Here, I offer a tentative exploration of Las Vegas as the stage set for tourist performance, focusing first on the site of Las Vegas as an omnitopian enclosure, second on post-tourist performances of Las Vegas, and, finally, the consequences of inauthentic post-tourist play as imagined by critics of "mere pleasure."

Las Vegas as the Capital of Omnitopia

Las Vegas is an enclave, a world unto itself. Visitors to Las Vegas have come to expect safe passage and fluid motion uniting an array of richly themed fantasies. Covered walkways, moving sidewalks, underground passages, and street-crossing bridges render each simulacrum—Venice, Paris, New York, and many others—into nodes of the same place, almost impossibly distant from the city beyond. A few blocks away, the continuum gives way to rundown motels, check-cashing businesses, pawnshops, and other allied trades. Beyond this perimeter, the day-to-day lives of city residents unfold with little connection to the gaming core. I am drawn to the older motels, many of which employ smaller theming technologies that reflect the vernacular of the region. Along with a plentitude of gambling references (The Lucky Cuss, the Pair-a-Dice, the Jackpot), one finds motels whose names and signs employ other typical themes of the western U.S. desert (Cactus Motel, Yucca Motel, Sky Ranch). There is no formal division between the omnitopian Strip and the disparate (and sometimes desperate) business "outside." Still, most visitors define Las Vegas by its Strip, an enclave within an enclave.

For years, Strip businesses struggled against the avalanche of walkers. They skittered between casinos, they contributed to local traffic, and they died by the dozens per year in car accidents. Today, however, the Strip is increasingly woven together by pedestrian bridges. At two intersections of Las Vegas Boulevard—one at Tropicana Ave, another at Flamingo Road—four-way bridges lift pedestrians above the road. These walkways provide portals between major Strip resorts, offering unencumbered passage over the traffic that flows along the road below. Hal Rothman (2002) describes the overhead crosswalks as "something out of Fritz Lang's *Metropolis*, futuristic and postmodern, the foot traffic of the future" (p. 255). The bridges draw together incommensurate themes, rendering them coherent to one another. For example, one may take a pedestrian bridge from New York–New York, with its dense *mélange* of urban grit, deco skyscrapers, and Lady Liberty statue, to Excalibur, with its golden chandeliers, medieval jousts, and fork-free eating. Lifting visitors above the streets and connecting them to fanciful places, the bridges contribute one component to the omnitopian enclave.

Beyond the bridges, the Las Vegas Monorail presents another level of enclave, which, by definition, requires some degree of exclusion. At a cost of $650 million, the monorail follows a lightning-bolt shaped path from Tropicana Avenue to Sahara Avenue. Single-ride tickets ($5 in 2008) enable passengers to ride 4.4 miles of the Strip. Rising a minimum of 21 feet above street level, the monorail's seven stations are most easily accessible from the large hotels. Indeed, I find only a single location where a tourist may park a car and hop on the monorail.

When I visit the Flamingo/Caesars Palace Station,[2] I find entering the monorail from street level to be impossible because each stairway, serving as an emergency exit, is enclosed and locked from the inside. I discover an elevator

Image 17: Las Vegas Monorail. *Photograph by Andrew Wood*

to an above-street entrance, but I am unable to use it because I lack a keycard from the nearby hotel. I return to the street and wander in frustration while monorail patrons stroll along a skyway to the station above. Walking under the monorail path beyond the hotels, I survey the backs of modest apartment complexes, an occasional resort timeshare property, a laborer moving from job to job, and the undeniable sense that this place is not designed to accommodate touring walkers. Crossing between some of the resort hotels, I must become an explorer, climbing 5-foot walls and dropping onto crumpled cigarette butts. In the sky above, a helicopter hangs in the air, perhaps monitoring traffic conditions for a local news affiliate. Outside of the comforting embrace of authorized places, I feel vulnerable and slightly illegal.

At last, I admit defeat and amble toward the Flamingo Las Vegas. Passing through the glass doors and riding the escalator, I am authorized, cleansed of my street distinction. Asking directions to the station, I receive friendly and patient service. Soon, I walk the skyway that previously rose above me. Inserting my ticket, compliments of New York–New York, I enter a clean and climate-controlled monorail. The ride largely parallels the Strip, but traverses construction zones, revealing the tops of service stations, the development of golf courses, and the tons of equipment used to build the dozens of condominiums rising nearby. I have found a paradoxical home in movement, after the dizzying meander outside. I have returned to the omnitopian enclave, to the swish of electronic doors and recirculated air.

Once inside, I search for New York–New York's America the Restaurant. "America" presents tourism as a series of secondary representations. Dozens of postcard epigrams line the long interior wall across from the register: "Having a wonderful time. Will be in Grand Canyon tomorrow. We are picnicking beside the road and sleeping in motels. Wish you were here." In America, wait staff wear blue button-down shirts with American flag ties. Superenlarged Curt Teich-style linen "large-letter" postcards, the kind with pictures in each letter, stretch across the upper walls: "Greetings from Milwaukee," "Greetings from El Paso," "Greetings from Memphis." Hanging over the main dining area, a 90-by-20-foot curved bas-relief map of the continental United States presents a 1950s-vibe of American Industry: oranges in Florida, oil wells in Texas, silver mines in Nevada. The menu offers a "carica-tour" of U.S. culinary delights: Baby Back Ribs from "Dallas," Rajun Cajun Pork from "New Orleans," Mom's Meatloaf from "Savannah," and "The Route 66 appetizer sampler" from "U.S.A." It's like being on the Eiffel Tower with its dizzying view. The map and the menu show it all, and the intoxicating rush is, again to quote the Irish rock band U2, "even better than the real thing." Leaving the restaurant, I spot a sign that says, "Thank you for visiting America."

One can become easily immersed in omnitopia; its performances and referents preclude meaningful or transcendent purpose outside of itself. The omnitopian locale is ever-present and pervasive, persuasive in its totality. Certainly, some places offer the illusion of depth, the possibility of multiple meanings. For example, Le Village Buffet in Paris–Las Vegas creates a convincing *mise en scène* with windows that reveal several receding layers, an outdoor walkway to organize the lines of hungry visitors, an inner courtyard style restaurant, and another outdoor façade to frame the serving stations. Despite its engaging and ironic play of interior and exterior worlds, the purpose of this place is to sell buffet style food to a large number of people who wish they could attempt a gastronomical *Tour de France*, but may never get the chance.

I perceive omnitopia as a series of apparently individual locales, each of which is designed to deposit me into the next. Every site is strange and fantastic in a vaguely disagreeable manner, ugly and exhilarating. I slip back a bit into Walter Benjamin's stroll through the Parisian streets, where the grand and ornate stores "form the eccentric frame within which the last privateers so readily displayed themselves" [M21a,2/455]. Constant and fluid motion—aided by light rails, monorails, sliding doors and moving pathways, and even fake tours through America the Tasty, France *La Bon*—the "eccentric frames" of themed environments allow me to ignore the burning desert expanse that encloses the city and to forget the mechanical process of consumer transfer that keeps those slot machines ringing.[3] This kind of place recalls the promise of Crystal Palaces throughout modern history, the ability to craft enclosed fantasies that play with natural impediments. Writing about enclosed shopping malls, Margaret Crawford (1999) offers another useful parallel: "Architects manipulated space and light to achieve the density and bustle of a city downtown—to create essentially a fantasy urbanism devoid of the city's negative aspects: weather, traffic, and poor people" (p. 22). A snippet of recorded audio playing at the Flamingo Hotel guarantees "a tropical paradise so lush, you'll forget you're in the desert." Inside omnitopia, I wonder about other tourists: How do they interpret this place? Are they trapped in a carceral state or a playground? Do they wander the passages asleep or do they resist? During my strolls, I find that tourists do indeed employ a range of tactics to craft their own performances, and yet the poles of commodity empathy and ideological struggle fail to adequately express their actions. I must attempt a middle approach, one illustrated by the concept of the "post-tourist."

Post-Tourists in Las Vegas

Visitors to omnitopia may unpack even the most totalizing enclosures knowingly, skillfully, and playfully. They may inhabit tourist traps, but not imagine getting trapped by them. Maxine Feifer (1985) defines these people as "post-tourists."[4] Post-tourists may be known by three qualities: They are freed from traditional tourist locales, they can perceive multiple perceptions of tourism, and they are self-reflexive about their roles in the co-construction of tourist sites. In this manner, one may argue that the post-tourist performs her or his role in a manner similar to that of the *flâneur*. Both adopt a stance that conveys recognition, even celebration, of the artificiality of the performance. Both also transform the totalizing spectacle of contemporary life into objects, snapshots, glances, and souvenirs, often in unintended ways, "dragging" new meanings on established ones, superimposing personal meanings on institutional ones.[5]

Most intriguing, both enact a paradoxical relationship of intoxication and ambivalence. Intoxication stems from the pleasurable fragmentation and overlap of sensory input, the heterotopian moment in which one becomes detached from the overwhelming narrative. Ambivalence stems from the nature of that detachment, the knowledge that one's identity and setting are artificial. After touring the Bavarian castle *Neuschwanstein*, a "real" site that inspired the design of Cinderella's castle in Anaheim's Disneyland, Paul Edwards (1999) describes the requirement for purposeful detachment amid such tackiness: "My ambivalence is a performance, produced and constrained by the site itself as I pass through it" (p. 273). For the post-tourist, ambivalence serves as a reminder: "Don't get too excited. This is not real." Performing ambivalence calls for a certain detached cool, a gaze that does not linger too lengthily on one site or another, a knowing smile that does not exude joy, but rather a sense of irony.

In New York–New York or Paris–Las Vegas, the post-tourist *flâneur* employs the well-practiced gaze of the mall shopper and the amusement park patron. Each attraction and each consumer opportunity is personal and individuated, grasped and perceived by its references to other media texts, in either the past or the future, not by their social context. One does not shop with strangers, although one surely may shop *for* strangers. Similarly, one does not perform the acts of the tourist for other tourists, but rather for those who accompany us or for those whom we might impress in the future. Put another way, tourists seldom experience their destinations with crowds, but as places that *have* crowds. Each place imagined for anonymous individuals who will likely craft similar memories is framed anew by pointed fingers and camera viewfinders of passersby. Most gazes are quick and superficially encompassing; each place text should be scanned briefly, not read intently.

In these ersatz places, the post-tourist *flâneur* engages in behaviors and utterances that enable transformation and performed "knowingness." Initially, I find that photographers and videographers demonstrate the most intriguing tactics of transformation.[6] After all, the photographer's gaze—the technologies of composing, editing, capturing, and discarding—enables a measure of control over the world, a means to transform it into one's personal collection of images (Urry, 2002). Chris Jenks and Tiago Neves (2000) describe this process as *détournement*: "the re-cycling, repositioning, or re-employing of the existing elements of an art work, or works, into a new synthesis" (p. 8). Often employed by photojournalists, *détournement* reveals absurdity and unplanned relationships: The walker can "playfully and artfully 'see' the juxtaposition of the elements that make up the city in new and revealing relationships" (p. 8). Manipulated by the photographer's gaze, places and even people become props, privatized for the purposes of individual pleasure. Here, "tourists are in effect acting protagonists who perform on the stages of tourism" (Noy, 2004, p. 116). This performance has marked the intersection of tourism and photography since its 19th-century inception when photography first transformed its practitioners into voyeurs, tourists watching the scene, but not acting as part of the scene. The viewfinder creates the means through which one may craft the "picturesque" frame of the natural world (Löfgren, 1999). Moreover, photographers using digital cameras supercede the traditional detachment afforded by older cameras. Rather than staring through an optical viewfinder at a person or object mediated only by distance and glass, digital photographers stare at a video reproduction of the image: a second order of detachment. In a similar manner, amateur videographers stroll the streets with eyes fixed on miniature screens that reduce even the most surreal fantasies to manageable proportions.

Reflecting on this, I recall sitting at the corner of one of the Eiffel Tower's four giant legs to watch the photographers and videographers. I notice that virtually everyone with some sort of camera stops to take a photo of the tower that rises above. One young girl tilts her video camera down from the spire of the Eiffel Tower to the ground before panning around to the small group of adults in her group. The tower has now become a family landmark, its position marked in relation to her loved ones. She then pans back around to a pair of men walking into the casino. One says: "She's filming your back, you know that?" The other, a guy in an Aloha-style shirt, laughs and replies: "Better get a wide angle lens, man!" This narrative becomes dragged onto the scene, the tourist site transformed into a post-tourist production: fleeting, intentional, and improvisational.

This improvisation calls for a performed awareness on the part of both photographers and their post-tourist subjects. Here I recall one evening under the New York–New York portico with its neon Aztec sun and the occasional idling stretch Hummer. A young woman in her early 20s waits for visitors carrying cameras. With her flowing gown, uplifted torch, and glittering crown, she works as a prop, offering a human personification of New York in Las Vegas. She wears a name tag and shares some relaxed banter with the doorman. She is official and authorized, and her smile is warm and inviting. Every few minutes, folks leaving New York–New York accept her invitation to pose for a photo. One man stands with her while his female companion frames the shot. Standing next to the human-sized Statue of Liberty, the man awkwardly holds his own camera, at first, at his side. A look of confusion crosses his face. He then hides the camera behind his jeans, presumably in hopes that the photo will look

Image 18: Las Vegas Statue of Liberty. *Photograph by Andrew Wood*

less staged that way. One might imagine his intuition that every added layer of artifice diminishes the value of the image he's framed, the picture he will share with friends of a stranger outside of a casino who happened to resemble the Statue of Liberty.

Wandering the streets of "New York" on another evening, I observe still more private performances, stylized and rehearsed exhibitions. Photo taking creates a specialized struggle given the omnipresence of crowds. Etiquette requires walkers to respect and quickly traverse the temporary zones of privacy created by the photographer's intended shot. Such decorum can result in odd courtesies. One evening as I stand on a bridge in order to shoot the New York "skyline," I decide to sit down in search of a more dramatic angle. A teenager

walks toward me unawares before nearly stepping on my feet. While I choose
to sit in a public thoroughfare and take the risks that behavior entails, it is she
who profusely apologizes. Standing (or sitting), of course, contributes only one
aspect of agency. *Moving* through omnitopian spaces, willfully and originally,
fleshes out the body of the tourist who would control a place. Elsewhere, I catch
myself in the gaze of another *flâneur*. One man leans against a light post, his
video camera viewfinder flipped up. He stares intensely at the image, his brow
furrowing. I look his way, figuring that I've entered his frame. He jerks the lens
to his left, and I am no longer part of his home movie. It appears that I committed a rookie mistake, spoiling the shot by staring at the camera. I'm fairly
certain that I was not the subject of the shot; tourists rarely photograph strangers
without some external context. However, I was clearly an object within the shot
and failed to perform my proper role.

Here, we turn to the notion of performed "knowingness," often through
ironic comment, that is so essential to the post-tourist *flâneur*. Here, the performance conveys that one knows the routine. To illustrate, I find myself sitting
on "Hudson Street" in New York–New York near the plate glass window for
"Mike's TV Repair": a jumble of old TV sets, one with exposed vacuum tubes,
some set to snow, and one running a local channel in black and white. The one
color screen reveals a shot of the alley where I'm perched. I see myself smoking
a cheap cigar. As folks walk by chatting and as people line up for photographs
of each other, I lean back a bit and suck on the cherry stogie. An older man
wearing business slacks and a dress shirt selects the table next to me and catches
sight of the TVs. He cranes his neck and spots the sign on the "second floor"
next to a wheezing half-sized air conditioning unit. Glancing my way, he says,
"Mike's TV Repair," and laughs.

In "Paris," I return to my café under the artificial sky. I catch folks gazing upward. One man stares at the faux ceiling, its fluffy white clouds mixing
with the shadow of an artificial tree, and remarks to his companion: "Sky blue."
She glances up and emits a brief explosive laugh. Later that afternoon, I find
another spot along the promenade, across from a "street" performer who sits
atop a short ladder. He is painted dull bronze and stands still, resembling a
statue. Invariably, folks walk by unaware before he touches them or blows a
kiss. The shrieks from surprised tourists inspire laughter from others who are
in on the joke. Across the path, I sit on a bench next to a real bronze statue:
a workingman in bronze overalls who rests next to a lunch pail and thermos.
Occasionally, folks come by to check his vital signs. One group ambles by, and
a young woman stops to sit on the man's lap. An infrared beam caresses them
both before a camera flashes.

Occasionally, a family will swarm around the statue, kids kicking and slapping at the metal surface. Later, a woman peels off from her group to touch the
metal man. She pronounces with confidence: "Not real." She laughs and repeats:

"Not real!" To my right, a guy in shorts and a silver pony tale stands with a smile, watching the show. After a while, I cannot help myself. I sit closer to the workingman, frozen in a similar pose, my arm hanging limply over the bench. I cannot convey the irony of my position: a relatively privileged academic posing as a statue for the gaze of others. My pose is potentially more artificial than "his" or the real workingman across the way: I can get up and leave. Even so, I revel in the pleasure of the occasional question: "Is *he* for real?"

The afternoon grows long, and I head for the doors that lead to the miniature *Arc De Triomphe*. Near the door, a small coterie in a ragged collection is intent on something, but I can't orient their gazes. Then I spot the mime. Of course, Paris–Las Vegas would have a mime. Armed with a curved plastic tickle brush, the mime waits for wandering folks to cross his path. He surveys the looks, some awestruck, but most blasé. He prefers the latter, looking for an opportunity to tickle them. The hapless walker invariably feels a strange sensation—a fly, perhaps?—and gesticulates cluelessly while the small crowd laughs. After a while, two or three dozen people are in on the joke, forming a thin conduit of gawkers who wait for the next victim. The pleasure of looking at those who do not know, laughing together at the inside joke, nodding at the photographers who try to capture the moments: These instances in this kind of place transform us all from strangers to post-tourist *flâneurs*.

Image 19: Las Vegas Strip. *Photograph by Andrew Wood*

Leaving Las Vegas

Viewing tourist locales as stage sets for performances provides a fruitful site for scholarly inquiry. After all, these sorts of places are adept at providing scripts and audiences, even as their cinematic apparatus are increasingly immaterial (Friedberg, 1993). Nonetheless, we find certain places to be so completely crafted, so totally rehearsed, that we imagine our roles as unassailably fixed. As we saw earlier, Fredric Jameson (1991) contributes much to this despairing account thanks to his baffling encounter with the Los Angeles Bonaventure Hotel, which "has finally succeeded in transcending the capacities of the individual human body to locate itself, to organize its immediate surroundings perceptually, and cognitively to map its position in a mappable external world" (p. 44). To Jameson, the Bonaventure's mirrored enclave disorients even the most practiced contemporary *flâneur*, rebuking Benjamin's reveries about the pleasures of urban life as being "both singularly relevant and singularly antiquated in light of this new and virtually unimaginable quantum leap in technological alienation" (Jameson, 1991, p. 45). Following Jameson's example, many scholars have bemoaned the disorientation that afflicts inhabitants in all manner of postmodern places.

Rob Shields' (1989) influential analysis of the West Edmonton Mall provides a useful example wherein post-tourists become replaced by *post-shoppers* who, despite their moments of ironic detachment, nonetheless become subjects of a Foucauldian prison: "Although the promoted image is one of freedom, unfettered impulse buying, and liminality, the reality is one of control, new forms of discipline, and surveillance" (p. 160). In his typically trenchant style, Zygmunt Bauman (1994) adopts a similar pose, noting that in the various "Disneylands" of contemporary life—casinos, malls, amusement parks, and other "dream houses of the collective" (Benjamin's term)—the *flâneur* wanders in a manner that may be considered "aimless," even while unconsciously affirming the designs of consumer society: "There was a goldmine somewhere in the modern urge to 'wander aimlessly'; the market found it and set to exploit. Disneylands are the mineshafts" (p. 150; see also Jokinen and Veijola, 1997). In these rebukes, we discover a determinist response to the types of sites found in omnitopia, the assumption that they compel us to submit to their designs. This is not the heady submission of intentional intoxication, but rather the mindless amblings of a zombie.

In my inquiries, I have responded that post-tourist *flâneurs* are not zombies. Instead, they enact performances whose winking irony contains the possibility of agency, if not resistance.[7] In this manner, I join a cohort of scholars attempting to study tourists in a more direct manner than those who only interpret representations of ideology. Initially, I am drawn to the intriguing work of Ian Woodward, Michael Emmison, and Philip Smith (2000), who take Fredric Jameson and Rob Shields literally when they describe the disorienting effects of late capitalist/postmodern enclosures, testing the hypothesis that people generally become confused in these consumer mazes. Aided by interviews and observations, the researchers found:

> Rather than being rendered passive and irremediably confused by such locales, they are able to learn from their initially disorienting encounters with complex built forms and develop pragmatic regimes for their navigation. Far from being written in stone, then, the influence of architecture is eroded over time and consequently the fatalistic vision of the mall scholars and postmodern architectural theorists is misplaced. (p. 350)

Woodward and colleagues add that many theorists of urban enclosures invariably confuse Walter Benjamin's notion of the *flâneur* with the related figure of the *badaud*, the gawker or the rubberneck.[8] I also hold that the *flâneur* is awake and aware, and cannot fairly be dismissed as a mere shopper. Beyond these empirical and etymological rebukes, however, I hope this effort contributes to an ongoing discussion about the relationship between authenticity and pleasure. Here, I have argued that the post-tourist *flâneur* does not condemn places that are artificial, but rather revels in the performance of inauthenticity.

Of course, the notion that tourism rests on an inauthentic foundation is hardly new. In his book, *The Image: A Guide to Pseudo-Events in America*, Daniel Boorstin (1992) dismisses the construction of pseudo-events (and pseudo-places) that are designed for tourists who flock to interstate highway sites such as the ubiquitous and anonymous motel, a location said by Boorstin to possess no meaning other than its service as nodes within a continuum of commodification: "They prefer to be no place in particular—in limbo, en route. . . . They feel most at home above the highway itself, soothed by the auto stream to which they belong" (p. 114). In his germinal research on tourism, Dean MacCannell (1973) gently rebuke's Boorstin's overly pessimistic rebuke by borrowing from Erving Goffman's front and back stages. MacCannell argues that tourists crave authenticity, even while they must often settle for "staged authenticity."[9] I have departed from MacCannell and his progenitors somewhat, returning halfway to Borstin's notion that tourists prefer the inauthentic. I hold that the post-tourist knowingly engages the façade, the surface, and the fake as a mutable substance that may be transformed into an individualized product of remembrance, a souvenir. In this way, I agree with Michael Harkin (2003), who states: "Tourists seeking casinos and kitschy public versions of traditional culture will greatly outnumber and outspend those seeking authenticity" (p. 583).[10] However, I also add that the performances of inauthenticity deserve as much attention as the places in which these performances occur.

This in turn speaks to an intriguing conversation within performance scholarship concerning the possibility (and the desirability) of resistance against inauthenticity. Indeed, my desire to wander the streets and pathways of Las Vegas was inspired by Tracy Stephenson Shaffer's (2004) essay on "constructing authenticity" in the performance of backpacking. Drawing from post-tourism scholarship, Shaffer positions herself as the kind of tourist many of us would like to be:

> I increasingly recognized my performance as transgressive, choosing and approaching tourist sites with the ability to take them at face value, recognizing them as constructions, and knowing that for everything I was seeing, there was much more I was not seeing. I was also able to impose my own counterhegemonic readings upon them. Although I was unable to get outside the apparatus of tourism, I attempted to revise it from within. (p. 156)

Setting off for Las Vegas, I assumed that an increasing number of visitors have begun to adopt a similar pose: transgressing as post-tourists, perhaps unable to escape the apparatus of tourism, but able nonetheless to challenge its limits. This school of thought proposes that tourists can (or should) become cultural critics, choosing to conduct the oppositional readings necessary to unpack discourses of oppression. Once more, Dean MacCannell (2001) provides an illustrative example: "I could summarize the central finding of all the research I have done on tourists as follows: the act of sightseeing is itself organized around a kernel of resistance to the limitations of the tourist gaze" (p. 31). From this perspective, a researcher must uncover signs of resistance, lest it turn out that tourists really *are* duped, or, worse, cultural theorists have been duped by an excess desire to confirm an ideologically driven hypothesis.

Admitting that the latter possibility richly resides in my own writing, I now find that searching for transgression (either in the stance of the tourist, the researcher, or the researcher who passes as a tourist) need not supply the only explanation for the performances we've observed. Here, I draw inspiration from Elizabeth Wilson (2001), who sympathizes with the plight of progressive scholars:

> . . . forever walking the tightrope of the elusive "third way," searching for compromise between two incompatible perceptions: the sometimes dour leftist apocalypse of a carceral capitalism from which there is logically no escape, and the alternative, a seemingly rather frivolous insistence on pleasure. (p. 71)

Brian Ott (2004) contributes to this conversation by adding a useful proposal for this "third way" by distinguishing between the ideological labor necessary to resist the hegemony of dominant meanings and the pleasure that simply reproduces the power of those meanings through submission. His "new space of pleasure" stems from paradox. Being simultaneously and *knowingly* aware and asleep, productive and passive, intoxicated and ambivalent: These reflect the performance of the *flâneur* and the post-tourist. This notion of pleasure, playful and ironic, calls into question the power of places and the permanence of our subject positions within them.

We rediscover strollers through the nodes of omnitopia that perpetually lead from one consumer ploy/play to another. We find that these tourists adapt the place into their kind of space, a stage set for their own performances. Drifting through the matrix, post-tourist *flâneurs* drag meanings from individual sites, commenting on them, framing them, and editing them on the spot or elsewhere. Here and there (and even in the "everywhere" of omnitopia), they counter what Nigel Thrift (1996) describes as the feared inevitability of a dehumanized world in which the "lifeworld is taken over by the system, 'authentic' spaces by programmed consumer spaces, tactics by strategies, and so on" (p. 5). To be sure, their productions of consumer places, fragmented, fleeting, and ephemeral, may not "challenge" them suitably, nor do they enable genuinely "authentic" relationships as imagined by the idealists among us. But these performances are meaningful enough; they affirm the potential to play in the landscapes of power (borrowing Sharon Zukin's redolent phrase). Sometimes playing is the most radical choice one can make.

Conclusion

Las Vegas is both the capital and borderland of omnitopia. As its capital, the city links together all manner of strange and impossible convergences of culture and commerce. As its borderland, the city marks an edge of omnitopia as structure. Beyond the horizon, we find only perception. As perception, omnitopia inevitably calls forth some choice of performance, to pass through corridors and walkways and terminals in an unconscious flow, or to meander or cavort or bop to one's own script, one's own device. The dimension of performance undoes the corporate structure and enables the personal rewriting of the walls into a personal graffiti that cannot be easily erased.

We should therefore play with technologies of personal performance such as Apple's iPod, a device that reveals the means through which mobile enclaves help us wrap ourselves within peripatetic geographies, rather than define ourselves by the planned pathways of architects and designers. This in turn reflects an increasingly potent colonization of our interior lives with corporate brands and devices while inspiring our imaginations of placelessness, a kind of freedom that may be genuinely revolutionary.

Notes

1. While convention attendance has begun to edge out gambling as the prime moneymaker for Las Vegas, those slot machines are hardly idle. Jeannine DeFoe (2004) writes that casinos raked in $6.1 billion in gambling revenues in 2003.

2. "Caesars Palace" includes no singular possessive apostrophe because its creator, Jay Sarno, insisted that *all* guests to this property could be Caesars.

3. Benjamin relates the intoxication of urban life to the mechanics of gambling, noting how the artificial stimulant of the game crafts an illusory sense that each moment offers the potential to overcome an impeccably constructed machine: "This state of affairs becomes decisive in the disposition of what comprises the authentic 'intoxication' of the gambler. Such intoxication depends on the peculiar capacity of the game to provoke presence of mind through the fact that, in rapid succession, it brings to the fore constellations which work—each one wholly independent of the others—to summon up in every instance a thoroughly new, original reaction from the gambler" (O12a,2/512–513).

4. See also Ritzer and Liska (1997) and Urry (2002).

5. Chris Rojek (1997) identifies how tourists and post-tourists "drag" signs from an increasingly sprawling index of "files," weaving them among their personal memories: "By encrusting the original object with secondary images, values and associations, these processes make us lose sight of the original meaning of the object. It becomes, as it were, co-opted to fulfill temporary, immediate personal or cultural interpretations" (p. 59). Like the *flâneur*, the post-tourist drags any number of meanings across the supposedly impenetrable façade, crafting personal meanings that may resist authority or, more frequently, play with it.

6. Here, I push somewhat against the boundaries of *flânerie* as imagined by Walter Benjamin. Concerned with the declining power of "aura," Benjamin's analysis of photography is well known. Yet, in his essay, "The Work of Art in the Age of Mechanical Reproduction," Benjamin (1968) admits that photography offers a powerful, even revolutionary, potential—once freed from the fetish of authenticity: "Here the camera intervenes with the resources of its lowerings and liftings, its interruptions and isolations, its extensions and accelerations, its enlargements and reductions. The camera introduces us to unconscious optics as does psychoanalysis to unconscious impulses" (p. 237). Susan Sontag (1977) adds that Benjamin constructed an almost cinematic montage of texts, employing much of the photographer's art/craft.

7. One might recall Judith Hamera's (2005) reminder: "That such doings may be banal rather than obviously subversive makes them no less meaningful or constitutive" (p. 95).

8. Benjamin quotes Victor Fournel's distinction between the *flâneur* who "is always in full possession of his individuality" and the *badaud* who is "absorbed by the external world . . . which moves him to the point of intoxication and ecstasy" (M6,5/429). Once more, Benjamin's ambivalence appears: this time, regarding the nature of intoxication. Throughout the *Arcades Project*, intoxication (sometimes related to hashish consumption, sometimes arising from Benjamin's interests in mysticism and surrealism) appears as a motive power to the *flâneur*, while other instances suggest that intoxication deadens the potential for detachment. This reading resides alongside Benjamin's concern for submission into commodity culture along with a similar submission he witnessed in the rallies of fascist Europe. In response, I imagine a kind of performed intoxication in which, to put it bluntly (with the aid of an American colloquialism), one takes a sip but does not drink the Kool-Aid. This manner of intoxication—not distraction—enables a slippage between the present moment and a range of parallel moments, each commenting upon the other. For Benjamin, "[t]hat anamnestic intoxication in which the *flâneur* goes about

the city not only feeds on the sensory data taking shape before his eyes but often possesses itself of abstract knowledge—indeed, of dead facts—as something experienced and lived through" (M1,5/417).

9. Dean MacCannell's (1973) notion of staged authenticity has inspired more than three decades of tourism research. He writes: "it is always possible that what is taken to be entry into a back region is really entry into a front region that has been totally set up in advance for touristic visitation" (p. 597). The cynics among us presume that the tourist is "taken in" by this pitch, from the desire for insider knowledge and below-market deals. One wonders, however, how many times the tourist recognizes the falsity of the scene and script but follows along regardless, paying for the privilege of being suckered, all to purchase the rights to a memorable story to be retold for years to come. The tourist does not require a clinical and detached awareness of the performance. But few are so entirely anesthetized that they cannot recognize the crafting of roles.

10. Mathew Spangler (2002) adds that "authenticity" becomes a contested terrain: "obscured, fragmented, confused, and ultimately lost in a complex web of signification that promises the genuine article but is always unable to deliver" (p. 126). See also Balme (1998), Kennedy (1998), and Fife (2004).

References

Balme, C. B. (1998). Staging the Pacific: Framing authenticity in performances for tourists at the Polynesian Cultural Center. *Theatre Journal, 50*(1), 53–70.

Barthes, R. (1997). *The Eiffel Tower and other mythologies* (J. Howe, Trans.). Berkeley: University of California Press.

Bauman, Z. (1994). Desert spectacular. In K. Tester (Ed.), *The flâneur* (pp. 138–157). London: Routledge.

Benjamin, W. (1968). *Illuminations: Essays and reflections* (H. Arendt, Ed.). New York: Schocken Books.

Benjamin, W. (2004). *The arcades project* (H. Eiland & K. McLaughlin, Trans.). Cambridge, MA: Harvard University Press.

Boorstin, D. J. (1992). *The image: A guide to pseudo-events in America.* New York: Vintage.

Crawford, M. (1999). The world in a shopping mall. In M. Sorkin (Ed.), *Variations on a theme park: The new American city and the end of public space* (pp. 3–30). New York: Hill and Wang.

DeFoe, J. (2004, June 17). Las Vegas hits jackpot with big conventions. *Seattle Times,* p. E1.

Edwards, P. (1999). Neuschwanstein or the Sorrows of Priapus. *Text and Performance Quarterly, 19*(4), 271–306.

Feifer, M. (1985). *Going places: The ways of the tourist from Imperial Rome to the present day.* London: Macmillan.

Fife, W. (2004). Penetrating types: Conflating modernist and postmodernist tourism on the Great Northern Peninsula of Newfoundland. *Journal of American Folklore, 117*(464), 147–167.

Friedberg, A. (1993). *Window shopping: Cinema and the postmodern.* Berkeley: University of California Press.

Hamera, J. (2005). All the (dis)comforts of home: Place, gendered self-fashioning, and solidarity in a ballet studio. *Text and Performance Quarterly, 25*(2), 93–112.

Harkin, M. (2003). Staged encounters: Postmodern tourism and aboriginal people. *Ethnohistory, 50*(3), 575–585.

Jameson, F. (1991). *Postmodernism: Or, the cultural logic of late capitalism.* Durham, NC: Duke University Press.

Jenks, C., & Neves, T. (2000). A walk on the wild side: Urban ethnography meets the *flâneur. Cultural Values, 4*(1), 1–17.

Jokinen, E., & Veijola, S. (1997). The disoriented tourist: The figuration of the tourist in contemporary cultural critique. In C. Rojek & J. Urry (Eds.), *Touring cultures: Transformations of travel and theory* (pp. 23–51). London: Routledge.

Kennedy, D. (1998). Shakespeare and cultural tourism. *Theatre Journal, 50*(2), 175–188.

Löfgren, O. (1999). *On holiday: A history of vacationing.* Berkeley: University of California Press.

MacCannell, D. (1973). Staged authenticity: Arrangements of social space in tourist settings. *American Journal of Sociology, 79*(3), 589–603.

MacCannell, D. (2001). Tourist agency. *Tourist Studies, 1*(1), 23–37.

Noy, C. (2004). Performing identity: Touristic narratives of self-change. *Text and Performance Quarterly, 24*(2), 115–138.

Ott, B. L. (2004). (Re)locating pleasure in media studies: Toward an erotics of reading. *Communication and Critical/Cultural Studies, 1*(2), 194–212.

Ritzer, G., & Liska, A. (1997). "McDisneyization" and "post-tourism": Complementary perspectives on contemporary tourism. In C. Rojek & J. Urry (Eds.), *Touring cultures: Transformations of travel and theory* (pp. 96–109). London: Routledge.

Rojek, C. (1997). Indexing, dragging and the social construction of tourist sights. In C. Rojek & J. Urry (Eds.), *Touring cultures: Transformations of travel and theory* (pp. 52–74). London: Routledge.

Rothman, H. (2002). *Neon metropolis: How Las Vegas started the twenty-first century.* London: Routledge.

Shaffer, T. S. (2004). Performing backpacking: Constructing "authenticity" every step of the way. *Text and Performance Quarterly, 24*(2), 139–160.

Shields, R. (1989). Social spatialisation and the built environment: The West Edmonton Mall. *Environment and Planning D: Society and Space, 7*, 147–164.

Sontag, S. (1977). *On photography.* New York: Picador USA.

Spangler, M. (2002). "A Fadograph of a Yestern scene": Performances promising authenticity in Dublin's Bloomsday. *Text and Performance Quarterly, 22*(2), 120–137.

Thrift, N. (1996). *Spatial formations.* London: Sage.

Urry, J. (2002). *The tourist gaze: Leisure and travel in contemporary societies* (2nd ed.). London: Sage.

Venturi, R., Brown, D. S., & Izenour, S. (1996). *Learning from Las Vegas—revised edition: The forgotten symbolism of architectural form.* Cambridge, MA: MIT Press.

Wilson, E. (2001). *The contradictions of culture: Cities, culture, women.* London: Sage.

Woodward, I., Emmison, M., & Smith, P. (2000). Consumerism, disorientation and post-modern space: A modest test of an immodest theory. *British Journal of Sociology*, *51*(2), 339–354.

8

—————— Convergence ——————

It gives the control of the journey, the timing of the journey, and the space
they are moving through. It's a generalization, but the main use [of the
iPod] is control.

—Michael Bull (cited in Kahney, 2005, p. 26)

In 2007, AT&T launched an ad campaign that illustrates the power of mobile
devices to enable convergence—that intersection of technology and performance
that allows its practitioners to carry a miniature version of the world with them
even to the point of ignoring the world through which they pass. AT&T illustrated
a fascinating expansion of convergence with its "works in more places" spots.
Here's a typical example: "You live in New York. You work in San Francisco. You
play in South Dakota. AT&T Works in more places like New Sanfrakota." The
name is awkward and confusing at first, but it undoubtedly grabs your attention.
Where is this place? Then you realize that the name is meaningful only to its
author. The place is a convergence of nodes designed to further an individual
ambition or corporate vision. New Sanfrakota—and other amalgams such as
Philawarapragueacago—are precisely not places for anyone else but their users.
Aided by technologies of convergence, we carry our own artificial worlds around
with us, tying together personalized nodes that allow us a more impenetrable
dislocation from the places through which we pass and the people by which we
walk. Conceptually, convergence allows us to craft our own hyphenated places,
which are rarely bounded by structure. Psychologically, convergence enables a
kind of global self that is both ubiquitous and solipsistic.

For many of us, public life is the convergence of communication media.
Their occasional harmonies amid frequent cacophonies signal that other people
are present, their opinions impact our own, and that we must cooperate with
them, at least occasionally. Our compromises and agreements develop through
shared watching, viewing, listening, and (sometimes) debating. Our communications define our social worlds in both practice and recollection. From this

perspective, I can hardly imagine the Second World War without visualizing a family sitting in some cozy parlor, gathered around a large wooden radio shaped like a cathedral, listening to one of President Roosevelt's fireside chats. In my memory (more accurately, the memory enacted by numerous media texts and reproduction radios currently on sale), the radio *was* the family hearth. Its vacuum tubes reflected the glowing light of a united nation facing its most dire existential threat since the Civil War.

Moving forward, I recall the gradual disintegration of that shared aural space. It didn't happen all at once. I recall the early 1960s in southern California through a lens created by George Lucas and his 1973 film *American Graffiti*. Watching this film again, I appreciate how the universe of young people in that era was bound and permeated with the music of strangers, emanating from houses and store fronts and roving car radios. Characters discuss the mythical persona of Wolfman Jack whose voice toys with them as much as it gives them pleasure and meaning. He is everywhere and nowhere at the same time. Some people think he broadcasts from a hidden station nearby while others are certain that he broadcasts from an airplane; his messages are so transgressive that he must stay constantly on the move. His influence is everywhere, his voice ubiquitous.

From the 1950s through the 1970s, transistor radios turned people into wandering radio transmitters. As many of us recall, the 1980s cannot be disassociated from the boom boxes that many young people carried on their shoulders. Media accounts from that era, however, conveyed a sense that things had gone too far. Boom boxes (many of my friends used the more pejorative term *ghetto blasters*) looked to be inextricably tied with race- and class-based outsiders, most typically poor Black males. Their unauthorized public performances of these devices became increasingly, ironically, antisocial, even threatening. The music of "others" contained a hint of menace, and the aural landscape began to shrink to the individual. This is no causal relationship, but the connections should not be dismissed. The collapse of the public into a disconnected amalgamation of private spaces reflects a broader assault on what Jürgen Habermas calls the *public sphere*.

Referring to Habermas in this way, I join a well-established conversation about the definition, extent, and potential death of the public sphere as a site of genuine and meaningful dialogue among strangers. Scholars such as DeLuca and Peeples (2002) define the public sphere as a means to enable "open access, the bracketing of social inequalities, rational discussion, focus on common issues, face-to-face conversation as the privileged medium, and the ability to achieve consensus" (p. 128). Yet they also note its unlikely appearance in contemporary life. Although some visualize the public sphere as a fantasy of the Athenian agora or the New England village square, DeLuca and Peeples depart from these nostalgic longings to propose that dissemination, not dialogue, reflects the dominant communication practice of contemporary life:

[T]he fondness for bodily presence and face-to-face conversations ignores the social and technological transformations of the 20th century that have constructed an altogether different cultural context, a techno-epistemic break [from] . . . deeply problematic notions: consensus, openness, dialogue, rationality, and civility/decorum. (p. 131)

Here, DeLuca and Peeples (2002) advocate that we study the *public screen*, presuming that new media call for new metaphors. They join scholars such as Wahl-Jorgensen (2001), who note an increasing degree of exhibitionism in public life, where the public becomes a "display of individual identities and opinions" (p. 308). Like DeLuca and Peeples, along with Wahl-Jorgensen, I observe a striking degree of exhibitionism in public places. When I ride the bus to and from work, I sometimes suffer at the sounds of self-absorbed mobile phone users who force me to suffer their private conversations in public places. Yet few would imagine speaking to a stranger whose mobile phone usage annoys us. We have not yet developed the necessary rituals and performances to support such a potentially awkward interaction.

We accept people and their media devices as sharing our places while being isolated in their own spaces. This singularization (suddenly the name of the mobile phone company Cingular possesses a new resonance) does not shrink our cognitive domain, however. As stated earlier, we are more connected to more people in more ways than any other civilization in human history. Yet even while respecting scholars who analyze our increasingly exhibitionistic age, I propose we should also consider the localized enclaves we create that reduce the "place" for potential interaction and that reduce the perception of place entirely. In this manner, I attempt to move beyond the study of airports, hotels, and malls to study the convergence of disparate "sites" that rid us of the need for place: the placeless enclave. This concept is best understood when related to the definition of omnitopia: a structural and perceptual enclave whose apparently distinct locales convey inhabitants to a singular place. An extension of omnitopia and a means to understanding its collapse, the placeless enclave is solely conceptual; it contains no structure at all. One may still move through space while within a placeless enclave. But when using this node, one need not even *experience* place.

I have chosen to focus on the Apple iPod as an essential site for understanding the placeless enclave. I should also add that an analysis of the iPod contributes to a larger purpose: to investigate how the omnitopian synecdoche for "the world" is being disassociated with specific nodes of the built environment and, instead, becoming associated with personal data/entertainment devices. My choice to analyze the iPod arises from the indisputable impact of this device on the daily lives of millions of people around the world. Michael Gartenberg, vice president and research director for Jupiter Research, states, "Apple has spawned something very powerful. The iPod is not just a consumer-electronics device, it's a cultural icon" (cited in Bulik, 2004, p. 1). Shipping 88 million units by the first quarter of 2007, the iPod is undoubtedly popular. But more important, it provides a powerful means to understand the rise of placeless enclaves and the impacts of that usage. To understand this phenomenon more fully, let us study the iPod more carefully, as an object of technology, the subject of advertising campaigns, and a sign of the struggle to create a new kind of etiquette.

Object Analysis

The iPod as an object is best understood as the culmination of efforts to create portable media devices that previously was epitomized by the Sony Walkman. Like the iPod, the Walkman promised more than music; it signified *singularity*. Writing an influential essay on the topic, Shuhei Hosokawa (1984) defines the Walkman as *musica mobilis*, a technology representing a larger trend in which society is marked by "an intersection of *singularities* in the construction of discourses" (p. 165; italics original). Hosokawa describes the Walkman as a notable example of miniaturization, singularization, and autonomy, one that allow its users to rearticulate the text of urban life for their own purposes. Gary Gumpert (1987) adds, "Each [user] moves in a portable acoustical bubble, and while the effect of the miniaturized unit is less political than the [boom] box . . . each of the users display some attempted mastery of his or her own moveable turf" (p. 91). In this way, the Walkman represented a radical shift away from its distant cousins, the transistor radio or boom box, by enacting a far less permeable membrane of social possibility than found in its predecessors. It was a small world, perhaps more of an island, but it offered freedom from the voices of others.

I remember my first Walkman, a plastic brick that clipped to my jeans. To me, the Walkman signified liberation from the deadening repetition of radio playlists. I rotated through my own collection of tapes, some purchased and others edited to create my own collaborations. I played my Walkman until the tapes broke. To me and millions of other impassioned users, this new medium conveyed a powerful message that even music TV could not overcome. A person need not be forced to listen to music programmed by strangers. A person could carry an entire world of choices in a pocket. Doing so was a sign of freedom and individuality, one that became a value unto itself. For a time, the Walkman represented the ideal illustration of this freedom. Portable CD players presented higher fidelity, but they skipped so incessantly that one could never be entirely free of one's surroundings. Every bump and jostle removed a listener from her or his enclave. Only the iPod could displace the Walkman as a truly revolutionary device.

The iPod manifests the famed "Reality Distortion Field" associated with Apple's Steve Jobs, transforming an industry backwater through design elegance and intuitiveness. Other companies tried to sell personal digital music players, but their efforts were met with little success. Their products were heavy in weight and light in storage, and they were expensive. Even more criminally, they were ugly and difficult to use. As is his tradition, Jobs instructed his engineers and designers to reconceptualize the digital music player, ignoring existing models and striving to create a device that was simple, beautiful, and (most of all) cool. The quantity of "coolness" possessed by the iPod is not a mere musing; it has been measured. Citing research from famed coolhunter Carl Rohde, Steven Levy (2006) announces that the iPod is nothing less than "the coolest thing in the world" (p. 55).[1] To understand why, one need merely hold one.

The first-generation iPod was a creamy white rectangle set on a stainless silver case; on the front, a grayscale screen and scroll wheel was ringed by four buttons. Within that wheel, a fifth button served as a selection device. The early iPod featured a plastic cover for the device's FireWire[2] connection that tended to dangle untidily, so this iteration was hardly the minimalist masterpiece that would appear in forthcoming generations. But the 6.5-ounce sliver was so much cooler than any device that had preceded it. This music player, advertising "1,000 Songs in Your Pocket," rightfully garnered immediate critical praise for its "emotional ergonomy" ("Apple Scoops," 2002, p. 6). Apple built this device to be integrated into a person's life, to become an extension of a person's identity.

The iPod's sensual touch ability inspired breathless acclaim. *New York Times* technology writer David Pogue (2001) called the iPod an "absolutely ravishing machine" (p. G1), while the *San Francisco Chronicle*'s Henry Norr (2001) declared it "gorgeous to look at" (p. G1; yes, the same page as the Pogue piece). Writing in *Business Week*, Stephen H. Wildstrom (2002) stated: "The iPod is proof that with enough care and concentration, designers can approach perfection" (p. 16). Each of these respondents, and the many others who commented on the iPod, also managed to discover limitations to the device, ranging from its steep cost to its lack of a belt clip. Even that sublime stainless-steel backing invited some scrutiny. The *Washington Post*'s Rob Pegoraro (2001) cleverly noted that the metal surface "couldn't collect finger prints any better if it were designed by the FBI" (p. EO1). The iPod—ravishing, gorgeous, almost perfect—could be viewed as sexualized technology, even while caressing one could lead to trouble.

I am an iPod lover. I use mine every day. Like other users, I gripe about its occasional hiccups, and I recall with some bitterness the battery crisis that afflicted my first machine. I also remember the scratched screen of my second. I care for my third with a concern ranging on the paternal. But I know that the caress of the iPod does not necessarily lead to enhanced *human* interaction. Although recent accounts of this device have discussed ways in which users have shared playlists or, at least, swapped ear buds, the iPod continues to be known as an individuating technology, one that dislocates us from others. Wendy Richmond (2006) notes:

> With this personal technology, we occupy an efficient, comfortable and
> entertaining private bubble. We are also more and more mentally removed.
> Our attendance in physical surroundings becomes more solitary, less shared.
> We are alone and separate in public. (p. 201)

I believe that the device contributes to that sensation. However, advertisements
that helped popularize the iPod enhanced the notion of the device as placeless
enclave. We now study how Apple sought to accomplish that feat.

Analysis of iPod Advertisements

Let us unpack three early iPod advertisements as a lens on Apple's popularization of a device meant to transform places into superfluous backdrops for our
singular activities. The first advertisement, launching the first-generation iPod,
presented a somewhat literal explanation of the music player's capabilities, even
while it demonstrates its more symbolic potential as a separating space between
computer- and noncomputer-mediated domains. The second advertisement, popu-
larizing the fourth-generation iPod, reflects the well-known "silhouette" campaign
that inspired a mini-wave of witty appropriations and satires that could inspire
scholarly attention beyond this project. But in the interests of brevity, I focus
my attention to the "silhouette" campaign's evocation of placeless enclave. The
third advertisement, announcing the first-generation iPod Nano, represents an
intriguing next step in iPod spots: the transformation of the city into a person,
which then becomes a placeless enclave.

Home Office

An October 2001 advertisement for the first-generation iPod begins with a man
typing on an Apple laptop computer. The creamy white icon glows in the center
of the frame. We see little of the man's face; only his glasses can be spotted
above the computer screen that fills about two thirds of the frame. The clicking
of the keys suggests a typical information worker banging out a memo. The
background of this scene is dark, lit only by a window that admits light through
Venetian blinds. Perhaps the man is working in some corporate headquarters. If
at some house or apartment, he is undoubtedly situated within a home office,
that depressing hybrid that represents the colonization of our private lives by
the disciplinary technologies of work. Faceless beyond his screen, he is simply
another white-collar drone. He clicks the keyboard once more, a sharp snap-
ping sound. This is a click with authority. Then the pounding rhythm of The
Propellerheads transforms the meaning of this scene. The tune sounds vaguely
like a snippet from *The Matrix*, all bass and machine gun percussion. The man's

head rocks, and his eyes look away from the screen, upward and to his left. He is here, physically, but elsewhere in a far more substantial way.

Things have changed: The frame clicks back to a broader view of the scene. He is indeed in a home office. Behind him are a square clock and a fireplace. But he is neither in his home nor his office. The man slips his glasses off; they now are better termed *shades*. The music is that cool, and now he is too. The man jerks his head even more sharply, left and right, in some sexually charged rhythm only partially found in the music. The camera view clicks once more; we are behind him. A red painting of a pointing gray object hangs on the wall; the depth of focus blurs its content. The head and shoulders of a man looking up? A giant middle finger? The scene shifts too quickly to see for sure. We now see his computer screen: that familiar iTunes interface. The man navigates through his digital music collection before selecting his song: "Take California." He clicks and drags, the screen reports, "Updating Songs on iPod." The frame follows a path from the computer to the device. A close-up: He detaches the FireWire cable. Silence.

The man then lifts the iPod and navigates to his song. His turn of the thumb wheel makes the same sound as a clicking keyboard. But his content is no corporate memo. The man selects the song and, figuratively, he "takes" "California." Now the music sounds different, richer, louder. It no longer emits from tinny laptop speakers. It pours into his ears, and it fills ours. The man departs from his desk and dances on the wooden floor of his room. He shuffles in white tennis shoes. He is Tom Cruise in *Risky Business*. He is Michael Jackson doing the moonwalk. He's not talented, but he doesn't care. The frame then fills with an adjacent coat rack that holds a red jacket. It's the same color as the background of that painting, a kind of burnt amber or rust. The viewer might be forgiven for noticing only now how muted and gray the scene was before the man found that red jacket. Grooving, rocking *out*, he does a sort of running man dance while heading for the door. The scene clicks to a close-up as the man places the white iPod in his jacket pocket. He turns to leave and slams the door behind him. The music stops in time for a reminder of what the product sells: "1,000 songs in your pocket." But the precise message, like those keyboard clicks, does not tell the entire story. This device contains more than music. It alters our sense of place.

Silhouettes

Fairly soon, the functionality of the iPod was known by enough of its potential purchasers for Apple to avoid an explanation of its workings at all. Later advertisements for the iPod depicted dancers listening to rock, hip-hop, or techno. We saw limited facial features, few clothing details, only the hint of any personal style at all. These "silhouettes" represented the potential for anyone to be cool, at least while performing their iPods. I use that phrase, "performing their iPods," intentionally. After all, these advertisements contained an unmistakable message. One does not merely "play" an iPod; this is not a passive device like a radio or even a Walkman, one that might allow some minor head rocking. One *performs* with an iPod, one abandons even the pretense of inhibition. You want just a music *player*? You've got the wrong device.

One illustrative spot released in June 2005 features "Technologic" by Daft Punk. The commercial illustrates the minimalist impulse that guided the design of the iPod. A tart-colored screen, a computer-generated backdrop, constitutes the only stage set for a series of iPod-wearing dancers. Each one casts a shadow while contorting her or his body to the electronic sound. One dancer's movements are fluid, organic, and nearly liquid. Another pops a bit more abruptly. Each silhouette figure is black, even as the actual race or ethnicity of the performer is impossible to discern. Each has some prop: a hat, a tie, some dangly earrings. But the most vivid image is the iPod, white and crisp against the day-glo colors and black silhouettes. Those cords whip and juke with the music; their y-shaped connections between brain and gut are signifiers of soul. Recalling this campaign, Steven Levy (2006) interprets these spots as being almost painfully cool:

> The white earphone cords—painstakingly drawn frame by frame by post-production artists—would shake wildly, a serpentine invitation to the aural bacchanalia provided to those who partook of the iPod drug. It was an out-of-control party in your head, which justified the neoepileptic fits of the anonymous baggy-pants dudes or miniskirted babes. (p. 64)

The "party in your head" invited the stares of others, but it hardly inspired inter-action. The silhouettes generally dance alone. Even when they dance in pairs or in larger groups, even when they mirror each other's moves, they remain locked into their aural singularities. For the iPod people, one need not inhabit the home office, the city, or even the world. One hears music without the distortion of others, no static at all. This is freedom of an almost elemental manner. The machine is so liberating that even the city might be freed, this time of people.

Music City

An early 2006 advertisement for the first-generation iPod Nano features Rinôçérôse's "cubicle" and portrays an explosion of album covers that unfold like origami paper to form a virtual city. As other patterns flip and unfold, a build-ing begins to form amid this image metropolis. The city contorts and mutates; it is a convulsing cluster of referents, similar to that found in *Dark City*. Soon our vision focuses on a central tower. The camera rotates around this building that grows and climbs, and we follow it upward toward the convergence of four album covers. Each album wall joins the others to form a sort of master cubicle at the top of the structure. The song reaches a shrieking crescendo, and each building begins to disintegrate. It appears that the entire city has been hit with an earthquake, the ground liquefying. But the towers do not disappear. Their album walls simply funnel into a narrow stream that pours into the top of an iPod Nano. The machine screen displays a rapid succession of album covers as the iPod captures each one. The device now contains the city.

The "cubicle" ad depicts a vivid blurring of corporate and corporeal bodies. The song's excerpted lyrics invite the viewer to imagine being locked within a corporate enclosure, suggesting that we enter this dismal place repeatedly and by choice ("This ain't the first time"). Because most of the song's sexually charged lyrics reside beyond the advertisement frame, we need not consider them in this commercial, but the pronounced rising and falling action found in this video suggest nothing less than the promise of sexual release. This city of office buildings is a club of dancers whose mutating fronts contain no internal structure or intention, only the undulating circuitry of perpetual transformation. But the city also contains rage, most obviously in the shrieking crescendo of the song excerpt. The hard rock beat suggests rebellion against the writhing city that imprisons its inhabitants. It is a city of bits, but it is even more a city of cubicles.

The rage against this city gains potency when compared with its bland counterpart: the beige doldrums of interoffice memos and three-ring binders found in the mythical office cube farm. The song excerpt refers to the cubicle as "little" because it is a *small place*, as described by Jamaica Kincaid (1989), a site where "[n]o action in the present is an action planned with a view of its effect on the future" (p. 54). This is not postcolonial Antigua; it is a corporate prison mocked in countless *Dilbert* cartoons. It is a place for young people who toil under the watchful eyes of wandering middle managers. By way of further illustration, we might recall the soulless, clueless supervisor in Mike Judge's 1999 film *Office Space*, whose practice of "management by walking around" transforms even the most banal exchanges like "Hello, Peter. What's happening?" into inquisitions and inane punishments. These white-collar wage slaves are nodes of the surveillance society, its victims but also its tools. They fantasize of escaping their cubicles, even as their only relief is yet another form of corporate incarceration, such as the nearby Chotchkie's "theme restaurant." Although real-life cubicle slaves are more likely to congregate at the corner Starbucks, the message remains: One must wrench freedom from the city, but one cannot escape it fully. This commercial packages the iPod as a means to unmake the cubicle in one sense even while it re-creates the cubicle in another. But how?

One presumes that the iPod enables the creation of a portable cubicle, one that is customized to the tastes and temperament of its occupant. The iPod represents a means to organize a world of digital consumer products into a personal domain. These products do not become the possessions of their consumers; they are merely localized nodes of intellectual property that reside elsewhere. What's more, now that some companies hunt for "pirates" with venom that parallels that of the IRS, can you imagine Apple rerunning its 2001 "Rip. Mix. Burn" campaign? But regardless of its relatively flimsy walls, the individuated city of music affords a persuasive sense of liberation and control. One may create unique playlists and burn them onto easily distributed CDs. One can stream purchased music over a personal Web site or even cast it via wireless connectivity. Following certain protocols, an iPod becomes a personalized radio tower. What remains is a realistic assessment of how often this potential transforms into practice. For most iPod users, their musical city remains a city of one.

I have chosen to analyze iPod advertisements by attending closely to their visual iconography. Studying a number of campaigns associated with the rollout of new models, I have noticed a consistent theme beyond Apple's delight at drawing from a random assortment of vaguely "cool" musicians to anchor their spots, playing to music that Steven Levy (2006) defines as "a brand new tune by a band that your kid has heard of but you haven't" (p. 64). Beyond the music, iPod advertisements tend to celebrate an image of an anonymous listener who inhabits a detached world and yet performs within that world as a dancer, exhibiting personal style with no need to interact with strangers. The choice of the dancer (and even the dancing city) is, to me, instructive. We find within Apple advertisements a listener who needs no specific place, no dance floor, no authorizing architecture needed to inhabit a disco of the mind. A home office, a subway, a bus stop, an airport terminal: Any of these enable sufficient space for one's personal performance. As Dylan Jones (2005) describes, TBWA\Chiat\Day, the firm that produced the iPod ads, employed an appeal to individualism that was relatively new for this kind of device:

> Unlike every other aspect of the computer world, the iPod had little to do with togetherness, had little to do with community spirit. The iPod was all about individuality and personal space, and its marketing would soon reflect that. Chiat Day's most successful ads for the machine revolved around "iPod-World"—a place that you, and only you, could visit. (p. 67)

Even if you have never seen an iPod listener actually dancing in a manner found within the commercials (and I never have), we might agree that the freedom imagined by these advertisements appeals to our desire to carry a sliver of rebellion and resistance with us, even if we do not act on that impulse. But I believe it is even more likely that we do not imagine an iPod-led contest with the places that define us, survey us, and even control us. Rather, we use these devices to render the places we inhabit (and the people with whom we must share our places) invisible.

This illustrates the meaning of placeless enclave. We carry our worlds in our pockets, now not even limited to 1,000 songs. Inexpensive hard drives allow us to carry all of our music with us at all times. We can carry more than that. The convergence of multiple media inputs, integrated by Apple's iLife suite of software applications, allows us to place books, games, photos, TV shows, and even movies on a device no larger than a pack of cigarettes. Let us not forget Apple's long-awaited iPhone. This tool, this toy, this consumer fetish object, nearly completes the convergence by allowing us to carry even our relationships around with us. This is the meaning of the placeless enclave. We need never interact with the strangers and places around us. We are connected to our worlds, each a synecdoche of "the world." In our own worlds, we can avoid threatening "others" that so defined previous generations' fears of urbanity. That's the idea, at least. In fact, the iPod has not rid us yet of the need to consider issues of courtesy. The introduction of this new machine into public life has raised a number of complex issues regarding the ways in which we mediate our tenuous encounters with strangers. For that reason, we conclude with a brief note on iPod etiquette.

iPod Etiquette

Let me begin with a story. On a warm winter day in northern California, no longer quite an unseasonable as it used to be, I watched a man riding his bike along a crowded traffic thoroughfare. He wore a ratty shirt and balanced on this bike precariously, but his most telling attribute was the transistor radio he held aloft. This didn't look right. When he pulled up to the bus stop and directed his music in our direction, I grew certain: This man was mentally ill. Who would stop his bike to play music to strangers on the road? I plugged in my iPod earphones and selected an Aimee Mann song about the hope and optimism of 1939 ("Fifty Years After the Fair") and bathed myself in irony, guilt, and regret. He passed me by, and the song's lyrics became all the more depressing.

I found myself thinking about the changes wrought by mobile technology on our public life. Rarely do we hear the music of other people, at least not as much as we once did. Certainly, a walk through an urbanized area promises the sounds of hucksters, artists, and street performers. Walk the main drag almost any Saturday afternoon in Santa Cruz, near where I live, and you'll hear a chaotic symphony of protest violinists, wandering drummers, professional guitar players, and beginning choral groups practicing for passersby. But these performances are intentional and largely fixed. We may also recall the cruising of cars whose thumping subwoofers create momentary desires for noise ordinances with life imprisonment penalties. But more and more, we are able to control our immersion into the urban cacophony, or at least we increasingly expect that we should be able to do so. The advent of cheap and lightweight earphones, and the gradual reduction in price of higher quality noise-canceling devices, promises to transform our human interactions even further. Our media enclosures protect us from the questionable auditory tastes of strangers, but they do so at some social cost. This is significant, but hardly new.

The introduction of new communication technologies have always produced profound jolts to the social orders in which they appeared. Often these struggles converge around debates over appropriate usage. Who can employ a new communication technology, in what manner, in what locations, and for what purposes? Frequently, these questions intersect with broader issues of access related to class, gender, and race, along with other dimensions. Questions of appropriate use are inseparable at first from questions of appropriate users. The early telephone, for example, was positioned as a business tool meant solely for a male-oriented economy. Frivolous "chatting" was deemed an inappropriate use, and women were designated as inappropriate users.[3] Eventually, the societal image of the phone's ideal user evolved. But rules of usage and courtesy needed to be negotiated first.

In a similar way, the iPod presented its own etiquette challenges that persist even today. The device allows us to disengage from our surroundings and from the people who occupy them; it is often far more interesting than our localities. One can imagine plenty of activities in which our choice to switch on an iPod is entirely reasonable: jogging, sitting on a bus, or just relaxing on the beach. But in any of these situations, the potential arises for those white ear buds to spark tension. Carl Wilkinson (2005) asks:

> [D]o you remove them when walking alongside someone you know a little? Can you continue to listen to your iPod while shopping in a supermarket? Can two iPod users stroll together through the park while independently engaged in their own playlists? Is it rude to interrupt someone listening to an iPod? (p. 2)

A common compromise to these questions concerns the usage of only one ear bud, leaving an open ear for interaction. Many users report that this approach signifies a willingness to engage in communication while subtly reminding potential interlocutors to keep their comments brief. But a number of respondents to my own unscientific inquiries on the question reject the tactic. One should listen completely to a person, they say, or not do so at all. The struggle here concerns the social tolerance for being even partially in a placeless enclave. Those iPod buds signify not being entirely present, keeping something of oneself in reserve.

My own observations of iPod users, not to mention my participation in the public performance of the device, lead me to imagine that age represents a key indicator regarding the definition of iPod etiquette. For many younger users of mobile technology, the ability to multitask one's interactions with text messages, e-mail, oral exchanges, and other stimuli is a natural part of public life. Focusing solely on one person and one interaction for an extended period of time can be done under extraordinary circumstances. But one can hypothesize that young people define their coolness by the multitudes of interactions they manage. Just as the number of contacts on a mobile phone signifies popularity, the number of simultaneous communications demonstrates social sophistication. Thus, the norms that may be imposed by older persons on the youth in schools and at work are not likely to endure. It can hardly be termed inevitable, but the expansion of placeless enclaves will increasingly alter our social landscape.

Conclusion

Attempting a brief survey of the iPod, its object design, its advertising campaigns, and its etiquette struggles, I have sought to unpack the notion of placeless enclave as a next step, perhaps a final step, in the evolution of omnitopia. At this point, a question becomes central: How useful is this term *placeless enclave*? Previously, I considered alternatives (media enclave, portable place), but I have chosen this term as the best illustration of the concept I hope to convey. I realize that, like most neologisms, *placeless enclave* runs the risk of being too clever to be useful. One might as well use the word *bubble* and be done with it. Like the bubble, the placeless enclave provides a semipermeable means of separation, mediation, and even navigation between its occupant and the world outside. The history of auto-based tourism represents the most useful predecessor to this concept. However, the placeless enclave reflects more than mere detached mobility; it provides the sense that one can carry one's world within a portable omnitopian node. From this turn I do not announce the death of specific places. We will be using airports, hotels, and malls for a long while yet. No amount of online gaming will remove the thrill of visiting Las Vegas for real. But a growing ubiquity of placeless enclaves transforms those places, rendering them as pliable backdrops, often ignored, always transformed according to our mobile perceptions. As such, even our extant knowledge of omnitopia demands a new iteration, a *transformative* iteration. This iteration signals at first the colonization of the omnitopian sensibility into our everyday lives. Yet in a manner both subtle and significant, it may signal omnitopia's end.

To better understand this possibility, we are wise to compare this iteration of omnitopia-as-placeless enclave with its predecessor, which was defined around physical places. Consider our passages through omnitopia as a conveyance to an enclave noted by dislocation, conflation, fragmentation, mobility, and mutability. Within these physical sites, we still imagine our habitation as being inside something shared. We perceive *this* place, and ourselves within it, as being one of many. We see crowds of strangers, and we package ourselves for their momentary consumption. We pass anonymous others, perhaps brushing their bodies as we walk by; we may nod or even smile. We learn to interpret people as texts; their logo attire conveys fragments of stories we alone read. Snippets of their conversations become lines of an aural poem. If we wish, we may detach ourselves from these texts and voices, entering a telephone booth, for example. This tiny enclave allows us to close a door on public life even in the midst of the city, at least for a while. But when is the last time you used a phone booth? They have disappeared from most public places in lieu of the placeless enclave of the mobile phone and the iPod. Some of us even mount them more or less permanently to our ears, emphasizing our perpetual connectivity, and our perpetual separation from locality. The places we inhabit become less important than the networks we occupy. In this way, we enter the placeless enclave, or, rather, we carry it with us. In this way, we may define the placeless enclave as a portable node of omnitopia through which we both detach ourselves from the surrounding locale and connect ourselves to worlds of our choosing. The portability of this enclave transforms the omnitopian function of mobility into its master theme. We do not merely move *through* omnitopia. We move *as* omnitopia, sometimes dancing, at least in our heads.

The iPod evokes the promise to become worlds unto ourselves, to be able to see everything at once, or at least to enclose everything that counts to us. But we must not forget that this premise existed long before the introduction of this "perfect thing." By way of illustration, consider Jorge Luis Borges' (1998) short story "The Aleph." In this story, the protagonist (presumably Borges) visits the house once occupied by a woman whom he loved, Beatriz, and is forced to endure the self-absorbed and boorish ramblings of her cousin, Carlos Argentino Daneri. Owing to his obsession with Beatriz, her palpable presence in the home occupied by her cousin, Borges tolerates Daneri. He even humors his recitations of a dreadful poem he's writing that attempts to summarize every minute detail of the Earth. Borges detests Daneri, but will suffer any pain to stay within the orbit of Beatriz's memory. Borges dismisses Daneri's stanzas as the ranting of a self-deluded failure. Being a writer of some note, Borges recognizes the self-delusion of this grotesque effort. But when Daneri reveals his possession of an object that displays the entire world in one place, implying that his poem stems from a real knowledge of the entire world, Borges decides that he must see it.

Daneri calls the object an "Aleph," recalling mystical visions of infinity, of Godhead. It is "one of the points in space that contain all points . . . the place where, without admixture or confusion, all the places of the world, seen from every angle, coexist" (pp. 280–281). The Aleph is *multum in parvo*, "much in little." The Aleph is so small that it can only be seen from a specific vantage point in the cellar of Daneri's house. Borges enters the cellar despite his growing confidence that the Aleph is nothing more than the apparition of a madman. Then, despite his doubts, Borges sees it for himself:

I saw a small iridescent sphere of almost unbearable brightness. At first I thought it was spinning; then I realized that the movement was an illusion produced by the dizzying spectacles inside it. The Aleph was probably two or three centimeters in diameter, but universal space was contained inside it, with no diminution in size. Each thing (the glass surface of a mirror, let us say) was infinite things, because I could clearly see it from every point in the cosmos. (p. 283)

Borges (1998) sees the Aleph; he knows that Daneri has spoken truthfully, but he decides nonetheless to mock him, he detests him so. He playfully implies that Daneri needs medical care, hoping to draw on the man's self-doubt. But Daneri will not be swayed, and he manages to publish part of his poem. Eventually his writing earns the kinds of accolades that Borges cannot attain. Our protagonist can only find some relief in continued mockery. Surely, he muses, the Aleph could not be real. If he *did* see the object, its visions could not be complete. Perhaps it was a false Aleph. In time, Borges begins to forget his vision of the world, all its myriad points and peoples in one place, just as he gratefully forgets his vivid memories of Beatriz.

For us, the iPod may be no more real a world than the Aleph. Music, photos, movies: These are shadows of the world, fleeting and playful. We cannot live within them. But we often wish we could. In this way, the iPod-Aleph represents both the culmination of omnitopia and a means to foreseeing its end. As a manifestation of late modern capitalism, omnitopia is a corporate construction, a theoretically inescapable milieu that connects disparate locales into one all-place. But as we purchase and modify our own miniature worlds, regardless of who builds them, we witness the means to disregard the larger one that has been built for us. The ramifications of this event call for careful consideration because they may signify a version of public life that is even more alienating (and more illusory) than the one we inhabit now.

Notes

1. Citing from Steven Levy's (2006) *The Perfect Thing* presents a peculiar challenge, given the author's choice to "shuffle" chapters of his book, resulting in several versions, each with its own order and accompanying pagination. As a result, the page numbers cited here do not necessarily correspond to the copy of his book that you might use.

2. Forthcoming generations of the iPod migrated away from the FireWire connection, employing the more standardized USB 2.0 connection.

3. Marvin (1988) describes how telephone usage became gendered quickly by the popular and professional press: "In the picture painted by electrical journals, the model of electric communication that came naturally to women and led them astray was the loquacious oral sociability of their everyday lives. Talkative women and their frivolous electrical conversations about inconsequential personal subjects were contrasted with the efficient, task-oriented, worldly talk of business and professional men" (p. 23).

References

Apple scoops D&AD gold award for a fourth year. (2002, May 30). *Design Week*, p. 6.

Borges, J. L. (1998). The aleph. In A. Hurley (Ed.), *Collected fictions* (pp. 274–286). New York: Vintage.

Bulik, B. S. (2004). The iPod economy. *Advertising Age*, *75*(42), 1, 37.

DeLuca, M., & Peeples, J. (2002). From public sphere to public screen: Democracy, activism, and the "violence" of Seattle. *Critical Studies in Media Communication*, *19*(2), 125–151.

Gumpert, G. (1987). *Talking tombstones and other tales of the media age*. New York: Oxford University Press.

Hosokawa, S. (1984). The walkman effect. *Popular Music*, *4*, 165–180.

Jones, D. (2005). *iPod, therefore I am: Thinking inside the white box*. New York: Bloomsbury.

Kahney, L. (2005). *The cult of iPod*. San Francisco, CA: No Starch Press.

Kincaid, J. (1989). *A small place*. New York: Plume.

Levy, S. (2006). *The perfect thing: How the iPod shuffles commerce, culture, and coolness*. New York: Simon & Schuster.

Marvin, C. (1988). *When old technologies were new: Thinking about electric communication in the late nineteenth century*. Oxford: Oxford University Press.

Norr, H. (2001, October 29). Apple's iPod has its charms. *San Francisco Chronicle*, p. G1.

Pegoraro, R. (2001, November 2). Apple gets it right with sleek, smart iPod music player. *Washington Post*, p. E01.

Pogue, D. (2001, October 25). State of the art: Apple's musical rendition: A jukebox fed by the Mac. *New York Times*, p. G1.

Richmond, W. (2006). The internal retreat from shared public space. *Communication Arts*, *48*(7), 200–201.

Wahl-Jorgensen, K. (2001). Letters to the editor as a forum for public deliberation: Modes of publicity and democratic debate. *Critical Studies in Media Communication*, *18*(3), 303–320.

Wildstrom, S. H. (2002, January 21). iPod: The designers got this one right. *Business Week*, p. 16.

Wilkinson, C. (2005, June 5). iPod: A world in your ear. . . . *The Observer*, p. 2.

9

Reverence

[B]uildings that are ruins in America tend to stand for increasingly short periods of time. They get torn down, not preserved, and the empty lots then get turned into Wal-Marts and strip malls. There is no such thing in America as a terminal cultural landscape, just real estate awaiting development.

—William L. Fox (2006, p. 144)

I began this project with a road trip from New York to California, endeavoring to portray life within an interstate passage of airports, rental car counters, convenience stores, fast-food restaurants, gas stations, malls, and rest stops. Aided by credit cards, Internet terminals, and mobile telephony, this cross-country, high-speed burn demonstrated a structural and perceptual convergence of disparate places into a borderless nation, a "place" marked by a peculiar mode of communication that allows strangers to maintain their personal enclaves even when packed into massive amalgamations. While organized around different nodes of omnitopia, the underlying theme of this effort has been to chart the rules of discourse within the chosen confines of a metastasizing enclavic sensibility—markers not for what is said, but what may be imagined as sayable. Over a number of years pursuing this project, I have found that omnitopia renders the risk and delight of the unplanned meeting or the unscripted conversation to be difficult, almost unthinkable. I have further found that, although dismantling the totalizing design of omnitopia can be difficult and sometimes even dangerous, a certain degree of serendipity resides within and beyond omnitopia.

The means to that end lies in the realm of place and the ways through which meaning becomes inscribed in the built environment. It is simply too facile to propose that we (academics almost always excepted) are subject to forces beyond our understanding or control. We have already seen fruitful and playful limits to that thesis. In places like Las Vegas, powerful scripts that are ordered almost inevitably around the lightening of visitors' wallets render difficult the possibility of performance in moments of gaze, technologies of appropriation, and communities of insider knowledge. The place diminishes in the performance of post-tourism. Attaching Borg-like devices (such as personal media players) to ourselves, we abandon further the contours of urban geographer that would direct and order our behaviors. But we can still play in these places, and we can play *with* these places, especially when we carry with us pocket universes of our own bricolage. Aided by these mobile Alephs, we can repurpose places built by others or ignore those places entirely. Even so, we must not lose site of an inescapable dictum: All the world is not omnitopia. Very little of it is, in fact. Ultimately, to depart omnitopia is to renew the search for place.

Consider efforts by a *Washington Post* humorist, Gene Weingarten, to search for a certain kind of place that could not be confused with all the strip malls, chain hotels, theme restaurants, and shopping concourses of the world, a place defined by a peculiar sense of locale that none but one could claim: The Armpit of America. In an essay entitled "Why Not the Worst?", Weingarten (2001) detailed his search for the U.S. town or city that could justifiably earn that moniker. Some towns, he reasoned, are pretty awful, notable for miserable weather, bland surroundings, or cantankerous citizens. But, he wondered, can one place be called the worst hellhole in the nation? After a great deal of consideration, he decided that the gritty mining Nevada town of Battle Mountain may well deserve that name:

> Take a small town, remove any trace of history, character, or charm. Allow nothing with any redeeming qualities within city limits—this includes food, motel beds, service personnel. Then place this pathetic assemblage of ghastly buildings and nasty people on a freeway in the midst of a harsh, uninviting wilderness, far enough from the nearest city to be inconvenient, but not so far for it to develop a character of its own. You now have created Battle Mountain, Nevada. (p. W12)

Visiting the town, chatting with its underwhelming residents, its forlorn Chamber of Commerce director, and its dour newspaper editor (the one who refused to live within the city limits), he committed to his hatchet job. And then the September 11th attacks changed his plans.

Following a day of such awful violence that all Americans felt (for a while, at least) united under common fear and resolution to overcome the tragedy, Weingarten assumed that no town or city should be mocked. The physical and psychic damage done to the country rendered the clever irony of a well-healed East Coast journalist inappropriate, offensive even. Instead, Weingarten returned to Battle Mountain in search of an uplifting story, some affirmation of America's essential goodness that shines through even the most abysmal places and circumstances. Battle Mountain would become a post-9/11 feel-good story. Only one detail remained as he discovered during his return trip: The town is still a pretty awful place.

Weingarten faced a dilemma. Would he write a snarky story about a deso-
late town that lacked charm, character, and even a newspaper editor who would
tolerate living within its bounds? He had plenty of material:

> I'd seen age, but no quaintness. I'd seen buildings, but no architecture.
> There was a coin-operated community car wash, but no community
> park. There was a store that sells only fireworks, but none that sells only
> clothing. There was a brothel but no ice cream parlor. There were at least
> seven saloons, but no movie theater. (p. W12)

Weingarten saw an opportunity for a witty, down-in-the-sticks story that would
entertain his East Coast readers, but he also felt some guilt about his project. The
town lacked amenities, but its residents demonstrated pluck. The town included
some fairly rancid people, but it also housed loving families and dedicated
boosters. Weingarten felt that, after the September 11th attacks, *Washington
Post* readers might not appreciate such a downer of a story any more than the
unfortunate inhabitants of a town with the initials "BM." He pondered and he
fretted. It was a decision dripping with doubt and fraught with risk. Only when
his photographer spotted a Shell gas station sign whose lights only spelled "hell"
did he decide: Weingarten would name Battle Mountain the "Armpit of America"
if only to inspire tourism to an otherwise forgettable town.

   For a time at least, the article accomplished its goal, sending more and
more motorists off from interstate I-80 to visit the sad and strange town of Battle
Mountain. It is a place worth seeing. Sometimes mocked, sometimes trivialized,
and sometimes romanticized, Battle Mountain resides beyond the omnitopian
bubble. I know because I have visited the town several times over the past few
years. I've made a pilgrimage to the Owl Motel, one of the settings for the 2001
movie *Joy Ride*. I've wandered the town's backstreets and photographed decaying
homes and businesses, and some nice places too. I've dreamed of visiting Battle
Mountain's "Festival of the Pit," an armpit-themed celebration sponsored (for a
time) by Old Spice antiperspirant. I've chatted with local folks who still debate
whether it was worth all the hassle to accept Weingarten's nickname, people who
wonder darkly whether their town has much of a future. I still search for more
of these sorts of locales, these places imbued with time and character, beyond
the super-slab.

   I've spent a lot of time on highways, in airports, and in countless Starbucks
coffee bars, exploring the ways in which omnitopia integrates individual places into
a synecdoche of the world while distilling that potentially globalized community
into an amalgamation of isolated individuals. Inhabiting these sites, as a passenger wandering terminal space, as a guest at conference hotels, as a consumer of
shopping malls, I've found that we generally leave little of our ourselves in these
places, and we rarely take much with us: maybe a souvenir, but little more. Our
passages are authorized, surveyed, and temporary; we pass through a fluid current

and inhabit a perpetual now. That's the idea, anyway. But this conceptualization of omnitopia confronts daily a healthy and fortunate dilemma: the existence of places like Battle Mountain that call forth questions of past and future, of people and emotions. In fact, you can surely remember a place, no matter how generic, no matter how interchangeable, no matter how constricting, that became a locale. The process may be joyful: a reunion of loved ones at an airport. The process may be painful: the departure of a loved one at the same gate. Such a place hums thereafter with meaning. Everyone can remember a moment in a checkout line, an hour waiting at an airport gate, or an evening in a themed restaurant that erupted into significance. All of us claim some places as our own, all evidence to the contrary: This is *my* local airport. This is *my* weekend hotel. This is *my* neighborhood mall. Despite being integrated to national and global networks of commerce and transportation and media, these places can easily, if not intentionally, become marked by times and character of their own.

I have proposed localization as a method of sorts through which one may transform a borderless enclave into something meaningful. This is a performance of place. In describing localization, I have drawn from the writings of Walter Benjamin, who described the purposeful wanderings of the *flâneur* as one who writes the world by walking through its passageways. At first an empire of surfaces, a city expands as an open book to the *flâneur* who simultaneously reads and writes the text. Yet I believe we should eventually move beyond the *flâneur* gaze and begin to experience places as more than raw material for our own solitary musings. The goal here is to integrate the values of meaningful places into our senses of self—not just to pass through them, but also to pass them through us. In this manner, we search for places (or we help create them) outside the omnitopian continuum. We visit these places, we share them, we celebrate them, and we fight to maintain them. In this effort, we reconnect human communication to the built environment for purposes other than commerce. For as communication shapes our perception of certain places, certain places enhance our means of communication.

To evoke locality within omnitopia calls for performances of time as well as place. A typical performance of time is decipherable to anyone who has waited in an airport gate, peering anxiously at monitors for updates on a late plane. At once, would-be passengers transform their bodies into pacing, fidgeting, glaring performances of frustration and rage. With the undesired addition of time, omnitopia collapses into a prison for travelers who commiserate with one another or vow loud enough for all to hear, "This is the *last* time I'll fly on *this* airline again." Stuck in a place built to accommodate anonymous movement, we are supplied with well-worn scripts and audiences. However, and here is the broader point, we also witness the potential for more desirable, or at least meaningful, performances of time. Where omnitopia conflates past, present, and future into a perpetual "now," locality superimposes a discrete sense of time on the perception of timelessness, and it almost always requires meaningful human interaction. Taken together—the performance of place and the performance of time—one may sense localization. In this moment, a place becomes enduring or temporary or fleeting, but meaningful all the same.

Enduring Locales

Beyond the omnitopian enclave, we may search for enduring locales, but not permanent ones. To be permanent is to be lifted out of time in a manner best compared to transcendence. Reflecting on this, I look back on a day spent passing through a temple ritual, remembering that I had not seen a clock anywhere in this place. I asked about the absence of clocks and was told, "There is no time in the temple." The answer was proclaimed proudly and with confidence, and I was impressed. A place with no time, I marveled. No time zones, I imagined too. Passing through the temple threshold, discarding my street clothes and donning symbolic garb, I realized that I had sought to exit a geographic location and enter some sense of completeness. Each temple, I was told, did not merely "signify" a doorway to heaven; each temple conveyed its inhabitants literally to the same place—heaven, a world without end. Ours was a performance, the giving and receiving of words and tokens, the portrayal of a religious narrative that had never changed since the founding of the world. On a certain level, I knew that this temple had indeed changed, that some rituals had been altered through the years to accommodate various exigencies. But I was told that any such changes were superficial, that no change could alter the fixed and unmoving word of God. This, I've come to understand, is permanence. But it is not endurance. To endure is to preserve against a ceaseless flow of change, to be noticeably contrary to the raging torrent. To be permanent is to transcend time. To endure is to wrestle time or, more frequently, to stand in contrast to its flow, to reveal history amid *ahistory*. Enduring places include efforts at preservation that scrape off the patina of today's world to reveal a peculiar past.

Throughout the world, one may visit sites, districts, towns, and entire regions that attempt to maintain enduring locales through a combination of local boosterism, municipal restrictions, corporate sponsorship, and touristic support. In truth, no place endures without compromise. Yet the occasional removal or alteration or improvement of a place is a necessary and apparent part of its endurance. In contrast to some spiritual sites and traditions that try to hide their transformations, enduring places generally celebrate their improvements or at least bemoan them. Either way, their transformations are known, like penciled lines on a wall that chart the growth of a child. Touring a historical spot, a docent will discuss the ways in which owners and planners have employed or responded to change. A wall where once flowed open space, the discovery of a layer of paint that denotes a temporary fashion, even the introduction of air conditioning: These evolutions designate and evaluate the degree to which a place has endured. What parts of this house are original and what sections were added on? How much of this furniture is period and how much was used by the original owners? These questions reflect the script and desire of endurance.

Crossing through the southwest United States, we can find examples of this search for endurance in towns and burgs that have been bypassed by the interstate, particularly at the Blue Swallow Motel in Tucumcari, New Mexico. The famed town of 2,000 motel rooms (now advertised at 1,200) boasts a twinkling, glowing collection of neon motel masterpieces, such as the Americana, the Buckaroo, and the Palomino. But the Blue Swallow is a place like few others. The motel is pretty basic, an L-shaped assemblage of rooms tucked off Tucumcari's main street, with a clam-pattern stuccoed facade topped by glowing blue swallows. Yet this motel offers more than just a room to rest after a day on the road. Once a set of cottages built in 1939, now a holdout against interstate homogeneity, the Blue Swallow is one of the most beloved motels in the United States, thanks largely to the preservation efforts of Lillian Redman who operated the property from 1958 almost to her death in 1999. Visitors still recall her stories of traveling from Texas to New Mexico in 1916 by covered wagon, her work as a Harvey Girl in the 1930s, her motel's fading fortunes with the arrival of I-40, and her oft-stated belief that a motel should serve as a spiritual sanctuary for traveling souls. Lillian charged intentionally low rates (about $11 in 1996) for a simple room with hardwood floors and a black-and-white TV. Her motel had no phones and no frills. But you could park your car in a covered garage right next to your room, and you could sit out front beneath the glow of the blue swallow and watch the cars march along the tourist drag. Since Redman's death, new owners have sought to maintain the Blue Swallow, despite the proliferation of chain hotels, promising to protect the enduring memory of a small place that no one wants to change. Their efforts confront a gaping reality that, for all its nostalgic charm, the town where Blue Swallow resides remains a tired remnant that most folks would just as soon see in the rearview mirror. I could hardly be surprised when I once received an e-mail from a critic who claimed that the name "Tucumcari" actually stems from Native American words for "litter box." It was a joke, yes, but also a reminder that too much nostalgia risks an overly pungent smell. Nonetheless, I yearn to visit that quiet place every few years. To me, motels like the Blue Swallow become enduring locales because they offer the potential for a moment of history where all else is ceaseless movement.

Temporary Locales

To endure does not mean to persist endlessly. As we've seen, endurance requires the awareness of a frontier to the existence of a place, to one's life. Yet sometimes our performances of locality require impositions of temporary reality; some things are good because they come to an end. Think of a holiday that unifies your community, refashioning its rules and practices into something special. In my neighborhood, Halloween draws forth that powerful sense of place. I live in an otherwise typical bedroom community, where garages are bigger than porches and where home values trump most other items of value. But my neighborhood transforms itself for Halloween. Garages open up and become haunted houses. Neighbors compete to fashion the most ghoulish themes for their porches. Eerie music streams from houses that sometimes flash with strobe lights. Thousands of children stream along the curvy roads, bringing traffic to a cacophonous standstill. Halloween provides an excuse for our bedroom neighborhood to become a community. Other holidays inspire similar degrees of celebration, but Halloween stands apart. There's something potent and acute about the way that evening affects this little place, an excuse for adults to act like children and for children to navigate the dark recesses of life. Yet eventually the orange and purple lights must come down and the inflatable pumpkin must be returned to the garage. The next morning, the excuse to avoid raking leaves, the insistence that a layer of dead foliage on the lawn adds to the Halloween spirit, loses its validity. Halloween, like most special occasions, is special because it is temporary. Such is the nature of a temporary locale. It rests on a foundation of transience, the bittersweet pleasure of knowing that some things cannot last.

In this way, the temporary locale reasserts a heterotopian dimension to public life. Omnitopia contains a number of heterotopias, undoubtedly. Amusement parks, for example, are woven into the entertainment and tourist sectors of urban life. These sites offer the kind of social safety valves promised by parks and green spaces, places for various people to intermix without the tensions of the city. Movie theaters and video arcades accomplish similar goals, containing overlapping narratives of reality and fantasy, civilization and chaos, which allow the management of crisis and deviance. What cannot be found within these types of heterotopia, however, is a sense of community required to imagine ourselves beyond the omnitopian enclave. Within the omnitopian-constructed "other place," our experiences are typically solitary. Other people may observe a spectacle near us, as in a stadium-seating theater equipped to overwhelm us with sensory input. We may become spectacles for others, as when playing one of those dancing games in a video arcade or tackling Guitar Hero at home. But we rarely partake of these heterotopian pleasures together. Our gaze focuses on a spectacle of instrumentality. Outside of omnitopia, the temporary locale resides among the performances of people. We sense the lure of community in these places because we will surely not see each other in this way or in this place for a long time, if ever. We are thereby freed, even compelled, to share something of ourselves. It is safety that inspires such an offering, and it therefore can be viewed as being somehow inauthentic. But sometimes the roots of a community grow deepest where they grow most precariously.

Consider an example from Phil Alden Robinson's 1989 film *Field of Dreams*. The movie's portrayal of the timeless values of baseball, the enduring appeal of an American pasttime, is counterbalanced by a temporary locale located in Dyersville, Iowa, site of that mystical field that attracts lovers of the game (and the movie) even today. Getting to Dyersville and then finding the field, located on land once shared (not always amicably) by two families, requires a sort of pilgrimage. One cannot merely pull off the interstate to visit this site; you have to really want to get there. Upon arrival, at least when I visited some years ago, you find a field that continues to be maintained, where tourists are invited to play the game for free. Concessionaires sell trinkets, and they do good business, but the desire to toss the ball requires no currency for its satisfaction. Even so, my memories of this site do not center on the field. No, I remember most vividly the temporary nature of the game. As players arrive, their cars trailing a cloud of dust from the road, they survey the field and make friendly announcements and inquiries. "Is it OK if I join? Does anyone have a glove?" Players make room for newcomers, forming ad hoc teams that adjust themselves to occasional departures. There is no ongoing season, no league.

Although most of the players know the rules of the game, none knows the history of *this* game. As a result, the interactions of this place assume a vivid and meaningful tone. One does not become a pitcher by wearing a uniform; one becomes a pitcher through the acclimation of the people with whom one chooses to play. Moreover, because all the roles are temporary on this field, because everyone eventually will return to the road, players assume many roles. All is not well on the field, we know, whether in Dyersville or Cooperstown. One can hardly play the nation's pasttime without reminders of how much the game has been sullied in so many ways. A visit to the Field of Dreams site offers no guarantees against the unpleasantness that can arise in any amalgamation of strangers. Still, the temporary community of this sort of place possesses the potential for that serendipitous encounter with a stranger who becomes a friend, even if only for an hour.

Fleeting Locales

Along with enduring and temporary locales, we also observe the potential for place to be imbued with time and character where our encounters are most fleeting. Initially, this claim may appear counterintuitive. Think back on a brief walk you may have taken through some urbanized landscape. You may recall monolithic structures, imposing objects, colorful artwork, or symbolic designs. But your passageways through the city also detonate an explosion of fleeting

signs—billboards, video displays, newspaper pages, personal media screens, clothing labels, t-shirt inscriptions, and even the practiced glances of people who have
turned themselves into caricatured sign systems. We are awash in momentary
objects for our appraisal. Consider an example from the 2002 Steven Spielberg
film *Minority Report*, in which the protagonist passes through a shopping mall
concourse whose walls verbalize advertisements directed toward the character
by name. In this world, messages, once discretely located at a site (a box called
a "television," a device called a "computer") become ever-present, part of an
information city. More than the billboards that once lined interstate highways,
these messages do not simply interrupt the passage through a structure; they
are woven into the structure of everyday life so intricately that text and context
can hardly be distinguished. It is the fleeting nature of our decisions, flashes of
light without insight, despite their occasional import, that reflects so much of
contemporary life.

On occasion, however, a locale derives its meaning solely from its fleeting
nature. We become aware of this moment as being somehow meaningful when
we spot some form of communication attempted by a person or group that
manages to rip through the noise of our daily lives. Often this communication,
an unauthorized inscription on a wall, the cynical alteration of a sign, a scribble
of poetry on an overpass, acquires its significance through illegality. Unauthorized communication, such as tagging, observed but rarely read, reveals the
contours and divisions of public life. We read it quickly, at a fast trot or within
a moving vehicle, and we contemplate vividly, maybe intrusively, an otherwise
amorphous awareness of the world beyond the "world" we traverse. This fleeting
locale derives its meaning, also, through its imminent obliteration. Order will
soon be reestablished, and often thankfully so. We await the wash of paint, the
repair by professionals, and the tidying of messes (and masses), and we know
with certainty that an act of genuine social threat must either be co-opted or
eliminated. Yet the moment endures beyond the thing, the place well behind us
now as we renew our movements through the city. The fleeting locale has become
a marker of mortality, a totem to the persistent hum of florescent awareness that
we otherwise wish to obscure.

Makeshift roadside memorials represent, to my thinking, the essential
example of the fleeting locale. Almost always they reside between seconds in the
brief flash afforded by automobile gaze, a speck against the horizon. Witnessed
too fast to be read in a traditional sense, the roadside memorial burns itself into
memory in a more visceral manner than the written word. Yet anyone who has
plied two-lane roads or interstate highways likely has seen hundreds of these
monuments. We are wise to recall that such inscriptions have marked human
movements throughout recorded history; it is endemic to the species to speak
into the darkness of inevitable demise by leaving markers of our comings and
goings. But a new kind of meaning entirely surrounds the interstate monu-

Image 20: Roadside Memorial. *Photograph by Andrew Wood*

ment beyond its connotation of violent death at high speeds. In an age beyond the frontier, when all land is owned by someone, even if by "the public," the roadside monument becomes a fleeting act of privatization, an imposition of personal and spiritual locality on the homogenous world that stretches endlessly from off-ramp to off-ramp. This private performance of naming, of grief, does not form a community of readers. Yet the solitary driver recognizes a human connection to the author of this place all the same. We pass by this place and look intently or shake or gaze upward or even invoke some religious sentiment through a ritualistic gesture, and we contribute to a chain of being that stretches beyond any physical horizon. In that moment, we resist what Jorgensen-Earp and Lanzilotti (1998) describe as our "societal discouragement of public grief . . . [,] a widening rift between the individual and the reality of death" (p. 156). We accept instead a vivid connection to people and things beyond our tiny, roving realms. Regardless of the totalizing influence that we associate with omnitopia, we find in the roadside memorial the potential for place to burst into our lives.

Image 21: Route 66 Relic. *Photograph by Jenny Wood*

Conclusion: Reverence for Ruins

We end our journey beyond the borders of omnitopia with a certain reverence for the decaying monuments of older times, the detritus of modernity. When contemplating the need for ruins, I draw from cultural geographer J. B. Jackson's (1980) book of the same name, his analysis of monuments that commemorate "a private vernacular past . . . mementos of a bygone daily existence without a definite date" (p. 89). For those who would exit omnitopia, there is joy in the ruins of older places—abandoned houses, decayed storefronts, and relic motels. In these places, we discover props for the theater of reconstruction, figments of a narrative that may be reconstituted toward our own needs. But more important, we find something more vivid, more real about ourselves in this type of place. All of us keep some secret memory of lost places, harboring that mental totem as proof and affirmation of how far we've come. We need ruins even if we dismiss them publicly, to affirm the endurance of memory, the temporary nature of our lives, the fleeting moments in which we can choose who we are. Ruins also prove the ephemeral nature of powerful places. We need to know, too, the inevitability that the most totalizing enclaves will be breached in time.

Omnitopia contains no ruins. Or rather if it does, the ruins are scripted for the purposes of play and fantasy. Like its heterotopian predecessors such as the old English pleasure gardens, omnitopian nodes may reconstruct some whiff of age or decay to allow inhabitants to engage in consumer performances of nostalgia or even irony. Today at almost every manifestation of omnitopia, one may visit a tourist "Olde Towne," eat at a themed "50s" diner, or purchase a "distressed" t-shirt meant to look as if it has been worn for decades. Such is the temporal fragmentation found in most omnitopian nodes: themed and kitschy performances of "the past," rather than nostalgic critiques of the present. But the functional reality of omnitopia is one of a perpetual present. Omnitopia is fundamentally ahistorical. Once more I turn to John Stilgoe (1998), who offers an evocative illustration:

> The explorer wheeling behind the [interstate] motel, around the gasoline station, between the taco and pizza restaurants sees everywhere not just the signs of continuous, casual maintenance, say the pails and mops and squeegees devoted to gleaming entrance foyers and plate-glass windows, but the evidence of continuous repair and restoration. Almost every cluster boasts a structure being *fixed*, somehow stayed again against deterioration. (pp. 163–164; italics original)

Image 22: John's Modern Cabins, Rolla, MO. *Photograph by Andrew Wood*

In contrast to omnitopia is a search for age, for roots, and for wear and tear on the physical, architectural, and social fabric. Outside omnitopia, we return to ruins as anchors to a world we would call real. I write this in a Starbucks, but mentally I inhabit a patch of overgrown land on Route 66 near Rolla, Missouri, a location that can hardly be spotted from the interstate where John's Modern Cabins stand only because no one has bothered to tear them down. The six cabins (and two nearby outhouses) have suffered from decades of neglect, and the red sign that promises a piece of motel modernity reflects only mournful irony as the cars scream by. But the 1930s-era cabins offer a photographer's dream—if you visit quickly. A fan planted Burma Shave signs nearby that read: "Photograph these while you're here. The wrecking ball is looming near." This then is the role of a ruin as a counterpart to omnitopia. Within the enclave, we find safety, but only for a time. We search for continuity, but we tire of it soon enough. Eventually, omnitopia confronts a relentless frontier and a final reminder.

Omnitopia is only a desire; it is not a place.

References

Fox, W. L. (2006). The impossibility of ruins. In J. Brouws (Ed.), *Approaching nowhere* (pp. 140–145). New York: W. W. Norton.

Jackson, J. B. (1980). *The necessity for ruins and other topics*. Amherst: University of Massachusetts Press.

Jorgensen-Earp, C. R., & Lanzilotti, L. A. (1988). Public memory and private grief: The construction of shrines at the sites of public tragedy. *Quarterly Journal of Speech, 84*(2), 150–170.

Stilgoe, J. R. (1998). *Outside lies magic: Regaining history and awareness in everyday places.* New York: Walker and Company.

Weingarten, G. (2001, December 2). Why not the worst? *The Washington Post*, p. W12.

Author Index

Subject Index

Notes: (1) Named airports are grouped in Airports. (2) Named highways and numbered interstates are grouped in Highways and interstates. (3) International expositions and world's fairs (from 1798 to 1964–65) are grouped in World's Fairs. (4) Page numbers are duplicated when one refers to the text and another refers to a reference page.

CPSIA information can be obtained at www.ICGtesting.com
Printed in the USA
241050LV00002B/17/P